I0729653

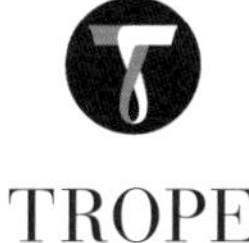

TROPE

TROPE PUBLISHING Co.

WHEN DO YOU FEEL FREE?

VOICES ACROSS AMERICA

RYLAND HORMEL

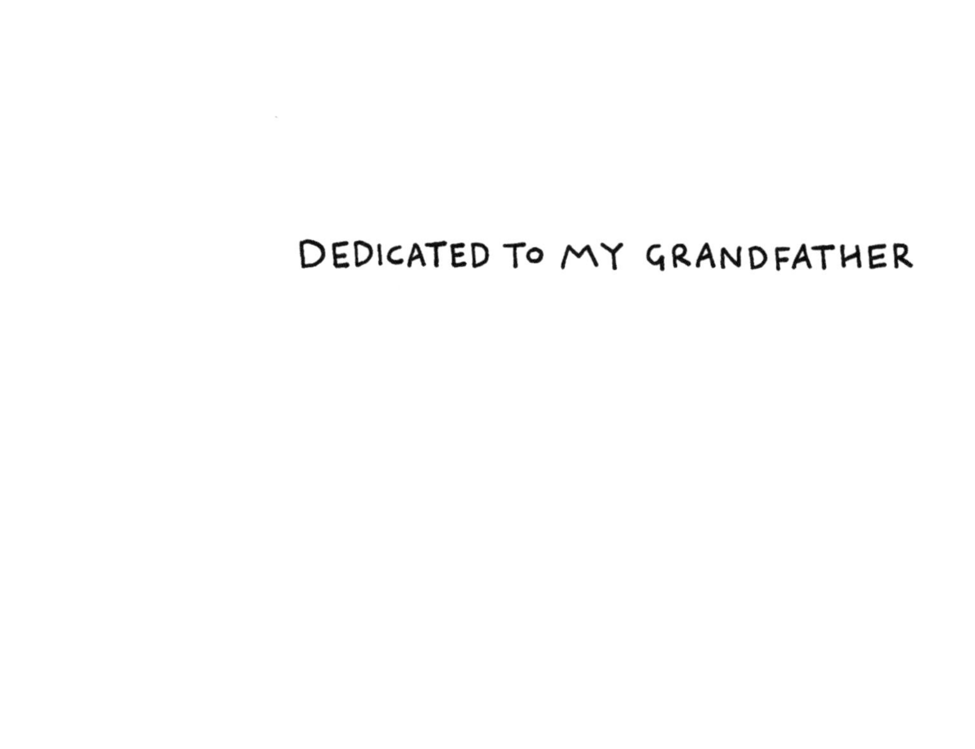

DEDICATED TO MY GRANDFATHER

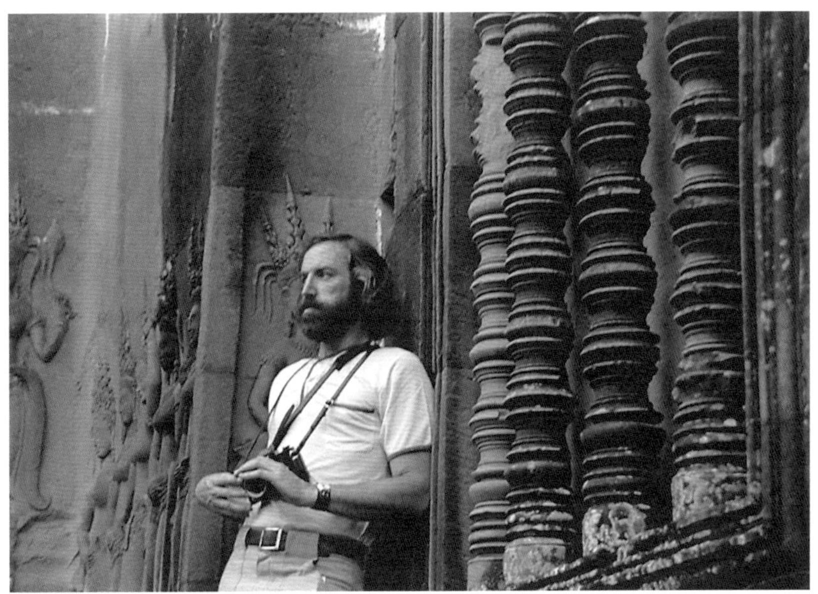

James C. Hormel
1933 – 2021

When I was seven years old, I watched you become the first openly gay ambassador of the United States of America to Luxembourg. You helped break down a wall of inequality that ultimately created more freedom for others.

I intended to take your portrait for this book. I wanted to interview you, listen to your story and learn about freedom from your perspective. There are so many questions I want to ask you. I waited too long—life had other plans and I missed the opportunity. As much as it pains me and at times fills me with regret, I find comfort in knowing that you have inspired me during every step of this long journey. I proudly dedicate this book in your honor.

I love you and miss you, dear.

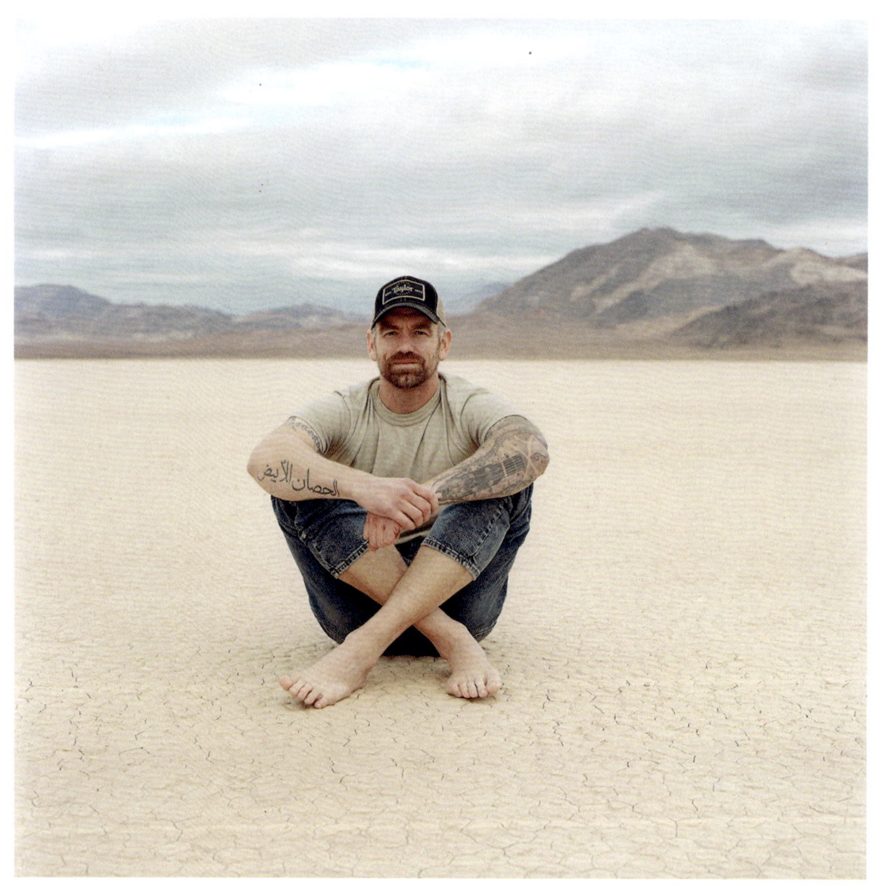

No one is free until everyone is free.

Sometimes it's best to say less about a creative work and let it speak for itself. This book is no exception. In it, you'll find a combination of portraits and hand-written messages which tell a story about the human experience of freedom. It's best to experience this for yourself.

As you read through it, know that Ryland spent many months on the road interviewing and photographing people to compose this work. He engaged in meaningful conversations about the feeling of freedom and took the time to get to know their personal stories. If this book feels distinctly human, it's because it was created in a distinctly human way.

By asking, "When do you feel free?," Ryland gives people an opportunity to reflect on freedom as a lived experience in time as opposed to an abstract concept or moral absolute. He's not as concerned with defining freedom as he is with feeling it. As you read through this text, this is an invitation to do the same.

By limiting responses to the space of a 3x5 index card, Ryland provides just enough of a creative constraint to unleash the philosopher and poet in everyone. Readers will find many of the statements in this work to be disarmingly powerful, distinctly grounded, and viscerally real. It's a work full of paradoxes and contrasts, beauty and simplicity, complexity, resilience, humor, and pain.

I'm confident that readers will discover aspects of themselves embedded within this work. Ryland gives us an opportunity to contemplate an important question about being and feeling free and it's in thinking through questions like these that we come to learn more about ourselves and what it means to be human. I invite all readers to take a full, deep breath, clear the mind, and reflect on what freedom feels like to you.

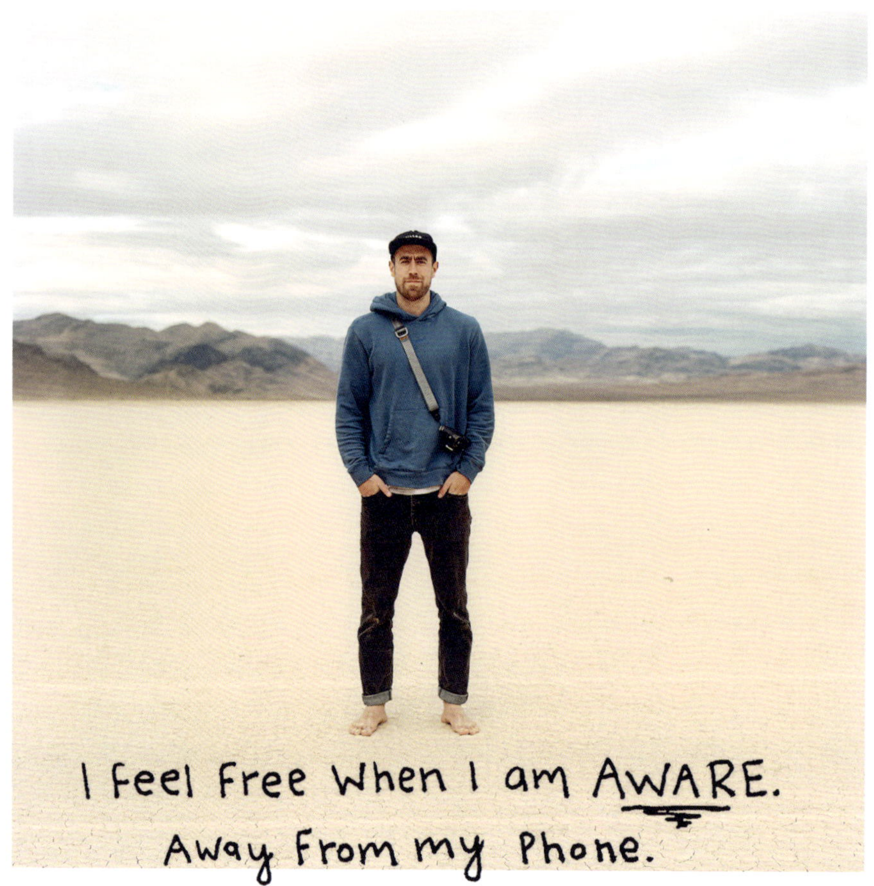
I feel Free When I am AWARE.
Away From my Phone.
NOTICING the beauty of life around me.
Enjoying the fleeting moment in
between my comfort and Fears.
Feeling called to create.
Whatever I am doing feels like
walking to the beat of a Song ♫

When do you feel free? I had just returned to San Francisco after spending three weeks living and riding with cowboys in New Mexico when the question first came up. My cousin Wes is a cowboy who lives on a ranch there, right off Route 66 amongst the open land and juniper trees. To escape the constraints of the Bay Area during the peak of the Covid-19 pandemic, I asked him if I could come down and document his life as a cowboy. He told me sure, but if I was to do so he would not only have to teach me how to ride a horse while carrying a camera, but I would also have to keep up. There is not much room in that line of work to be patient with someone who is getting in the way of accomplishing a day's job.

The first three days on the ranch I was thrown into the fire, learning how to gallop a horse and turn on a dime. This was a no-training-wheels type of lesson. Although my legs got cut up and bruised with scars that still remain, I had the good fortune of joining my cousin and other cowboys on a few jobs—one of which felt like it was out of a movie. We met ten other cowboys on a neighboring ranch with the mission to move over 100 cattle out of the open pasture and into their pens. We rode out in formation as the sun rose. My job was to stay somewhat behind the professionals and document with my camera. As we rode, a cow broke from the herd and headed my way. The cowboys yelled, "Fucking get 'em!" In a flash, my newly trained instincts kicked in. I strapped my camera to my backpack, kicked my horse and put myself directly in the cow's path. Seeing a 1500+ pound bovine run toward me at full speed and trusting it would move out of the way was one of the more exhilarating experiences of my life. I was the butt of many jokes that day, but I think I gained just a little bit of respect with that crew for being a city slicker trying to play cowboy for a few weeks. When the work was done, I got into my truck and had the most incredible feeling of freedom. The word "freedom" kept coming up every time I asked these cowboys questions about their lives. "We may not be rich but we're free to do what we want," they said.

The experience with the cowboys was the seed for this project. Weeks later, upon my return to San Francisco, my mentor and teacher Carolyn Cooke asked me, "When do you feel free?" The question sent a perspective-shifting wave through my body. I had always thought of freedom as a destination, not a feeling. Freedom was always a "one day" type of achievement in my mind. Now, I see freedom as a fleeting feeling, one that can be uncovered on any given day at any given moment by breaking away from mental constraints and attachments. The more I learned about my own relationship to freedom as a feeling, the better I got at being able to lean into the things in life that create it for me.

During that time, I was selling my photographic prints at farmers markets alongside Ian, a collage artist and friend. One day, I decided to set up a table with the question "When do you feel free?" printed next to a stack of note-cards and a Mason jar filled with pens. I asked people to write down their answers. These early, anonymous responses appear throughout the book. The same people came back to my booth at the farmers market week after week, less interested in my photography than in talking about freedom. The question seemed to have a mystical power, provoking deep reflection. It was around this time I decided to travel across America taking people's portraits and collecting their handwritten perspectives on freedom. I wondered how people from different communities and parts of the country would respond.

My first stop was Southern California to spend time with my grandma, Amie. My cousin Robbie had recently discovered that our grandfather, Granby, had a vintage Leica M6 analog camera sitting in his closet, unused. This camera is simply beautiful, difficult to use, and demands a level of stillness and awareness to unlock its full potential. Knowing I would be interviewing people across the country and listening to their stories, I decided film was the way to go. Film demands trust. There is no way to see what was captured until it is developed, which allows me to be present with the subject and to listen to their story. I believe film photography can amplify authentic connection. I used a range of analog cameras for this work, including the 35mm Leica M6, a medium format Hasselblad and even a Kodak disposable camera that is sold at any local pharmacy. The entire project was shot using Portra 400 film stock. When I went to collect the Leica, Amie became the first person I photographed and interviewed for this book.

From Southern California, I flew to Alaska. For ten days, I spent time with fishermen who were connected to my friends Barkley and Georgia. Something cowboys and fishermen have in common is their hard, brutal work. On the other side of this work is freedom, usually experienced and enjoyed with a can of beer and conversations after a long day on the range or on the open sea.

Now that I had my sea legs, I continued the work in the best way I know how: on the open road. I am somewhat of a ramblin' man at heart, and driving long distances makes me feel free. Although I have driven across the country three times and at one point in my life lived in a van for six months, I had never taken the route starting in California and driving through all of the southern states to finally end on the east coast. This was my course. On December 6, 2021, I packed up my truck with my cameras, a cooler full of film and all else I felt I needed to survive. With my dog Moose in the backseat, I hit the road. Over the course of nine months and 20,000+ miles, I interviewed and photographed hundreds of people, all starting with the question, "When do you feel free?"

My first stop was Death Valley, to see my friend Josh Mantz. In addition to being a breathworker, Josh is also a former Army officer who actually died for 15 minutes when he was shot by a sniper in Baghdad and was brought back to life. This made being in a place with death in it's name all the more interesting. I met Josh at 4:30am in a state of profound doubt that I was the right person to do this work—or even what "this work" was, exactly. We drove around the unforgiving landscape for nine hours talking about life, death and everything in between. Josh was critical of my question—his own answer was "No one is free until everyone is free"—but he encouraged my journey and helped me see more deeply into my purpose, for which I'll be forever grateful.

I kept driving, to Denver, then Santa Fe, and finally returned to the ranch where this project began. My next stops were in Austin and other parts of Texas. From there I visited New Orleans for the first time. My dad played music professionally there in his 20s and I connected with his old band-mates, Red and Tommy. Both of them are featured in these pages.

In New Orleans, I met Jerry as he sat on the side of the road with his dog. We struck up a conversation and he asked if I wanted to see where he lives in his tent by the Mississippi River and meet his pet gator. For some reason I felt I could fully trust this stranger, and agreed. Jerry walked me across the railroad tracks and down through the swamp to his tent. Sure enough, there was a gator right there—not actually his pet, but an animal he had come to know…at a distance. We sat by his tent and talked for an hour. Jerry, a veteran, does not have much in the way of money or possessions, but embodied an enviable sense of freedom. Jerry told me, "Just helping others when I can and doing the right thing makes all the difference in life."

Next, I headed to a horse farm in Ocala, Florida, where I met Mr. Ralph and Mr. Freddie while they were selling peanuts right off one of the main roads. I sat with them in the boiling heat with my truck running the AC to cool down my dog Moose. From there, I drove to Atlanta for two weeks and eventually made my way to Savannah, Georgia, mostly so I could satisfy my ego and say I went from coast to coast on this trip. I then began to make my way back west and stopped in a few more states before I got back to the Bay Area to conclude this work.

Who am I to ask strangers when they feel free? As I mentioned, during my time with Josh in Death Valley, anxiety almost stopped me from pursuing this work. I remember looking at all of my gear packed up three days before I hit the road and questioning if I really wanted to do this. I was afraid of pissing people off and confronting my relationship to freedom in such an intimate way. By nature of my background and identity, I have a very different relationship and access to freedom than most people in this book. This project, in part, was designed selfishly, to learn about my individual freedom and the responsibility I have in being a part of this world. We all share different experiences, and my personal experience provides me with a lot of mobility which I did nothing to earn. Feeling safe driving across the country by myself is a freedom. I remembered the conversations I had at the farmers market and what the power of listening can do. This reminder helped me get into my truck and put it in drive.

Every single person in this book became my teacher. I have met people on this journey who at one point in their lives had no money, who were living on the streets, and who had to work harder than I can ever imagine. I listened to stories of people coming out of the closet and sharing their true identities with the world in a society that still doesn't make them feel safe to do so. Stories of people who had to fight their way out of prison. Stories of people who were abandoned by their families. All I can do now is stand in complete awe and admiration of these individuals.

Most of this work was about listening and using the camera as a tool to do so. I had some very hard conversations that challenged my beliefs and perspectives. I learned that what I'd thought of as freedom is a privilege, and that true freedom is the feeling and experience that comes from breaking away from constraints and/or attachments. A lot of times it's facing our fears. Sometimes freedom creates room for choice and causes pain. No matter what, the feeling of freedom is fleeting and not absolute. Getting off the couch and going for a walk outside has the potential to create the feeling. Experiences of freedom are as varied as the human beings who contributed to this story.

What this book is not: telling you what freedom is. I am by no means trying to define freedom or tell you how to feel about it.

What this book is: a collective conversation about freedom through the fragmented perspectives of individuals across America. The people in this book are the real teachers. Please listen to them with an open mind, as I did. Celebrate the moments when you find your perspective is challenged or changed.

These conversations taught me that we don't all live in the same America. Freedom as a right is not distributed equally. Freedom as a feeling is. Let that sink in as you look into the eyes of the people in this book, listen to their perspectives and feel the heartbeats from a variety of communities across the country. I invite you to slow down, let go of your limiting beliefs, and connect with humanity.

WHEN DO YOU FEEL FREE?

VOICES ACROSS AMERICA

I feel free when I am in good company with good conversation & feel safe enough to be myself.

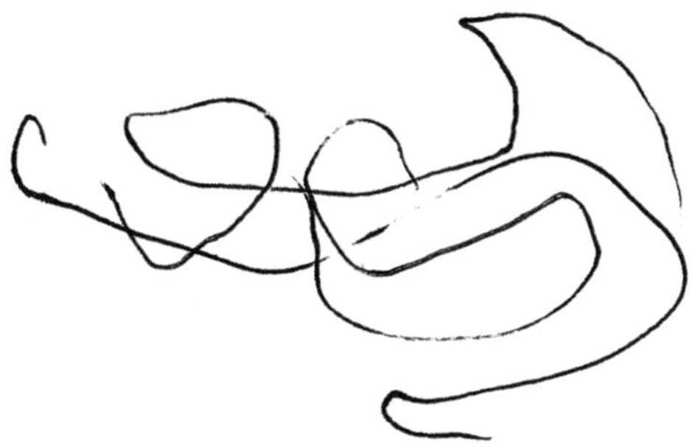

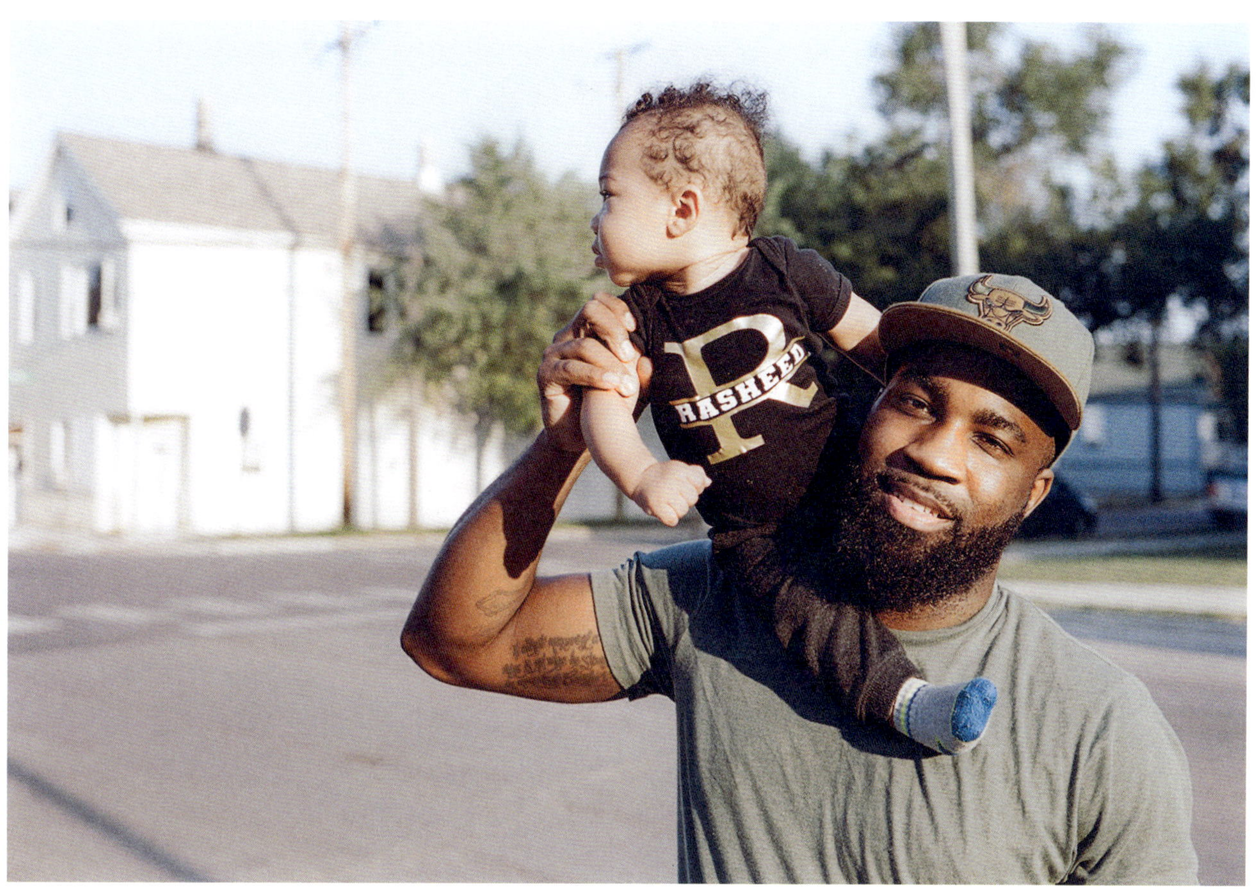

Rasheed

Chicago, Illinois · August 2021

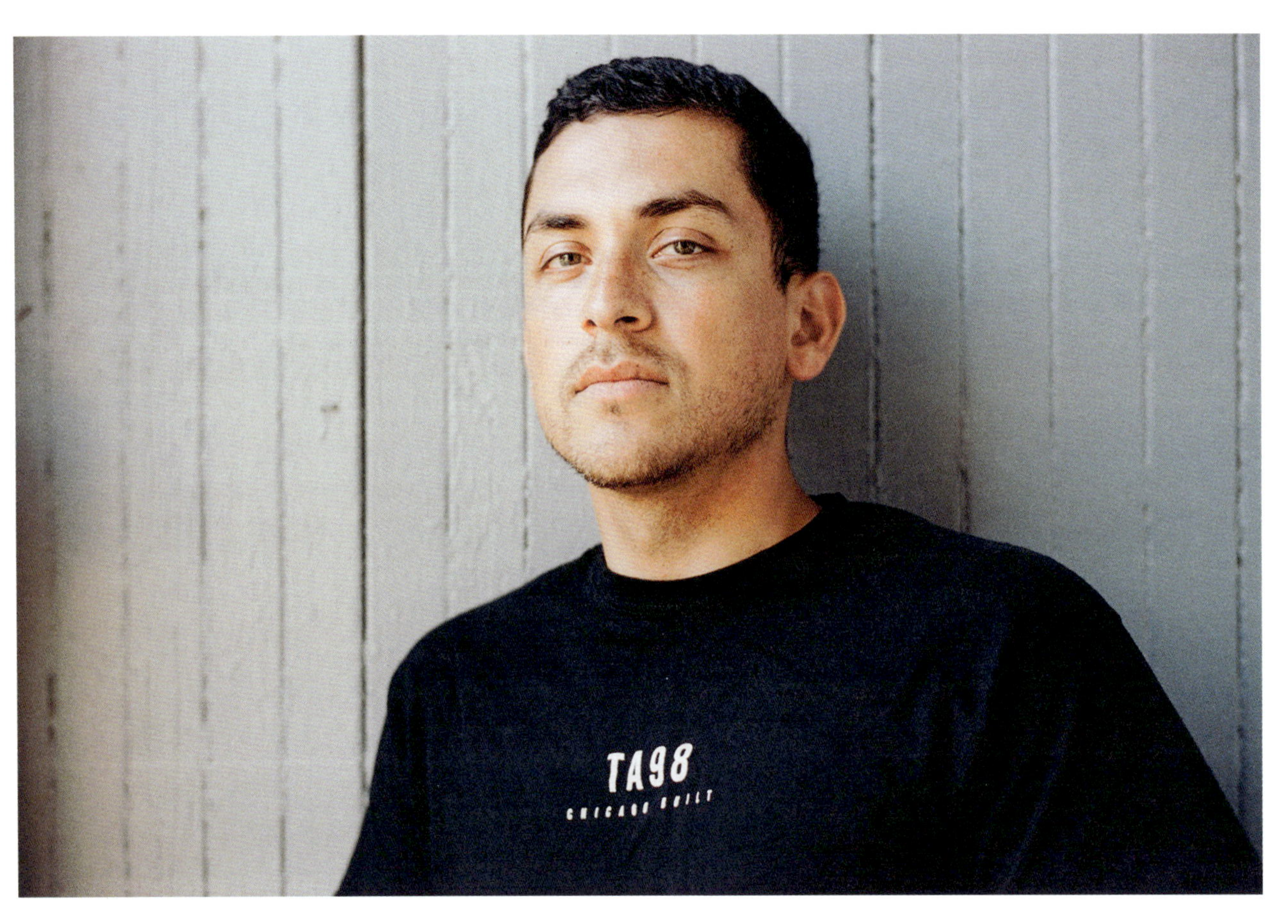

David Rojas JR.

I feel most free when
I eat my moms homemade
salsa, and foods she makes
with memories of her mom.

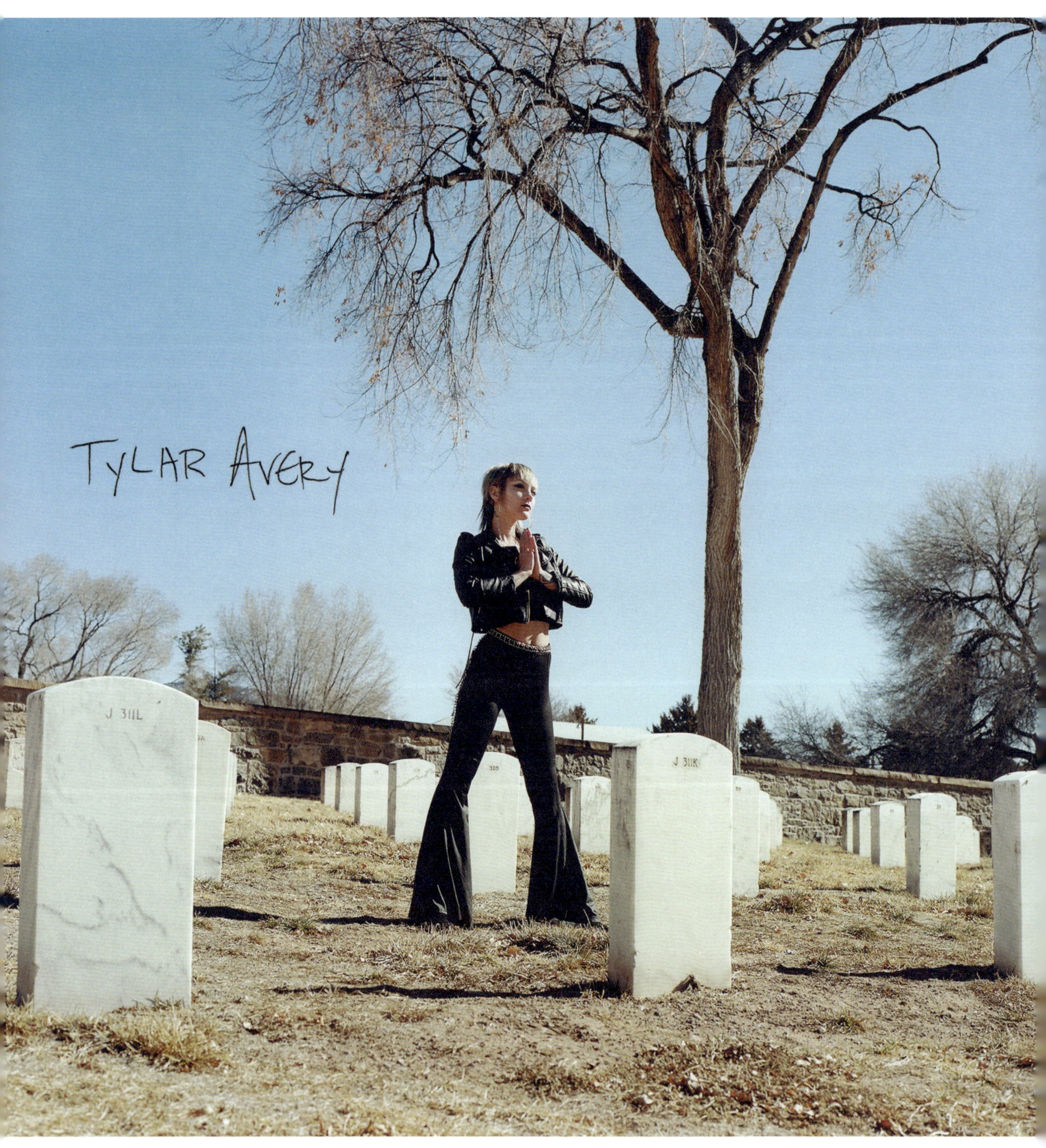
TYLAR AVERY

I FEEL FREE
WHEN I DON'T
    NEED
ANYTHING.
TO CHANGE HOW
I FEEL.

ITS NEVER TO
LATE TO
HAVE A GOOD

    CHILDHOOD

ONE SHOULDN'T
HAVE TO FIGHT
FOR FREEDOM

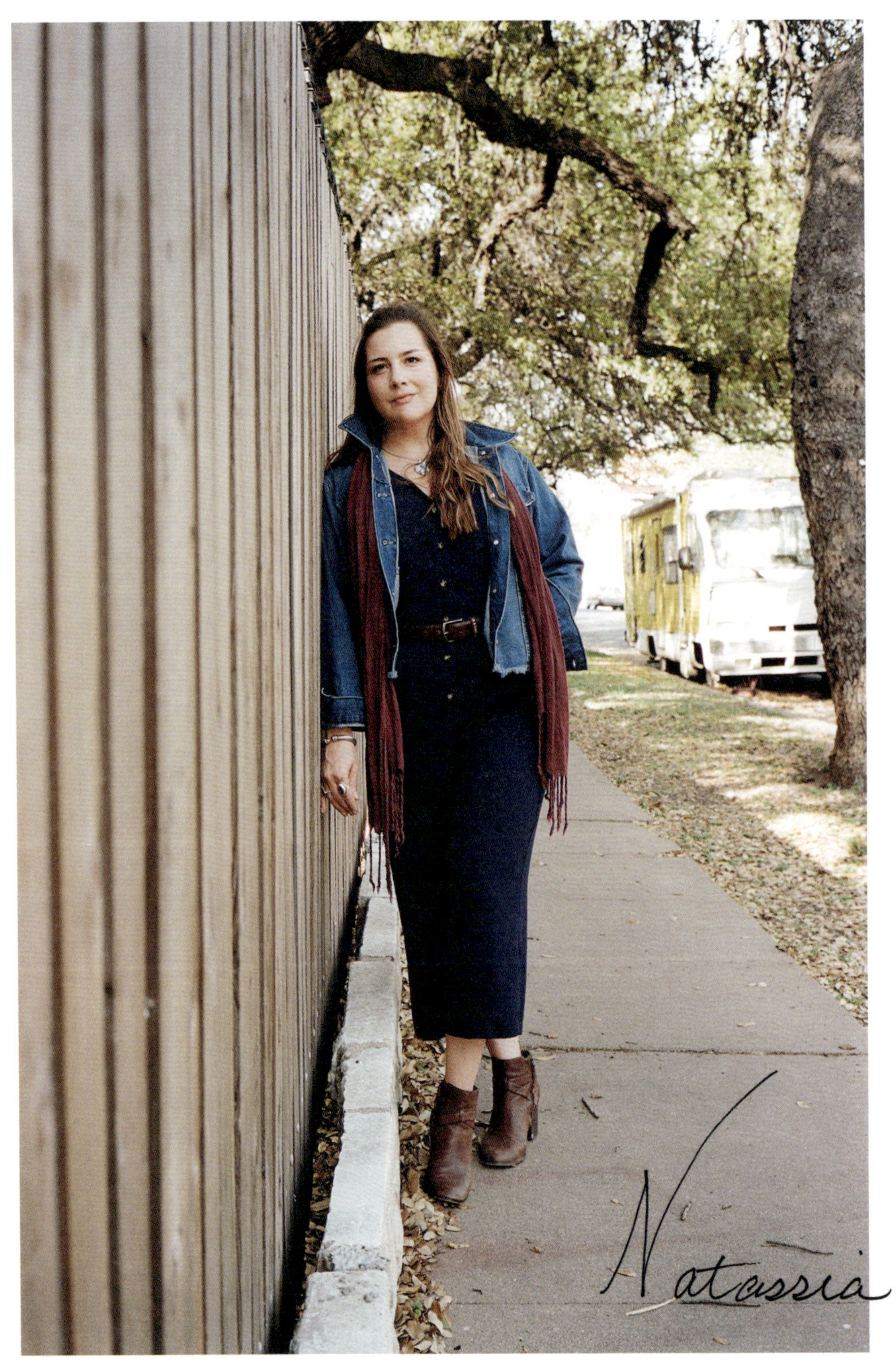
Natassia Wilde

When do
I feel free?

These days I feel free
all the time. Making a
living doing what I am most
passionate about is the ultimate
expression of freedom to me. Also when
I am in my creative flowstate; Behind
the camera or putting together a color
story while I curate a show,... I
feel like it is an experiment
in controlled freedom. My
art is about this. My
life is about this.
That is where
the magic is.
The divinity is
in the moments
between.
✳

I feel free when I do
personal styling & shopping
for people. It makes me feel
good and I like to make
the person feel good also.

I Feel free when I go to
A cafe on a nice day and
Get some sun.
I feel free when I do
Meditation
I feel when I go clothes
Shopping

San Francisco, California · September 2021

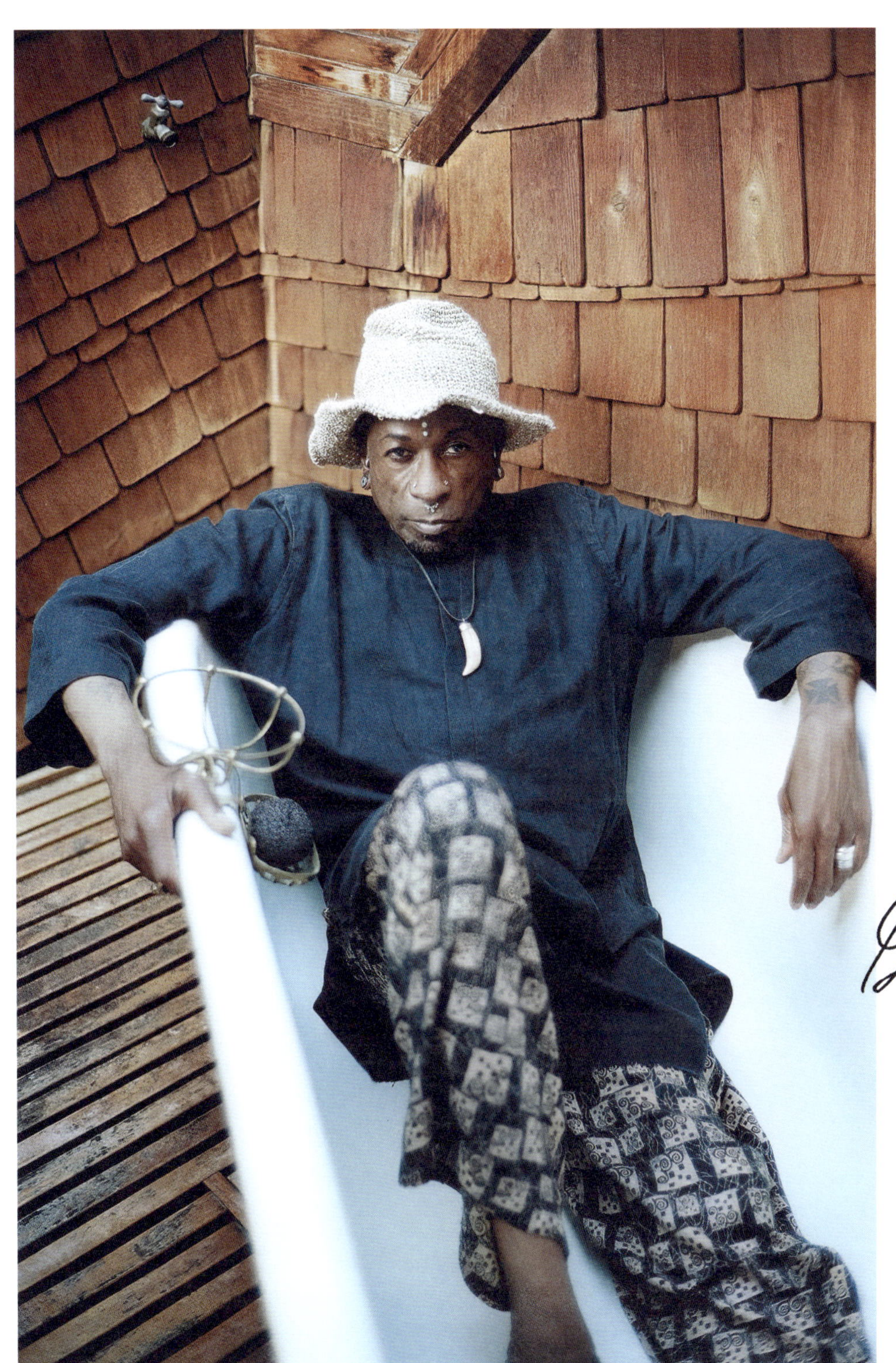

When do I feel most free?

I feel most free with the lady and dogs, taking a nice long walk deep into the woods.

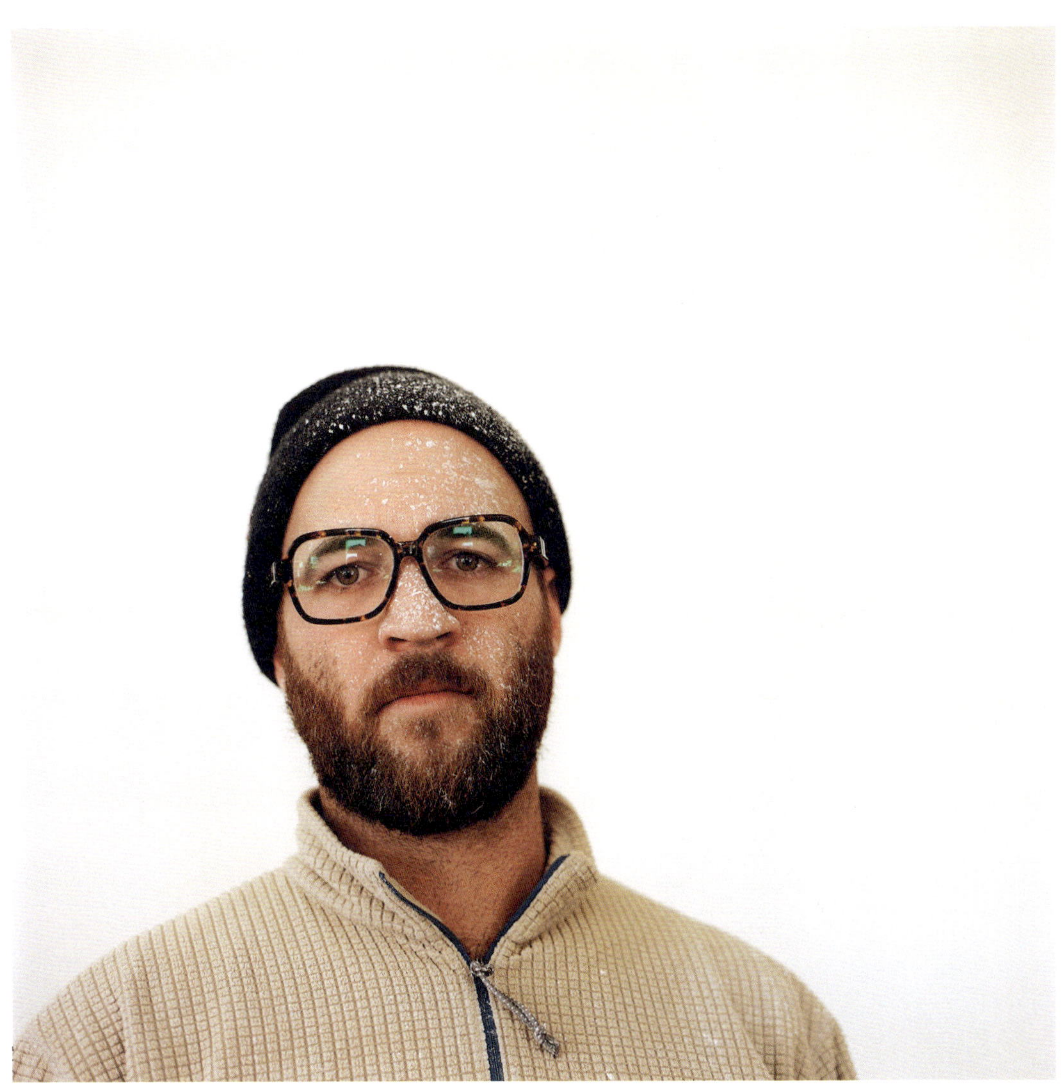

Gary

27

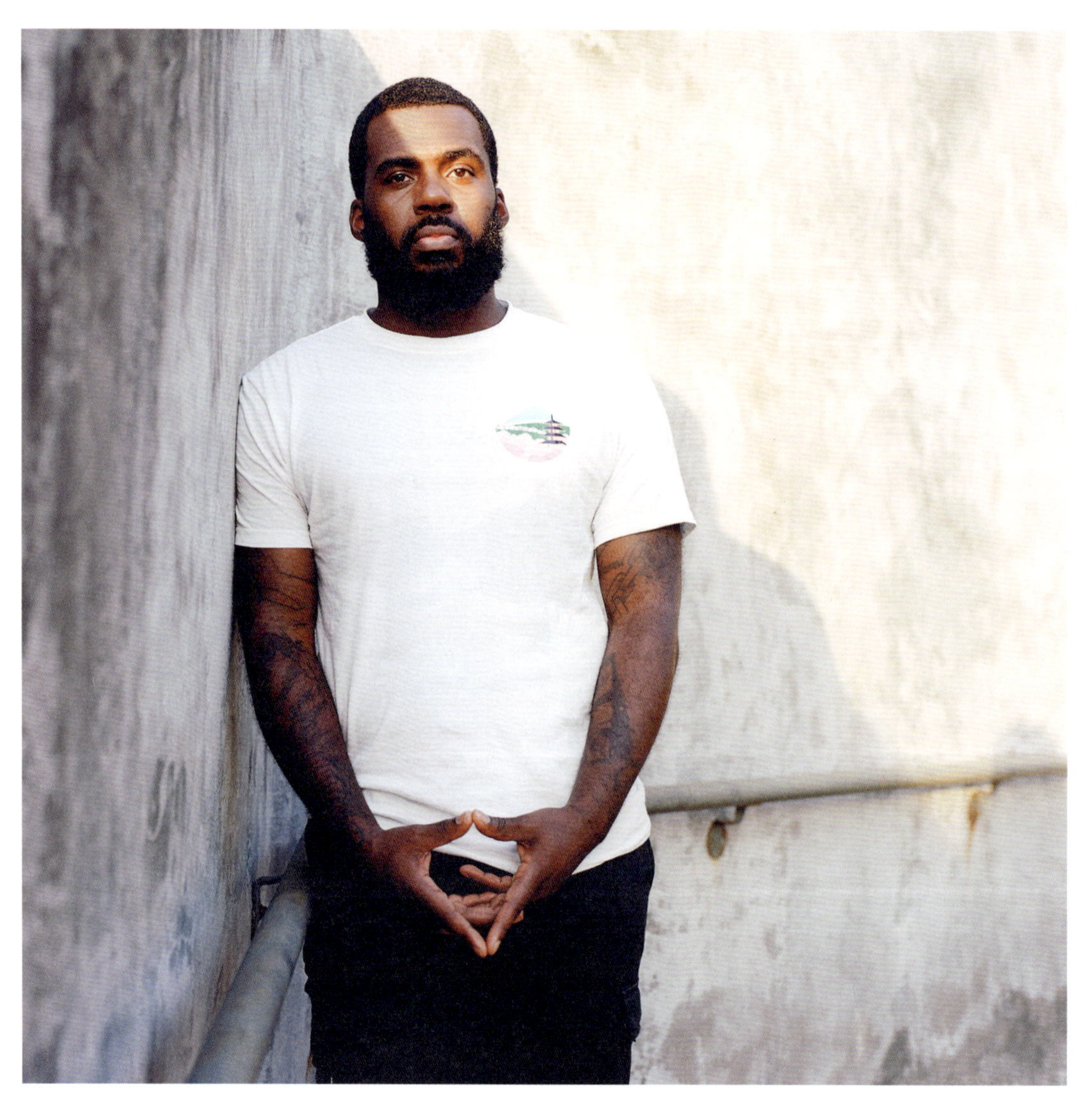

André
" W.Y.ZÉ. "

I feel free when I am creating
Or when I'm in nature. Creating
Shows me what is in my control.
Nature reminds me to be still
& to move with purpose. I feel
free when I realize that my only
job is to be uniquely me and to LOVE.
—WYZE

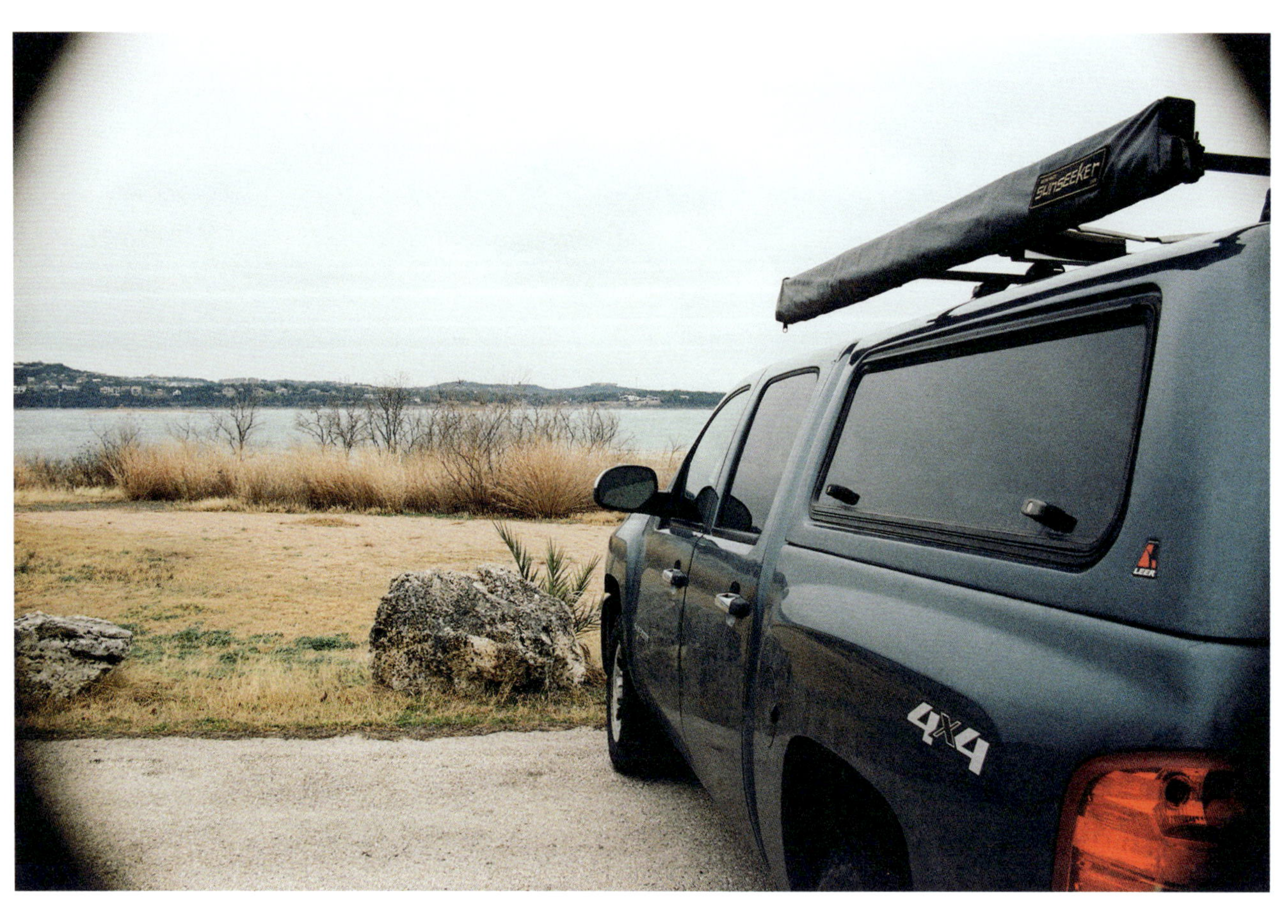

at the beach,
watching the
sunset w/ friends

When I am doing something
I love like sports or talking
about someone or something you
care about.

PLAYING BASKETBALL MAKES
ME FEEL FREE. IT REMINDS ME
OF WHEN I WAS A KID, BEFORE
I KNEW I WAS GAY. BEFORE I REALIZED
I WOULD HAVE TO HIDE MY TRUE SELF.

PLAYING BASKETBALL MAKES
ME FEEL FREE.

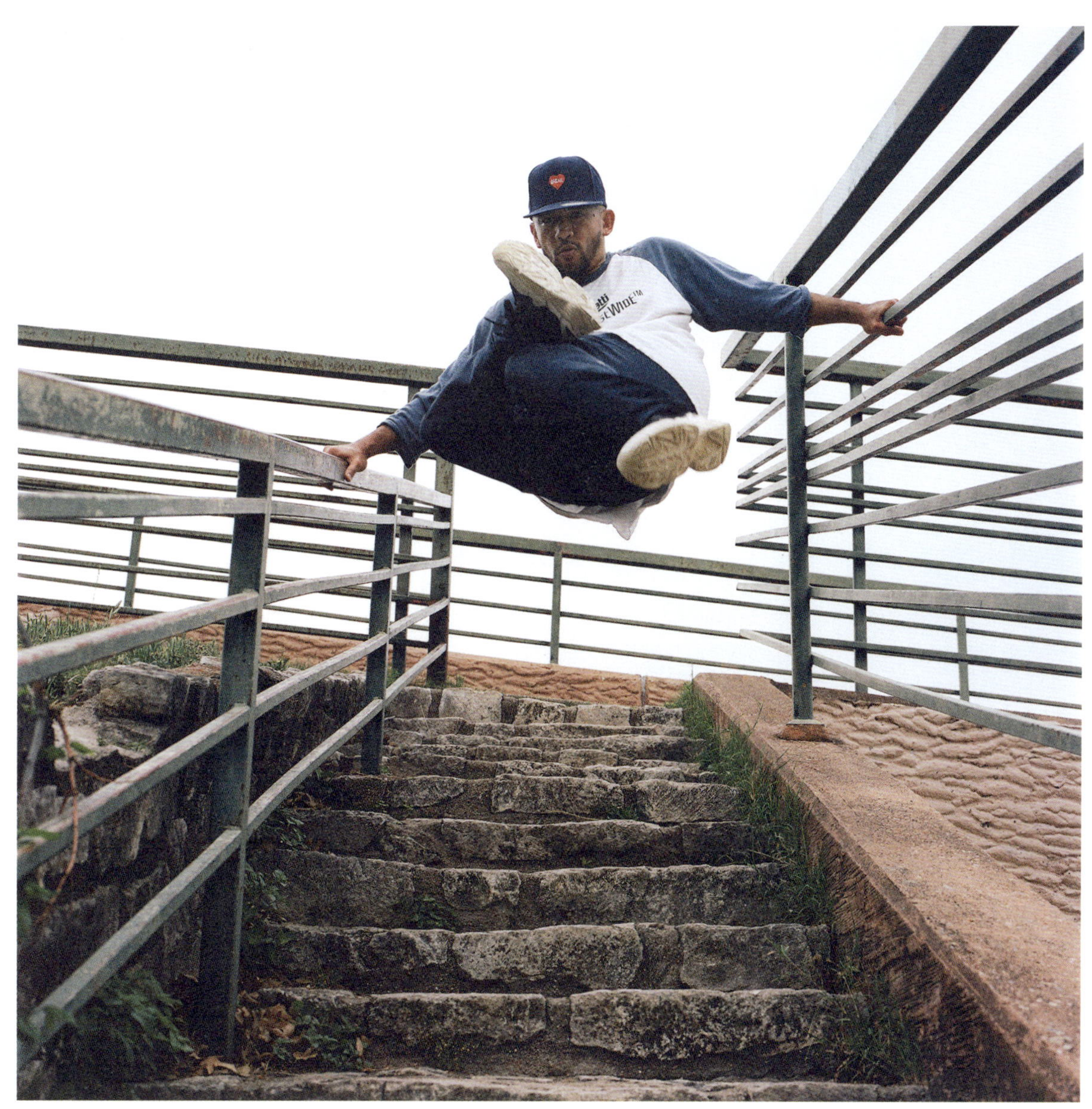

Austin, Texas · April 2022

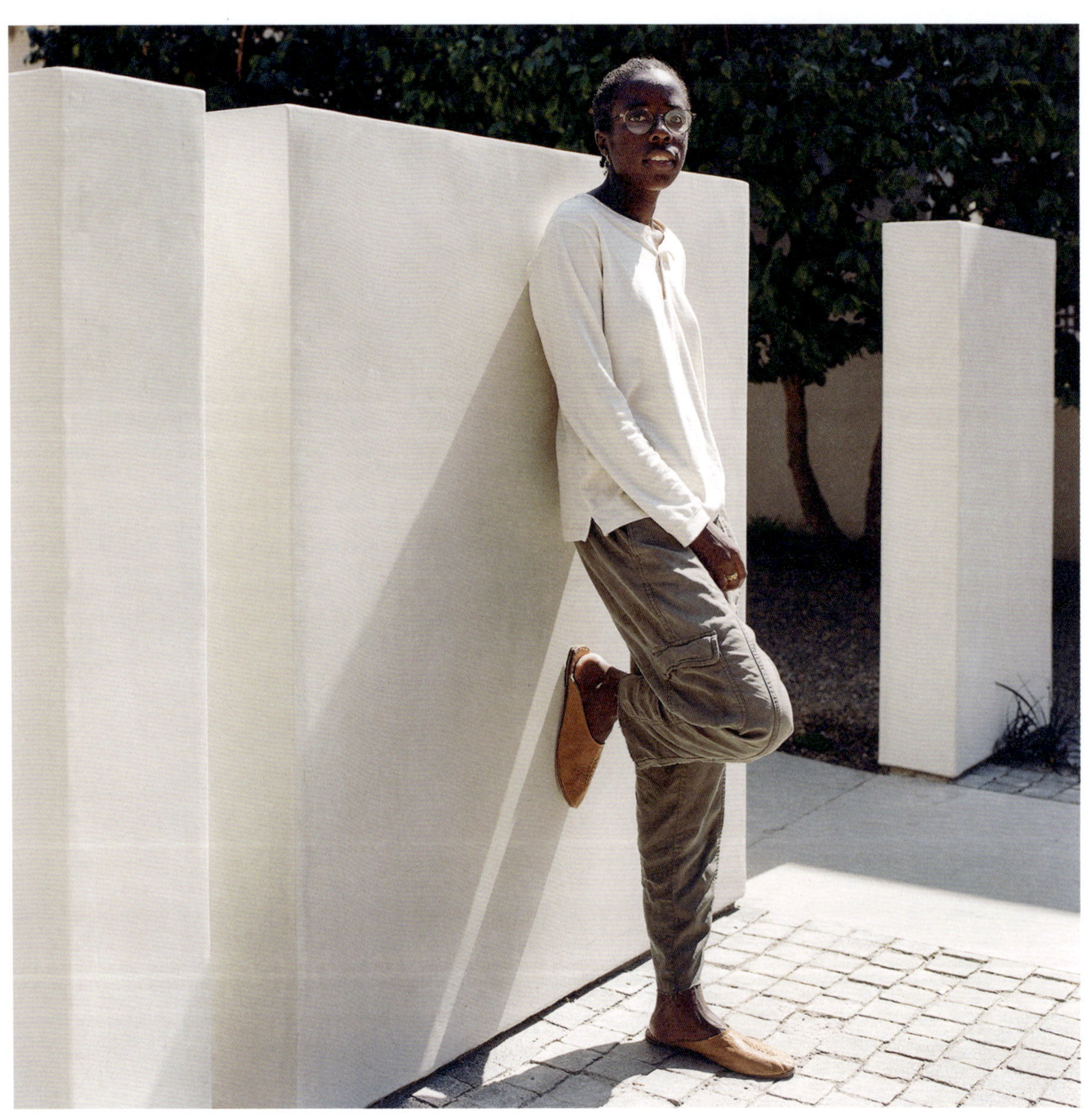

Aurora Maxwell

I feel free whenever
and wherever
Spaciousness exists.
When there is slowness.
when there is quiet.
where there is humor.

Berkeley, California · September 2022

I feel free when I'm part of a symbiotic relationship on this planet

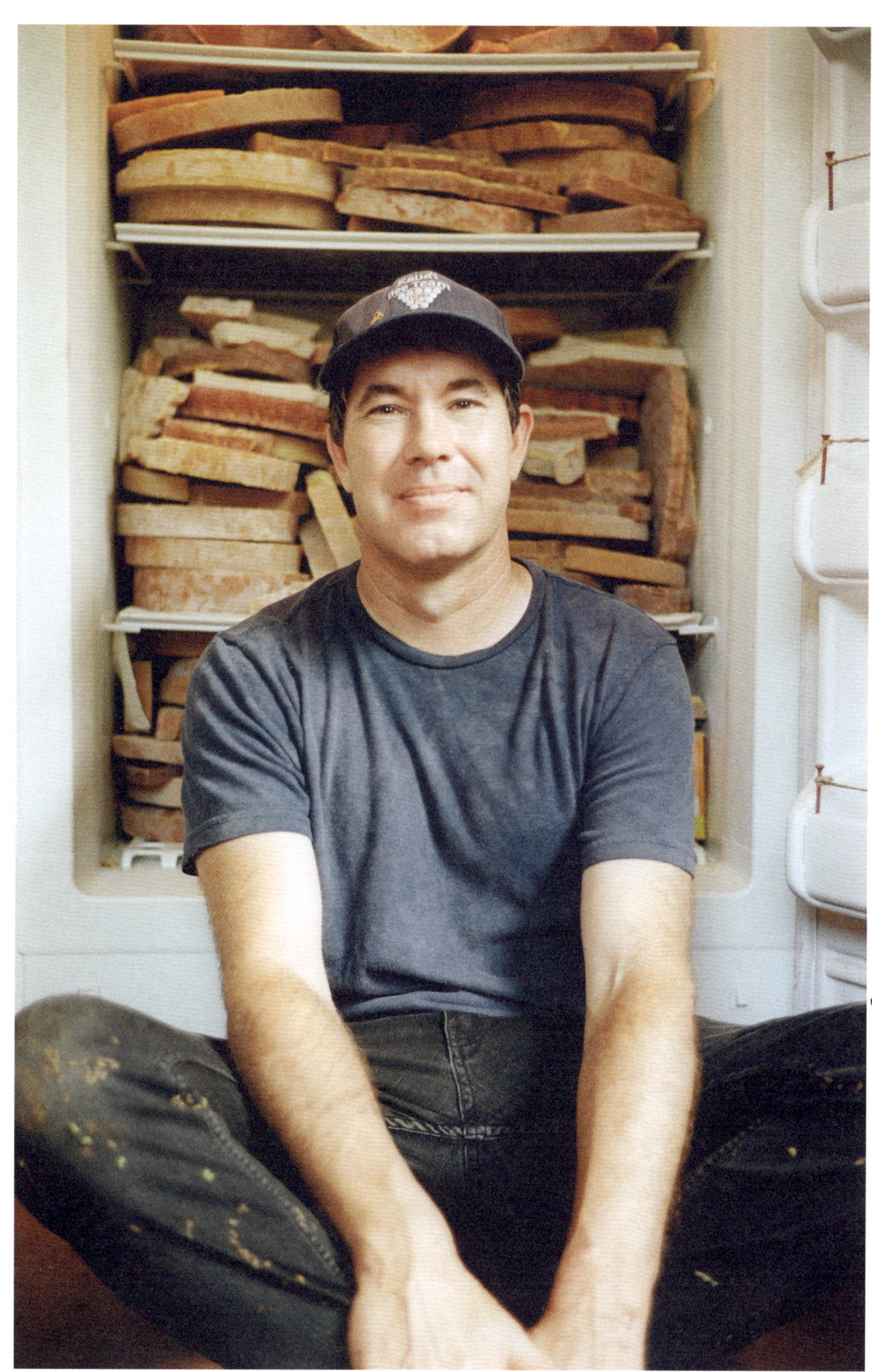

Ryan Tourstein

Libertad es sentirse libre de algo malo

Cuando uno se siente atrapado en algo y no puede

superarlo, eso es muy preocupante. Pero uno tiene que

superarlo. La verdadera libertad, es llevarse bien con las personas.

Santiago Beltran

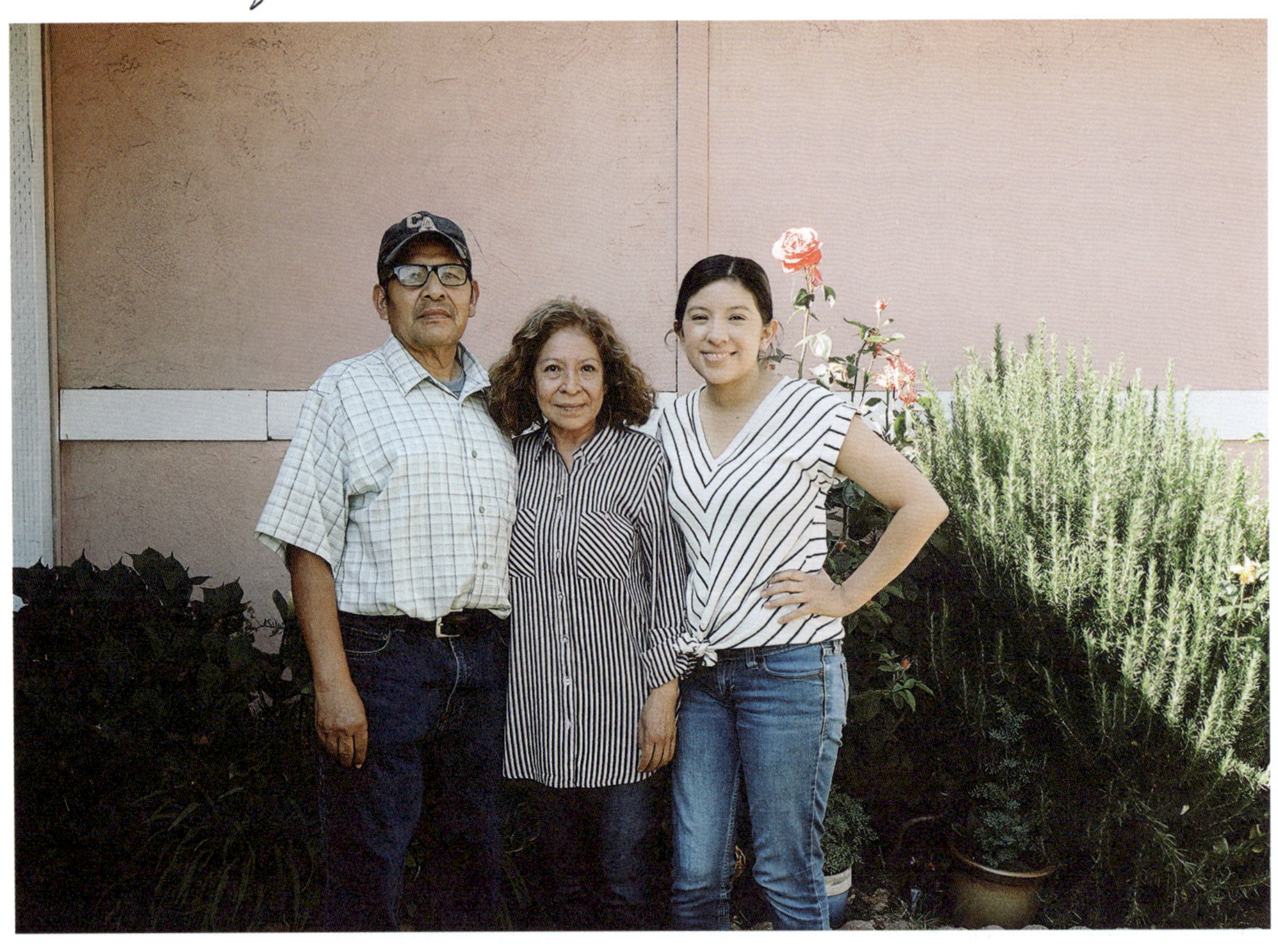

Libertad Para mi es Tratar de vivir la vida en Paz
a Pesar de las dificultades que la lamísma vida Trae.
no dejarse llevar Por emociones negativas.
vivir en armonia unos con oTros

Dominga Meleludr

Freedom to me means not feeling restrained to anything
that does not make you happy. Having the ability to keep
reinventing yourself as a person. Also having no limits
and knowing that you accomplish anything you set your mind
to.

- Lily Beltran.

I AM FREE
I AM FREE
I AM FREE
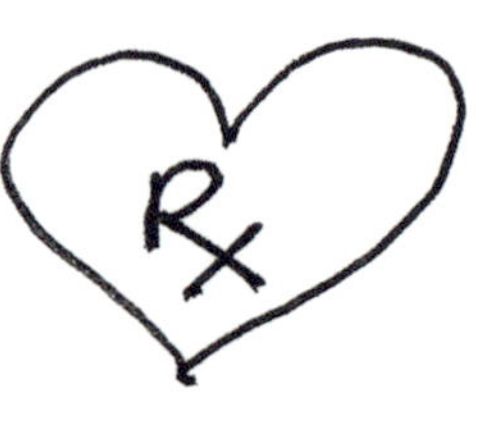
THE TRUTH SHALL SET YOU FREE.
I AM THE TRUTH, THEREFORE
I AM FREE.
FREEEEEEEEDOM!!

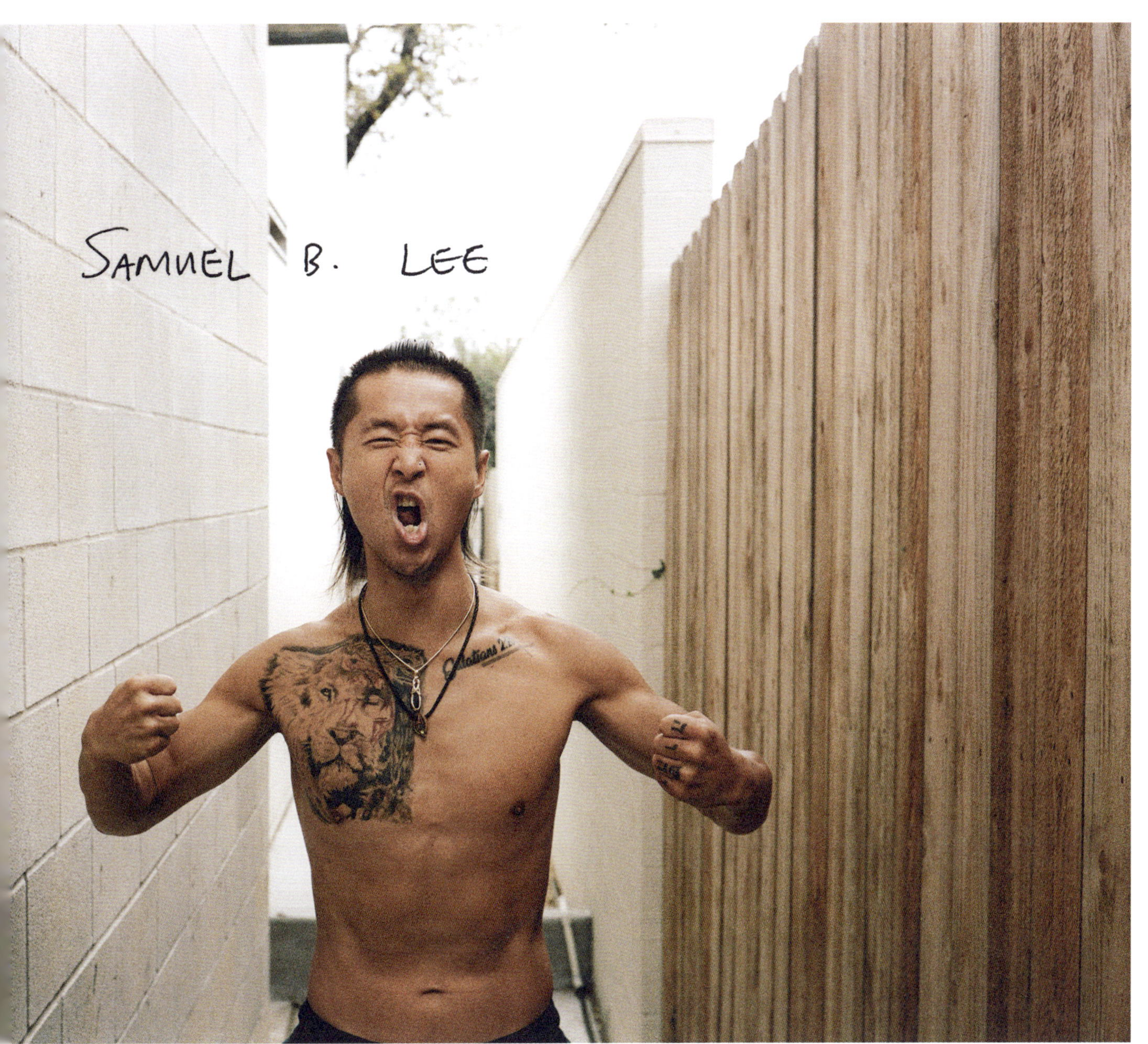

Austin, Texas · April 2022

I feel very free when
in the garden around
the flowers and
birds and beautiful
clouds above in
the sky.

Grandmother
amie

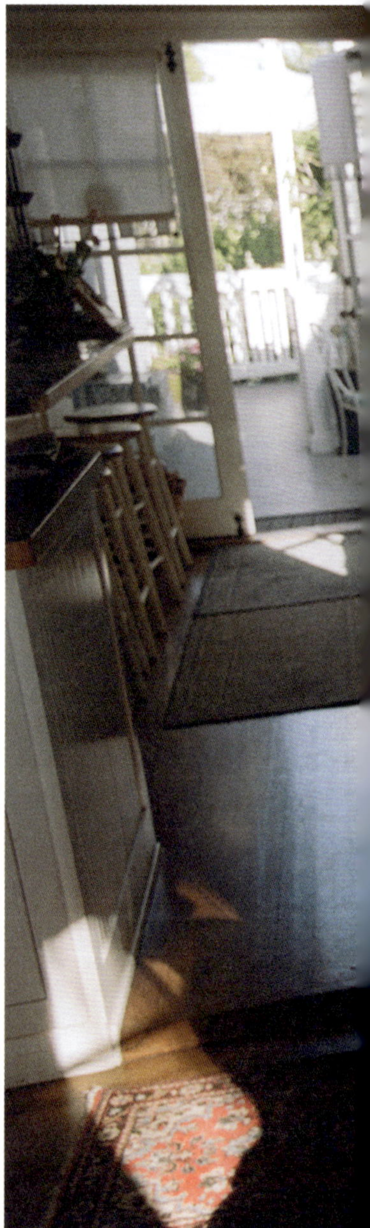

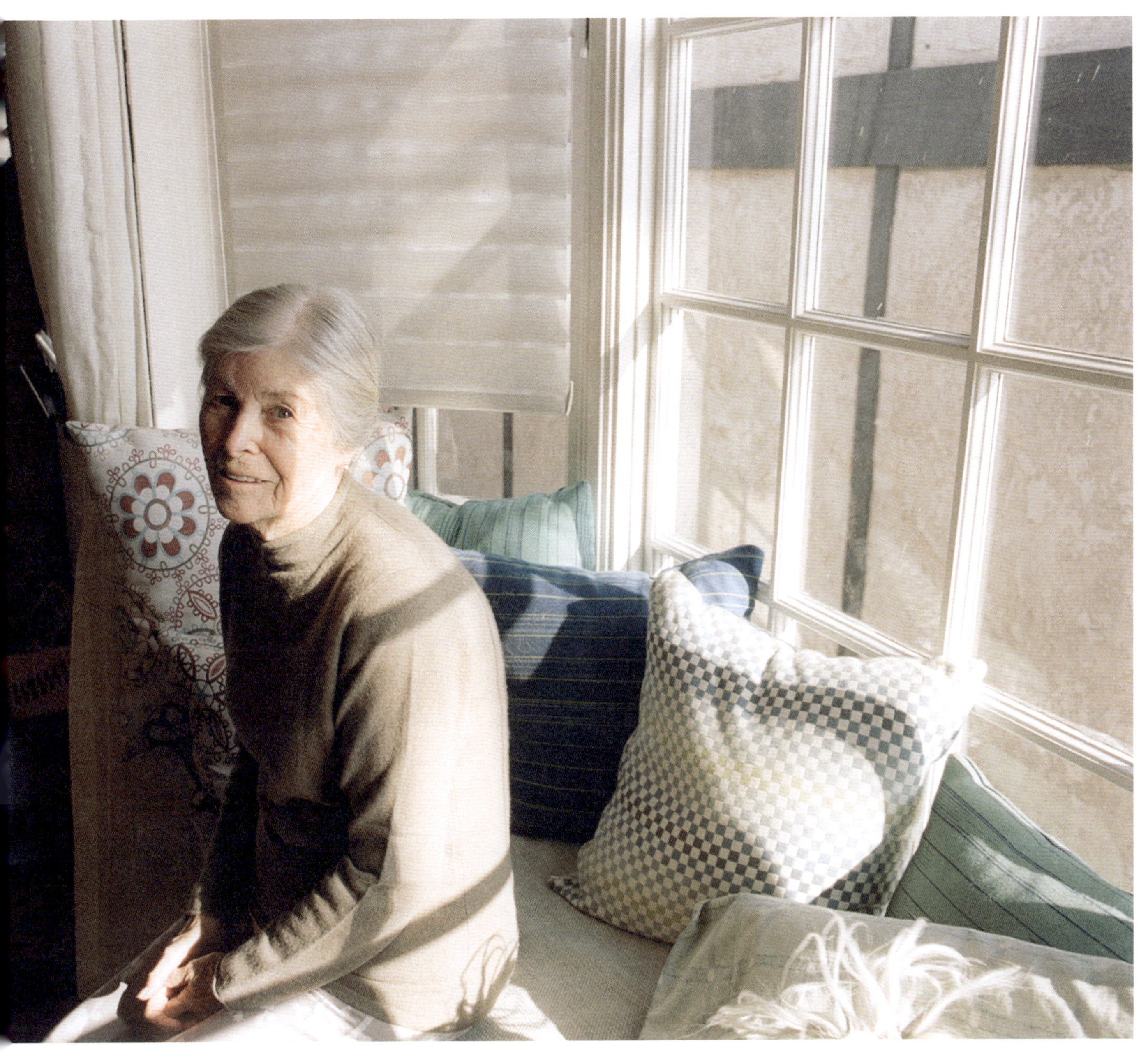

I feel free
when I am
operating The
F/V Falcon
on Cook Inlet
Alaska !
&
I Also feel Free
on The open Road
To Alaska

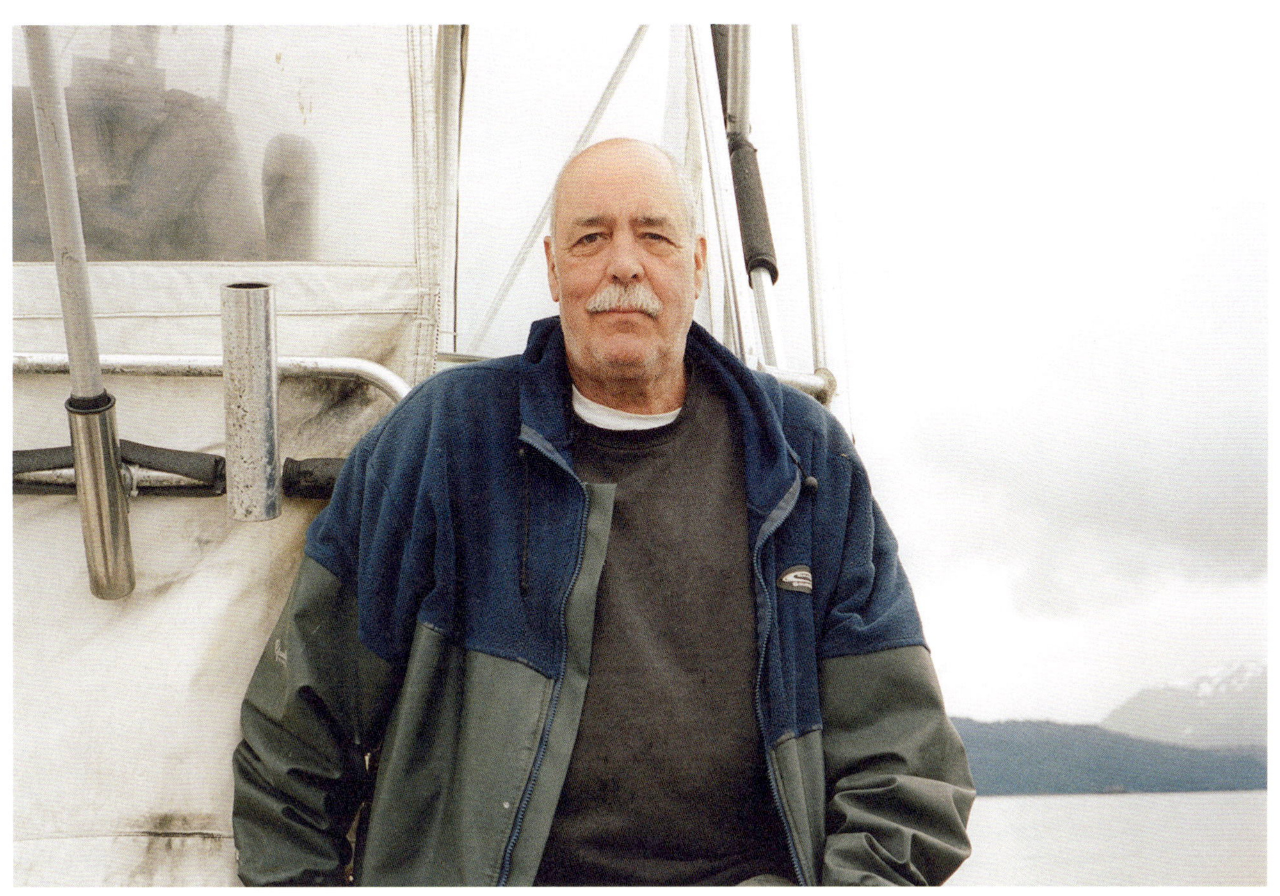

Homer, Alaska · June 2021

Saye - I Feel Free when I am playing, drawing, biking, Fishing, dancing
Climing

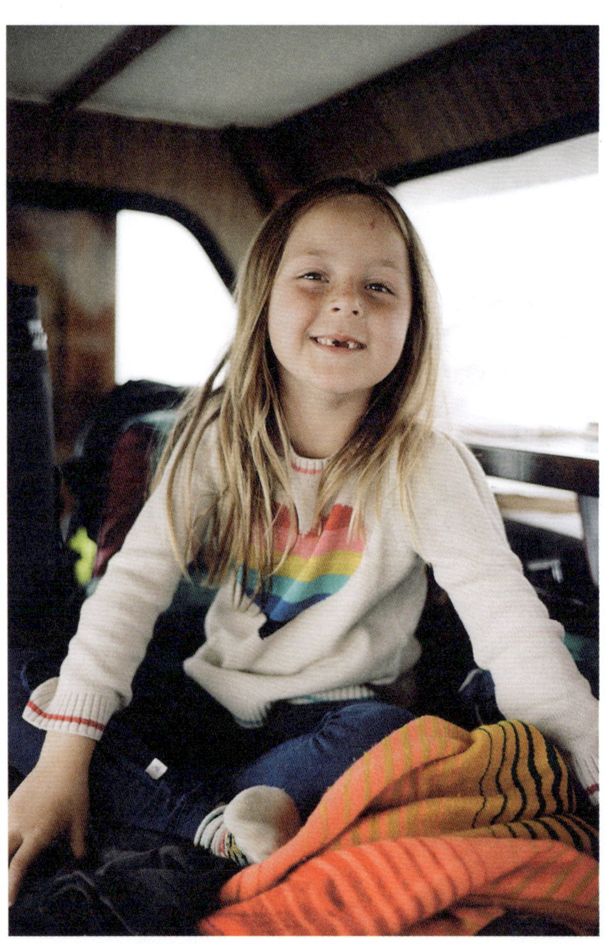

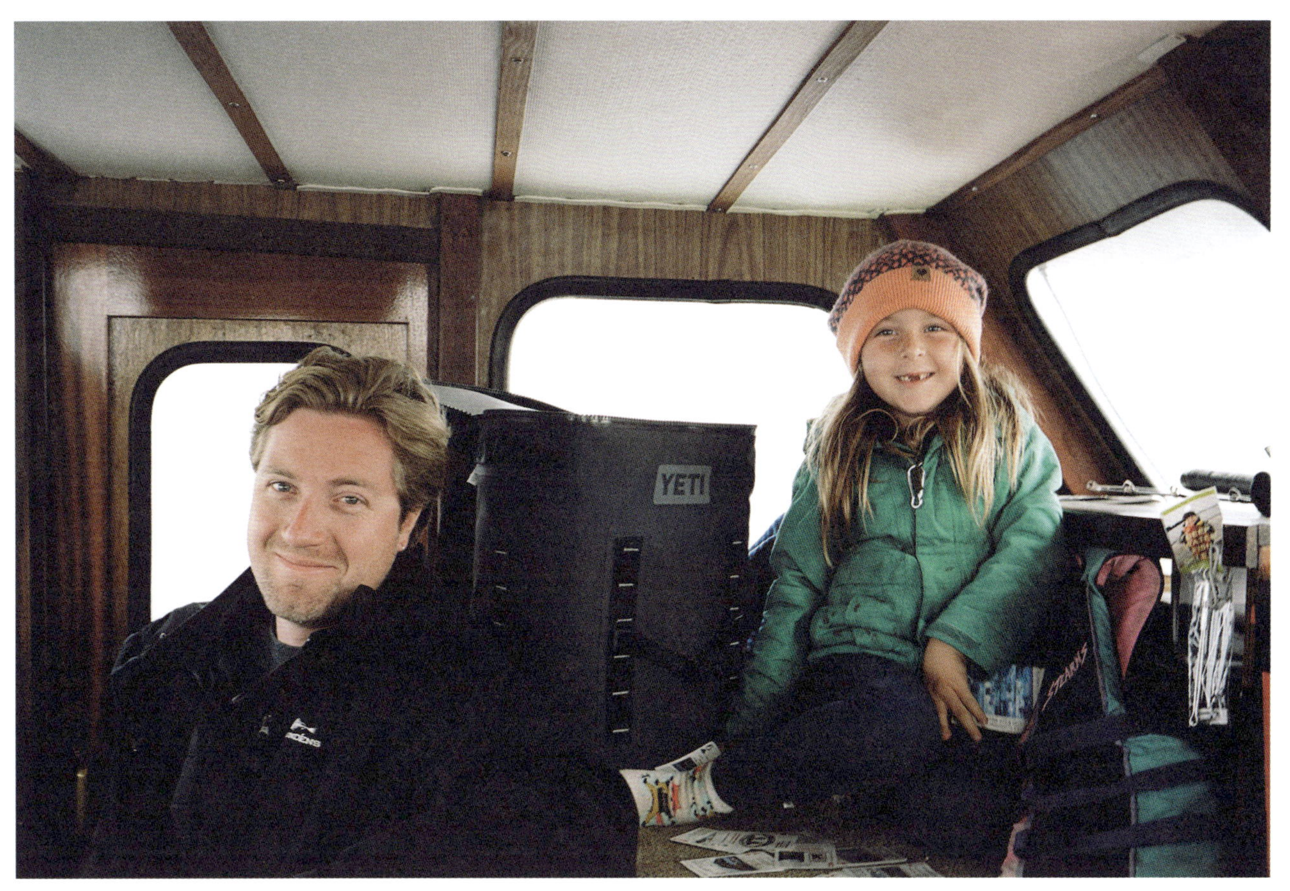

I Feel Free when enjoying
the out doors with Family & Friends
Cooking, camping, Fishing, Hiking, biking,
Working outside with my hands and
helping people Learn

                    Avery

When I'm traveling alone or
in a challenging situation and
I find a beautiful and quiet spot
where I can sit, close my eyes,
and feel the wind on my face.

Chelsea Schmitt

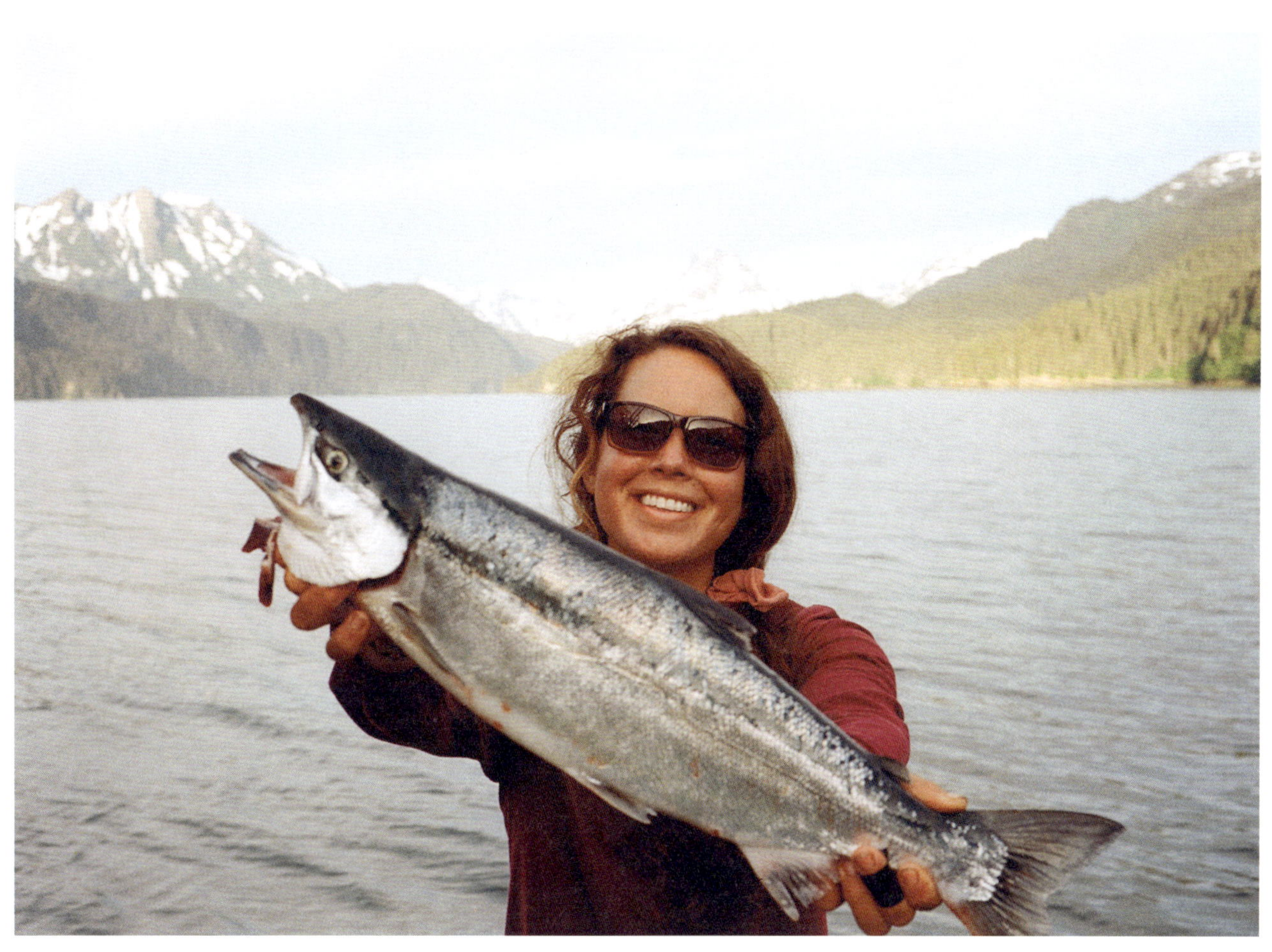

Homer, Alaska · June 2021

When I am creating
something beautiful for
Others to enjoy.

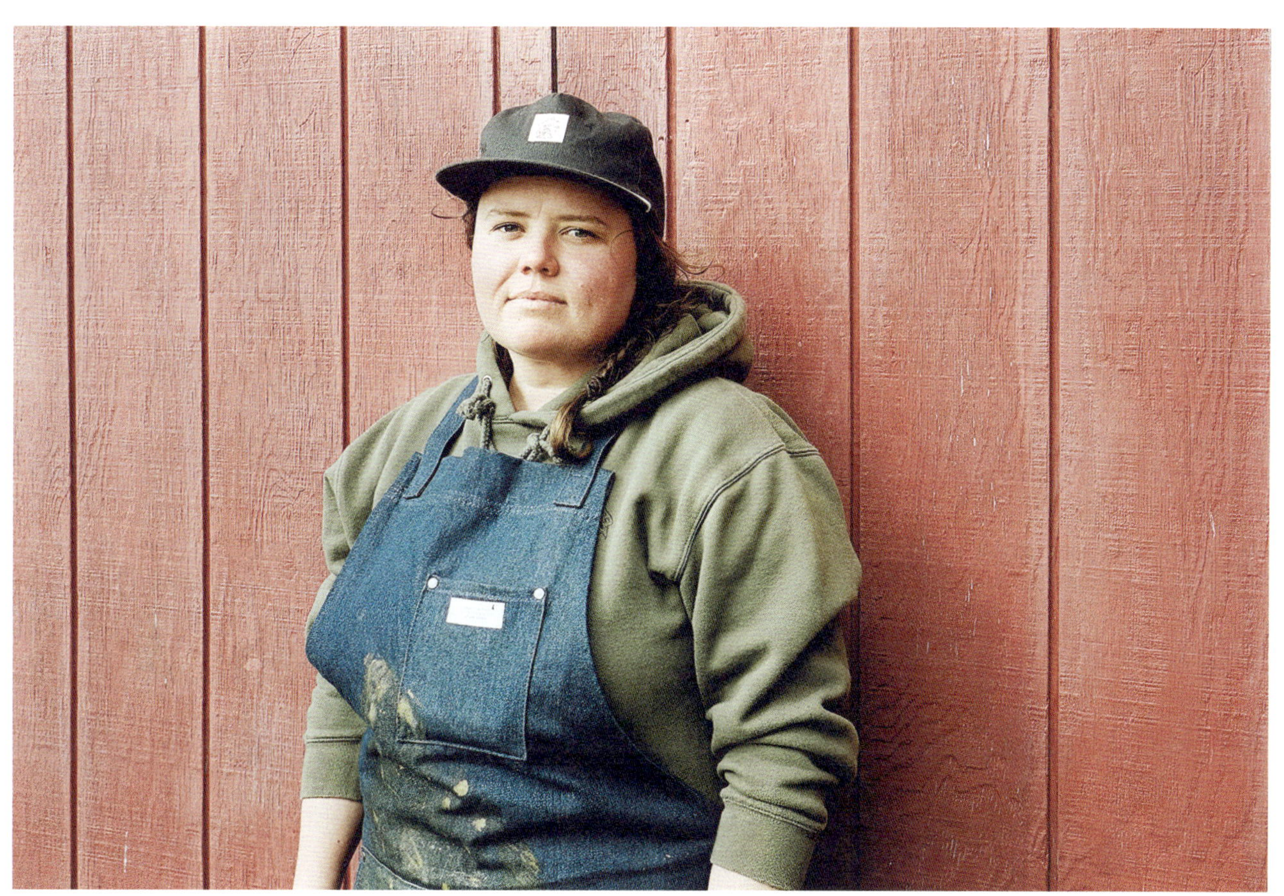

Lindsey Kenton

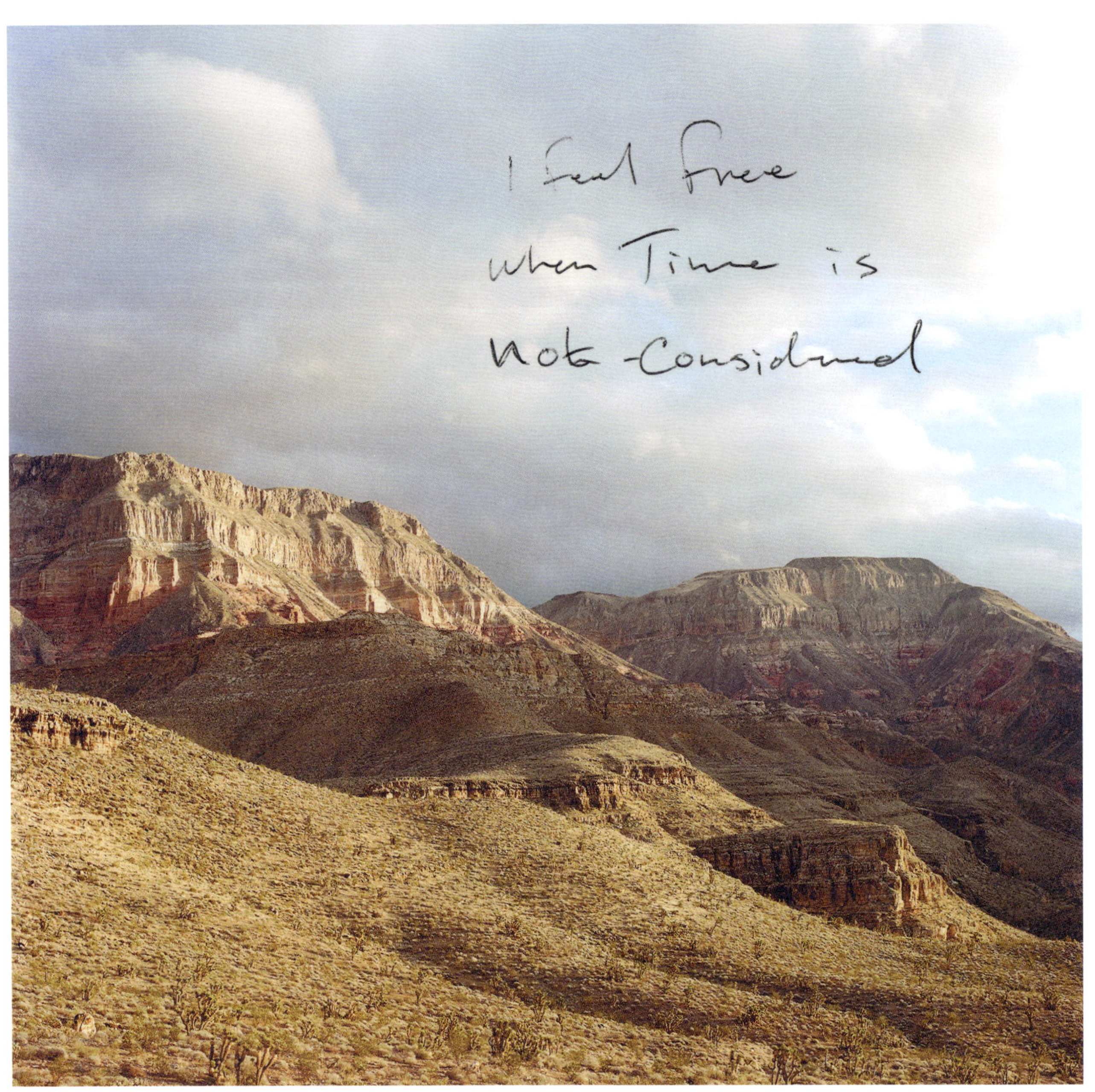
I feel free
when Time is
not considered

when I stare at the
sea

Freedom to me is accepting you cannot learn or experience everything, but also knowing you can still choose.

I think it's easiest to feel this when meeting new people. Every interaction is a new chance to learn, to be reminded of your ignorance, and to choose to learn more anyways.

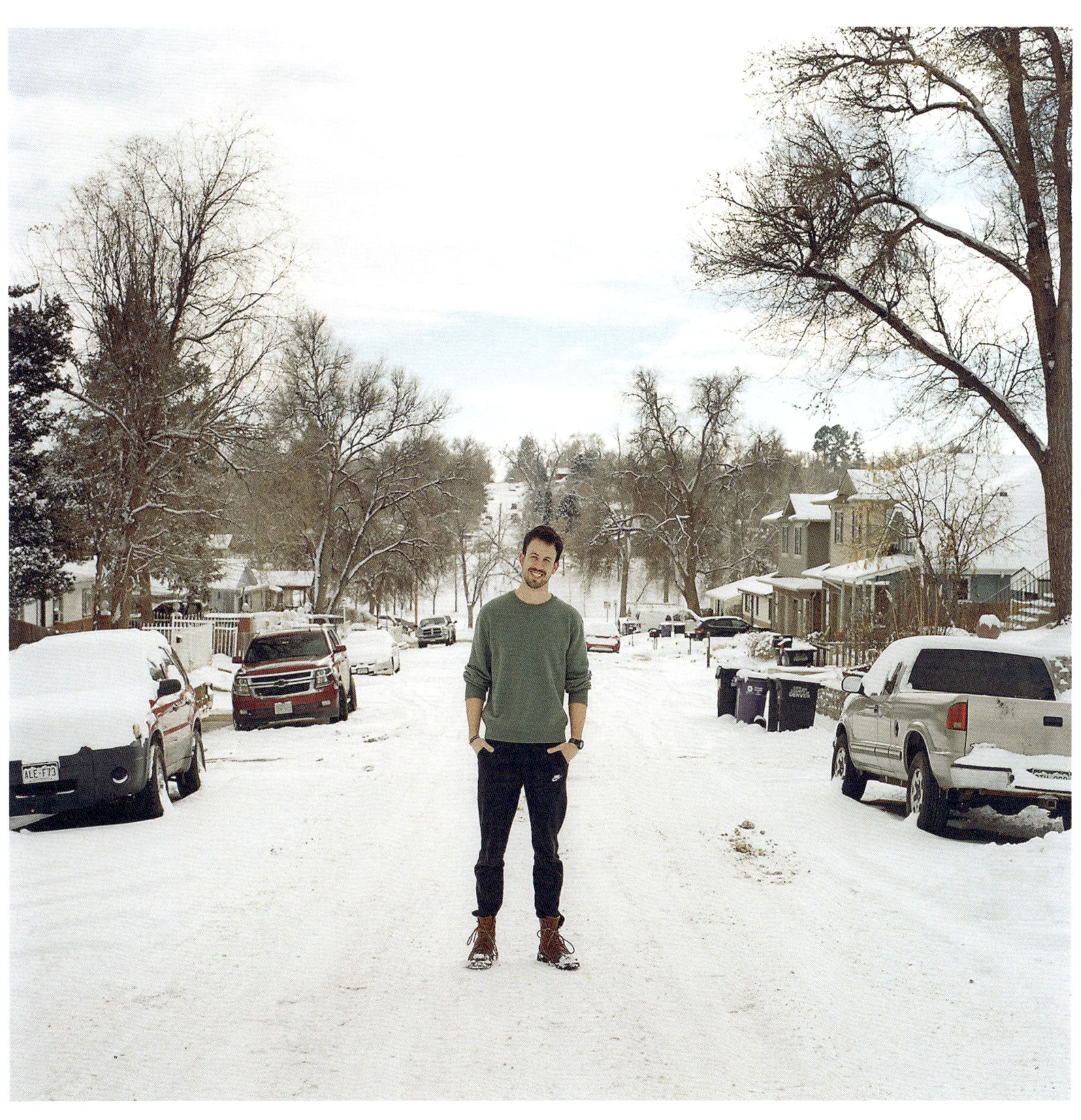

Doug Fair

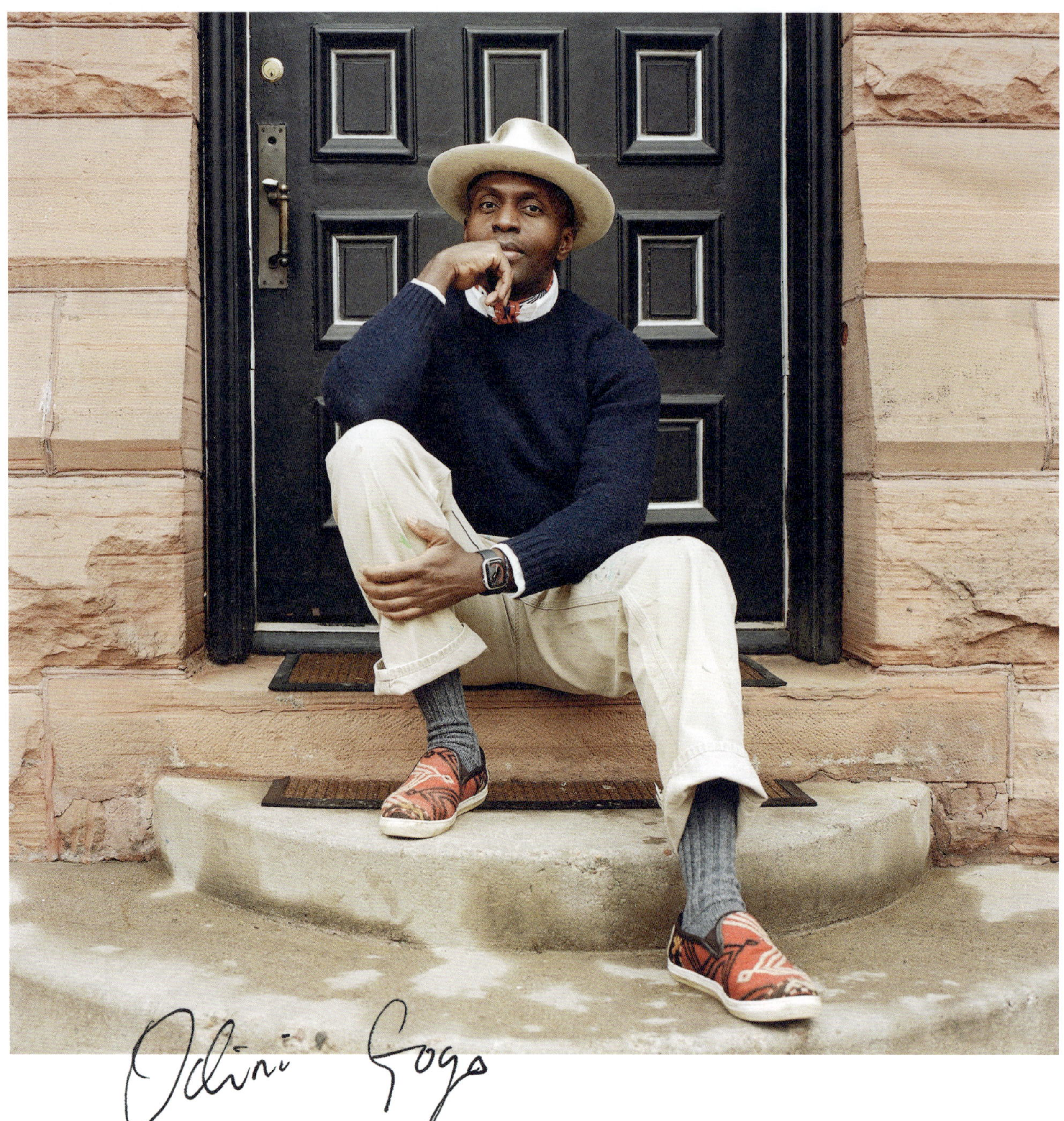

Freedom is when I am all of myself,
with the person (or people) I Love
and in a place where my
Soul is at Peace.

Aspen, Colorado · January 2022

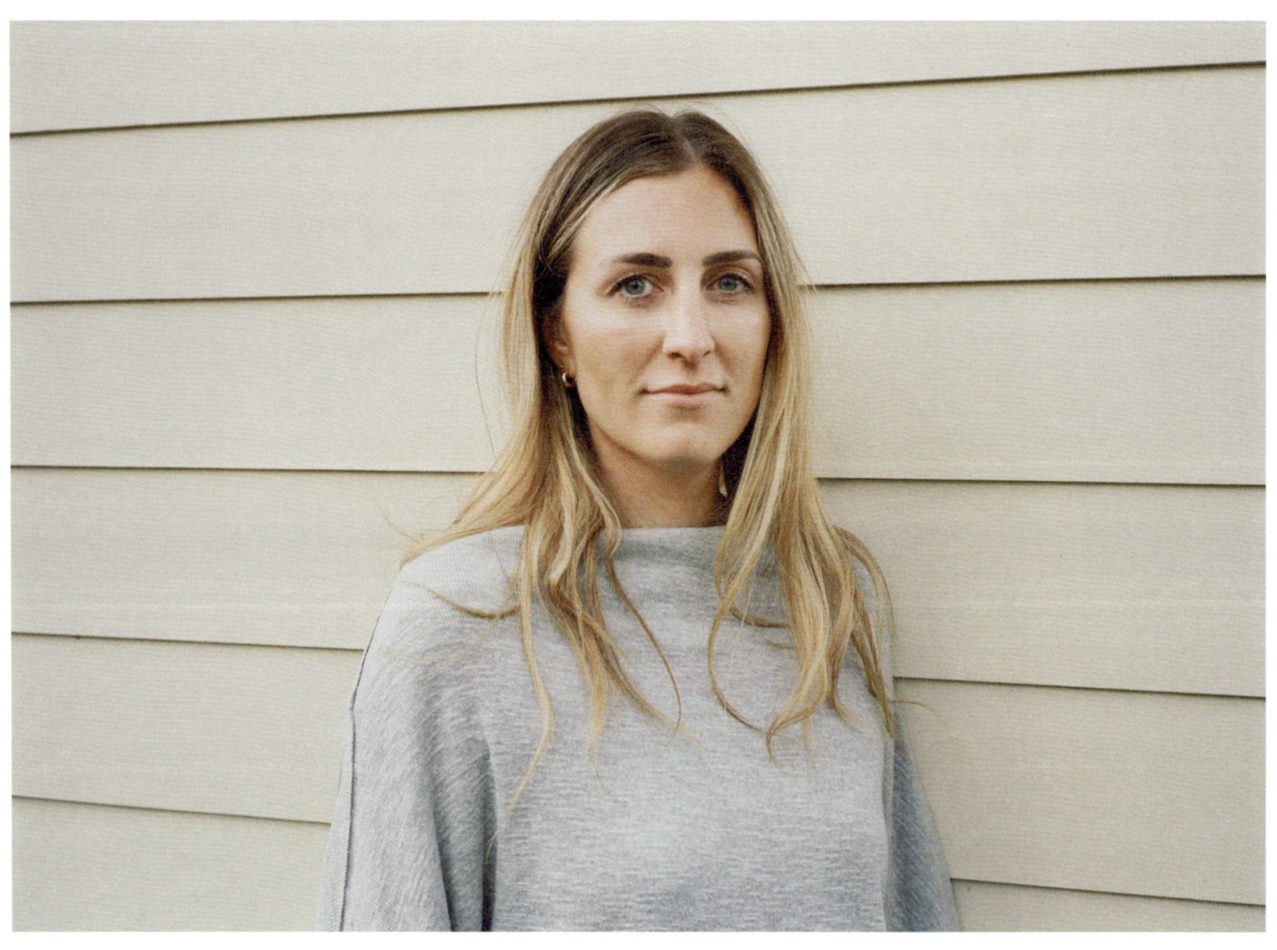

Anna Wilson

I feel free when I am focused on the present. I have ADD. Freedom to me means the rare moments when I engage in an activity where the distractions melt away. I have the freedom to focus & not worry about anything else around me. This is why I love skiing — it's the time I'm most focused on the present moment. The freedom to think, feel, and engage with the world in exactly the way I feel in that moment.

Denver, Colorado · December 2021

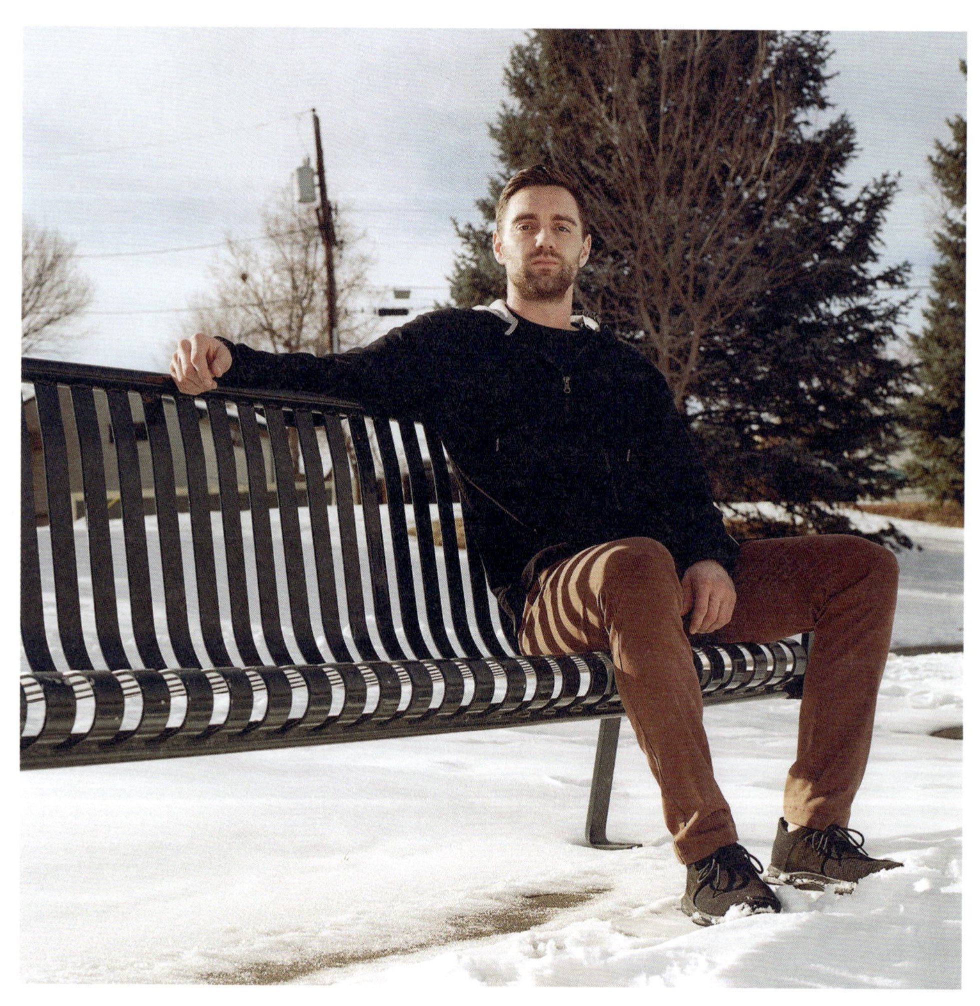

Sam Moore

I feel free when
I trust myself to
have my own back.

Denver, Colorado · January 2022

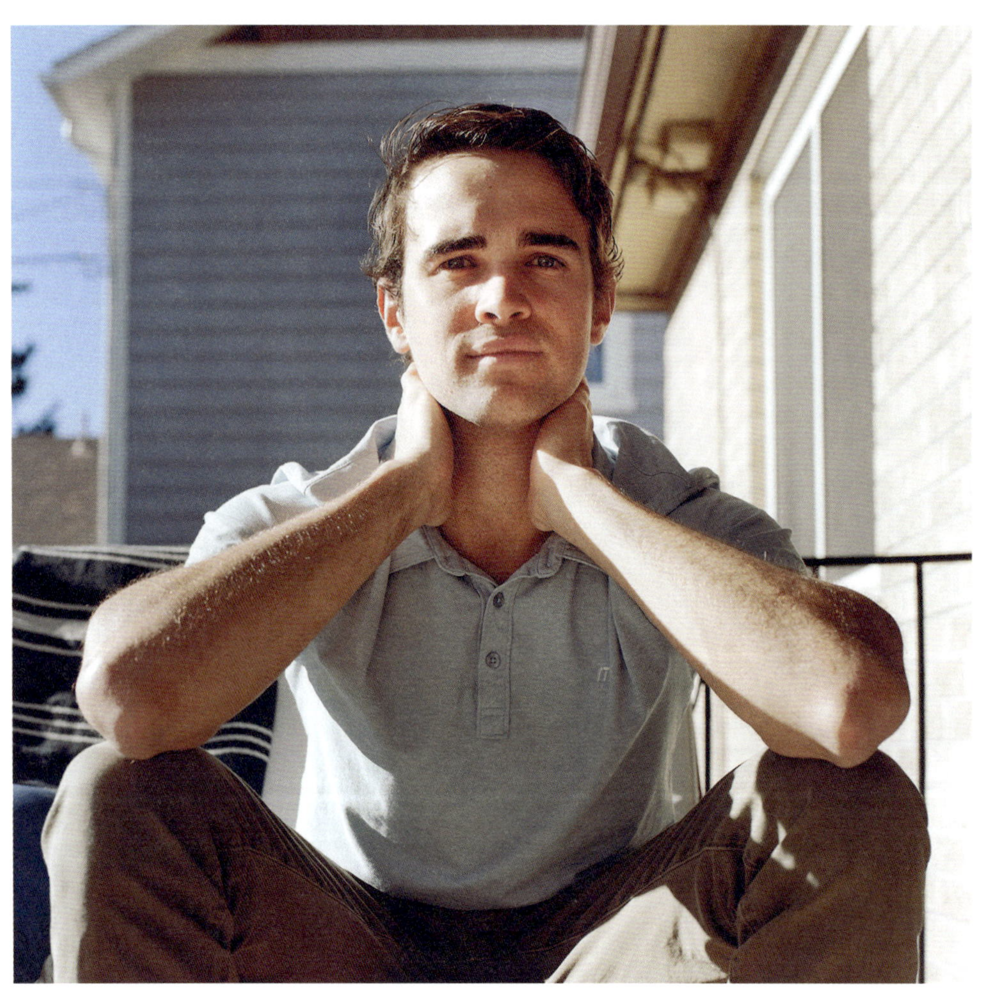

Jack Pillsbury

I'm very fortunate to live a life that gives me many opportunities to "feel free". Embarking on an epic road trip makes me feel ~~free~~. Chasing friends down a ski hill, dirt biking through the high desert, sipping whiskey by the fire on a backpacking trip with no cell service makes me feel free. Sharing a home cooked meal and glass of wine with Taryn makes me feel free.

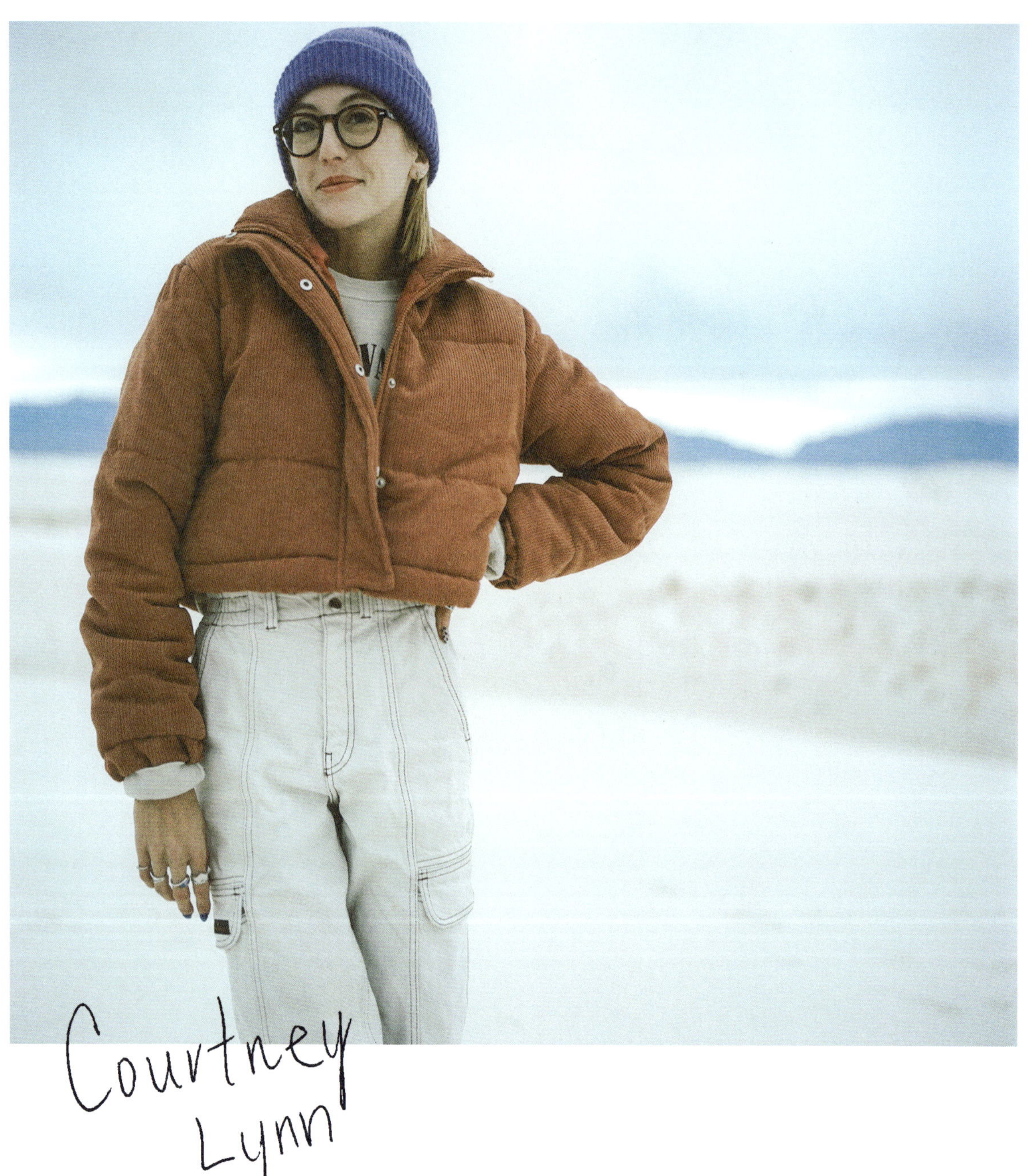
Courtney
Lynn

freedom exists within
presence + being present.
Moments of silence where
quiet and loud intertwine.
When light and dark
    Meet, but don't touch.
Space + togetherness
    all in one.

Chase your light
    Stay Open
        xoxo

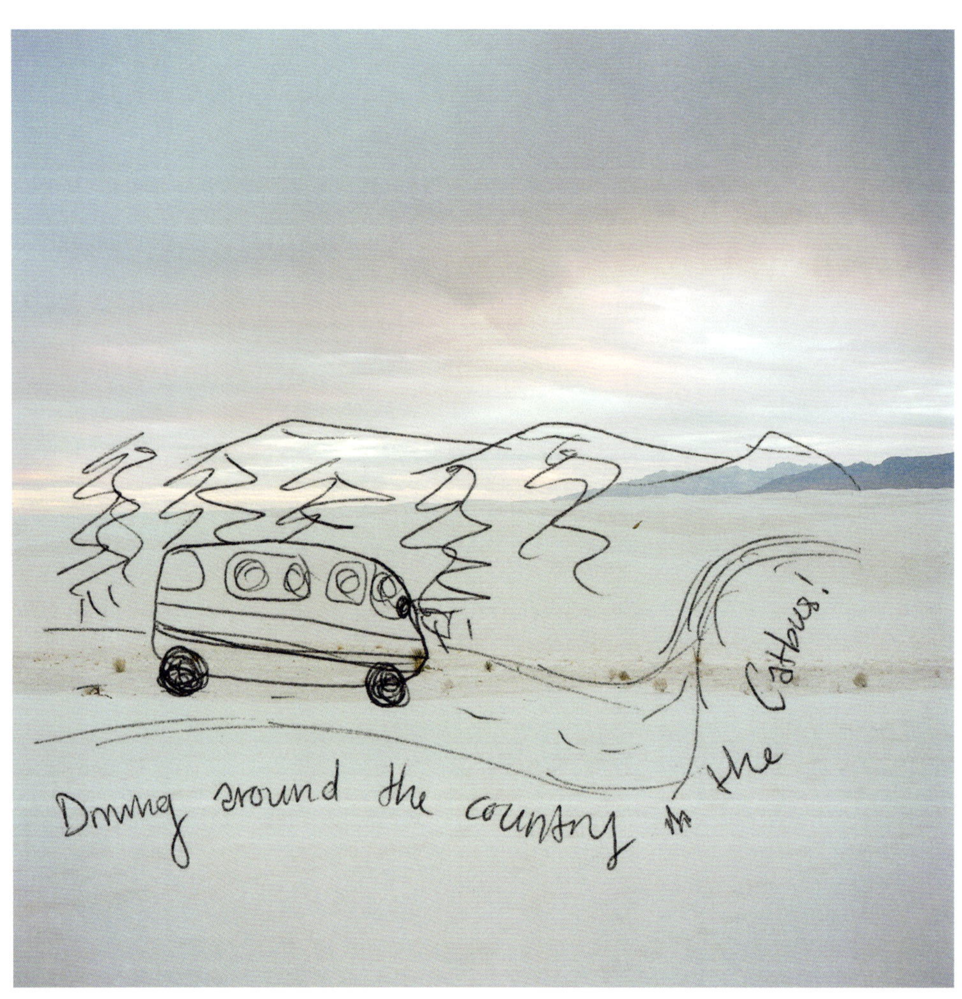

Driving around the country in the Catbus!

SWIMMING

sky diving

I feeL Free when
I wake up!!!$

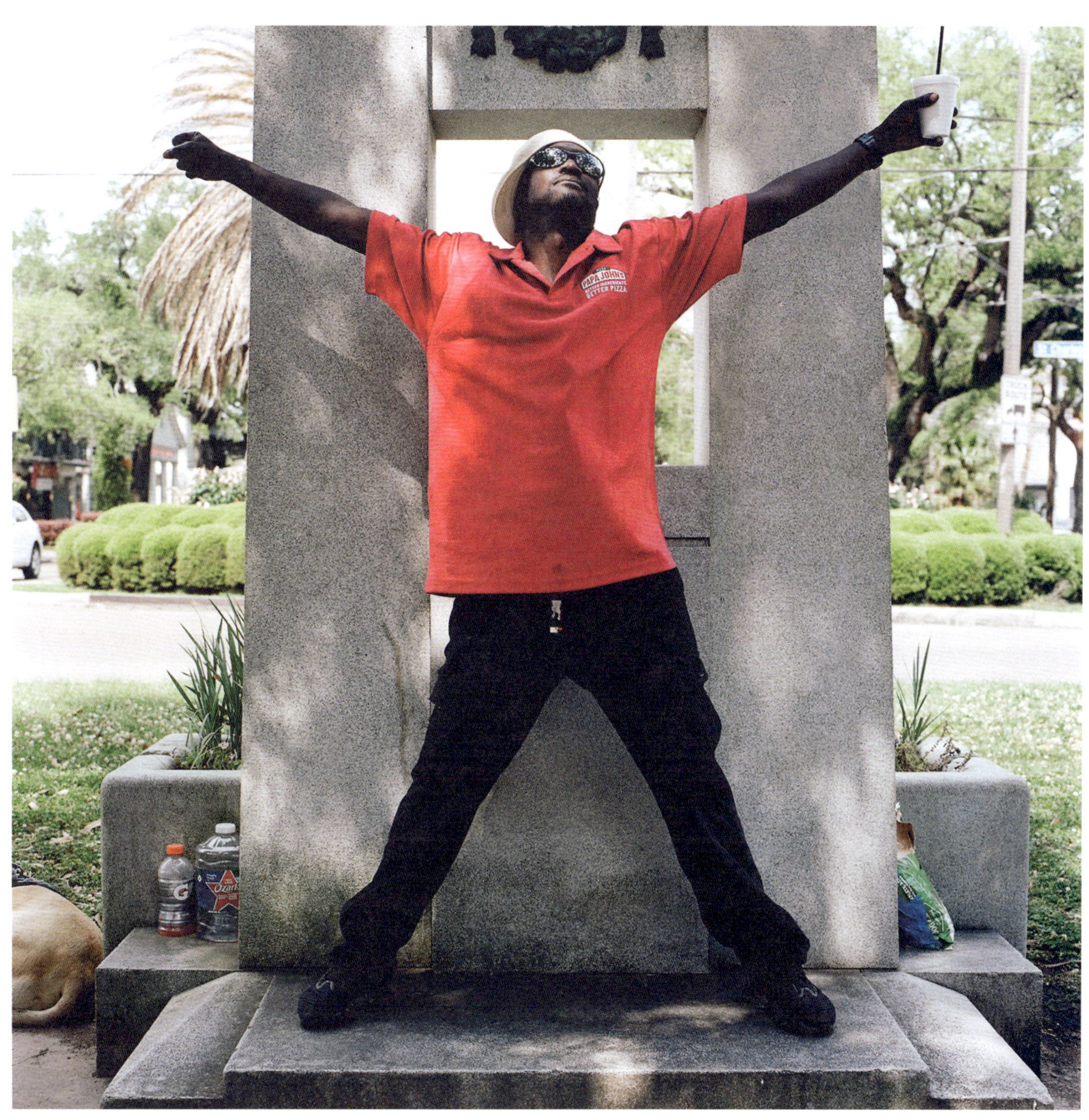

TRAVIS TAYLOR

When I wake up knowing I'm exactly where
I'm supposed to be. Doing the things I love
doing. Building community with the people I love
supporting — and who love supporting me.

I've spent many years chasing dreams that
weren't mine. Living in places that weren't home.
Bailing water out of sinking relationships.

Life has a way of trapping you I guess. Or
at least that's what we tell ourselves. It's
never too late to change course.

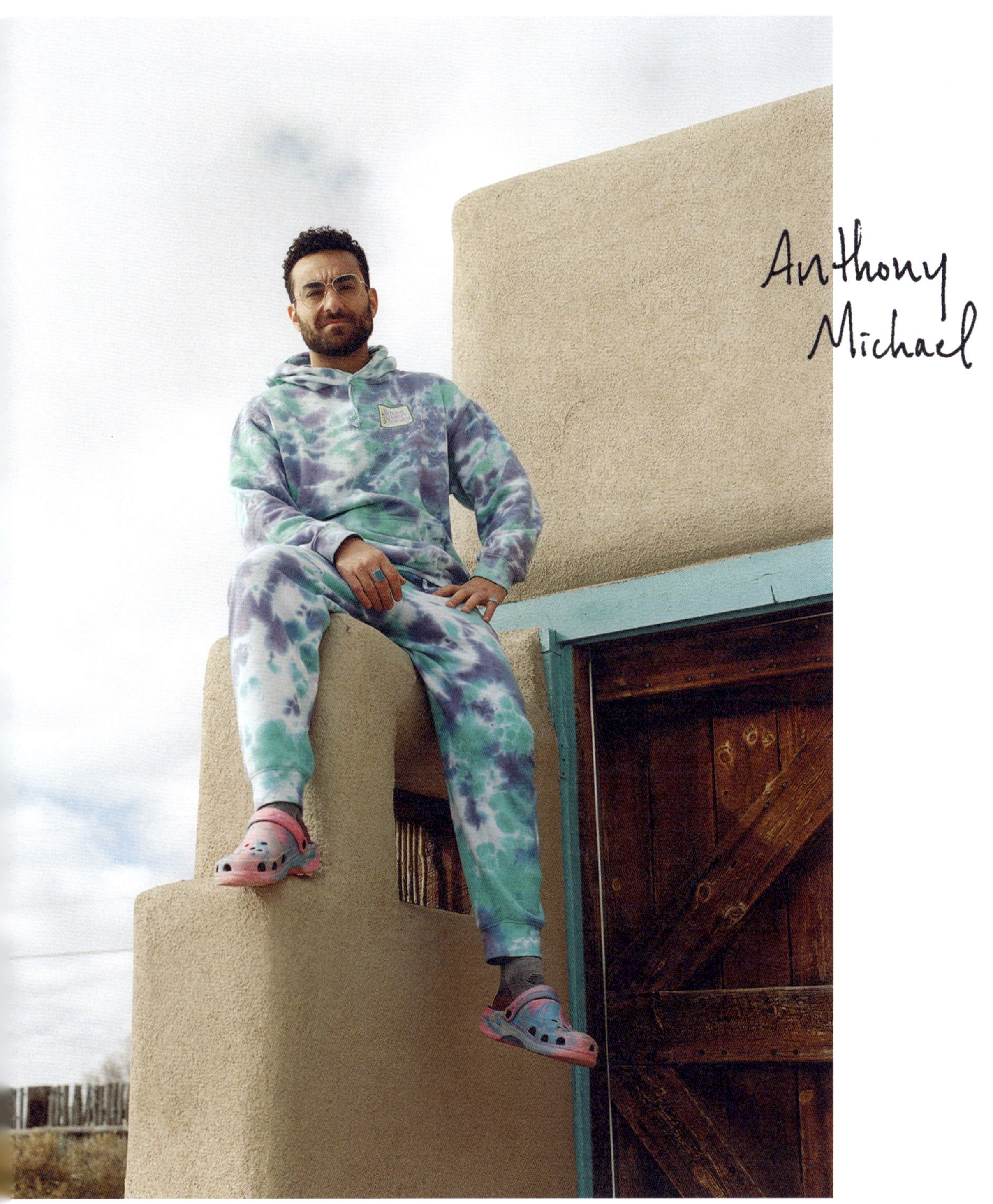

Taos, New Mexico · January 2022

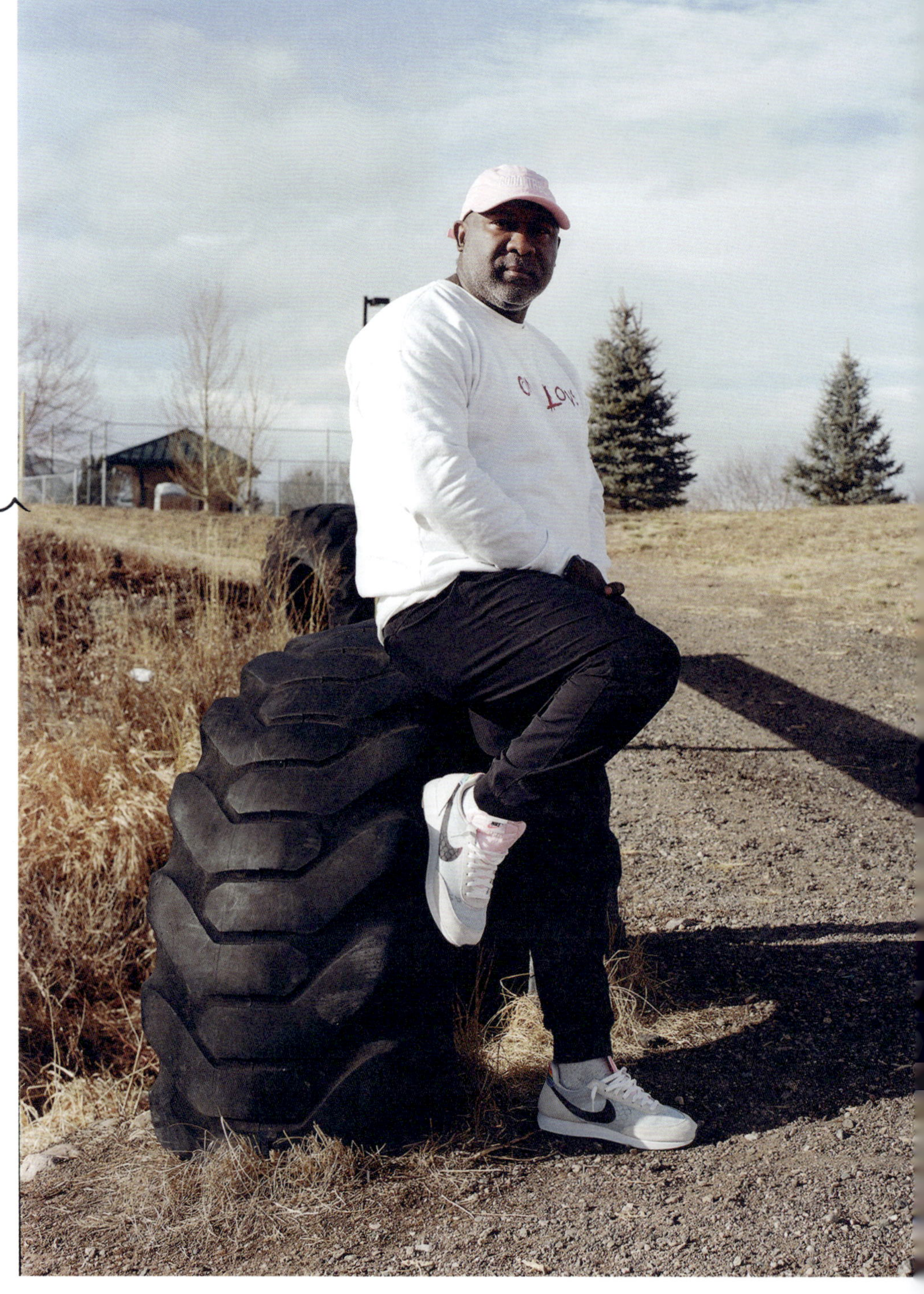

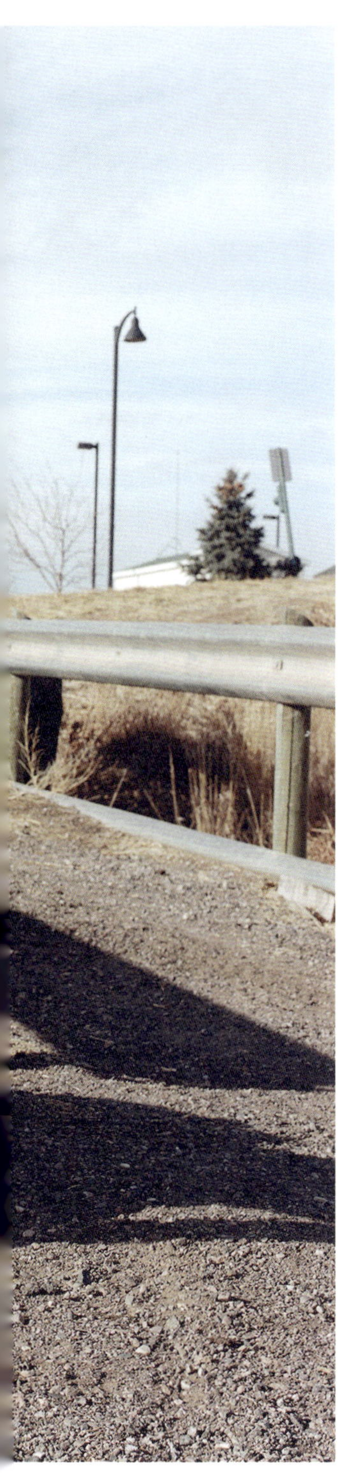

I feel most free when
I am putting my heart
& soul into people & ideas
that I love. ♡

Fort Collins, Colorado · December 2021

I feel free when I am in the position to assist my parents and siblings in times of financial need. It gives me much joy, inner peace and freedom to be that helping hand to my close and love ones.

I feel free when I am alone and cooking. That is where I have my ultimate freedom. It allows me to escape reality for the next hour or so and just focus on the food that I am making and being at peace with myself.

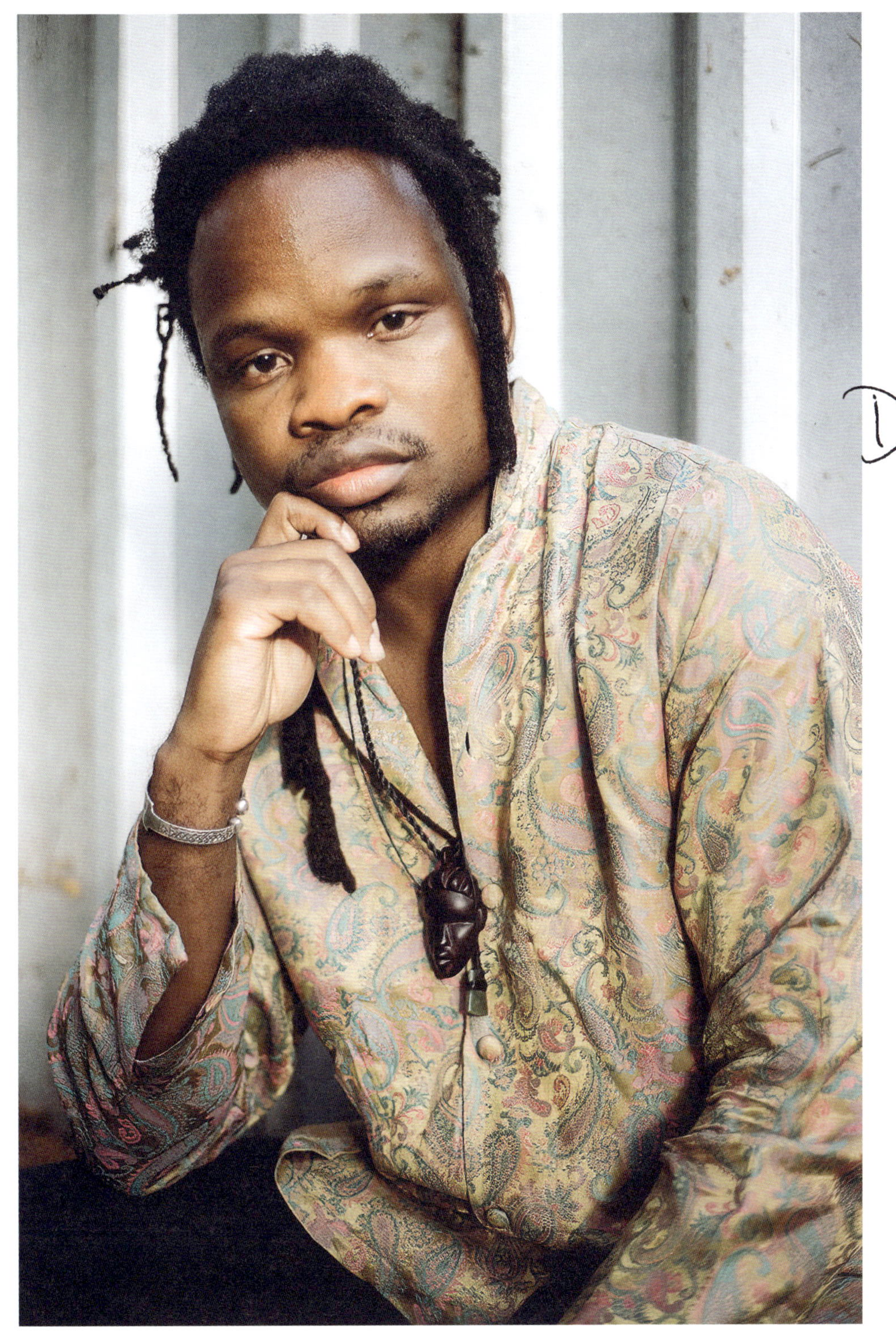Darlington
Martor

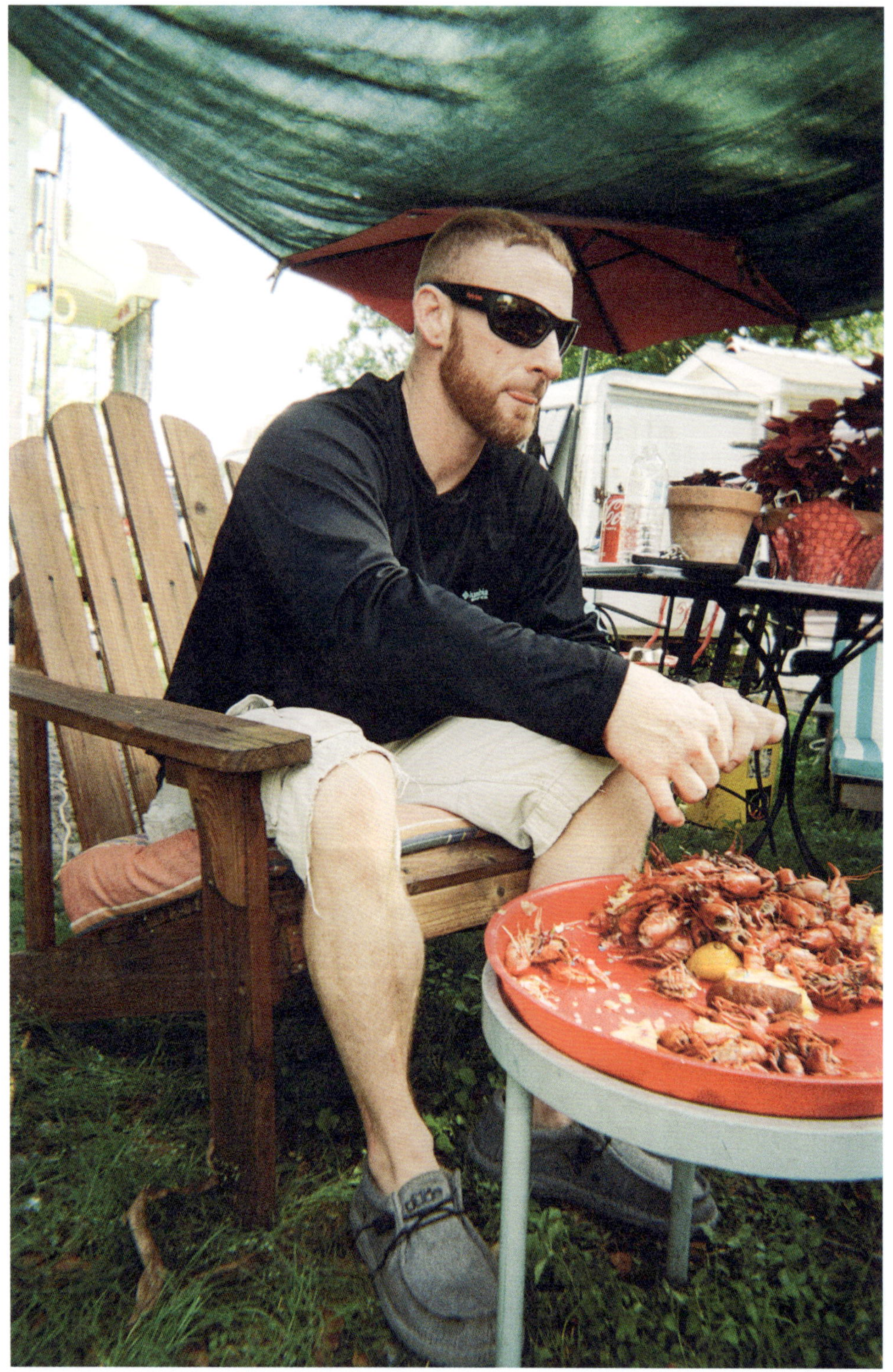

I feel most free when I'm <u>fishing</u>. In this case anything I'm doing for fun in the outdoors!

Luke Gautreau

"Luke Gautreaux"

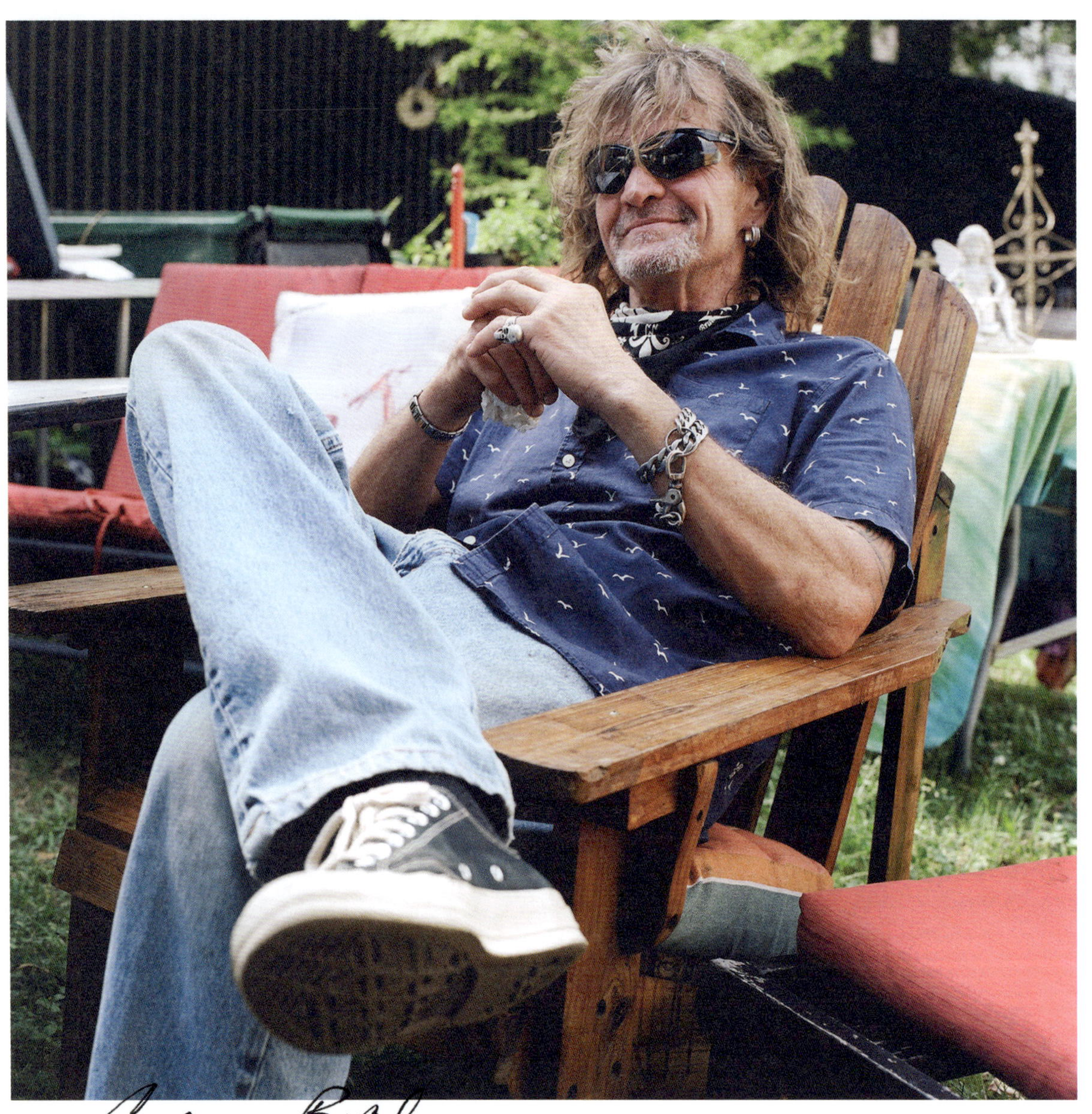

Greg Byrd
also know as
"gabby the Gabster"

freedom =
to me is Many
things or instances, circum
stances
The Cruest time for
Me is Standing in the
Rain or Looking Above

at the Stars and the
Night Moon, When your
Not allowed to view the
Stars the Moon, or Not
allowed to Stand in the
Rain your're Lost freedom
freedom, or Something you
Don't wanna Lose Greet
man

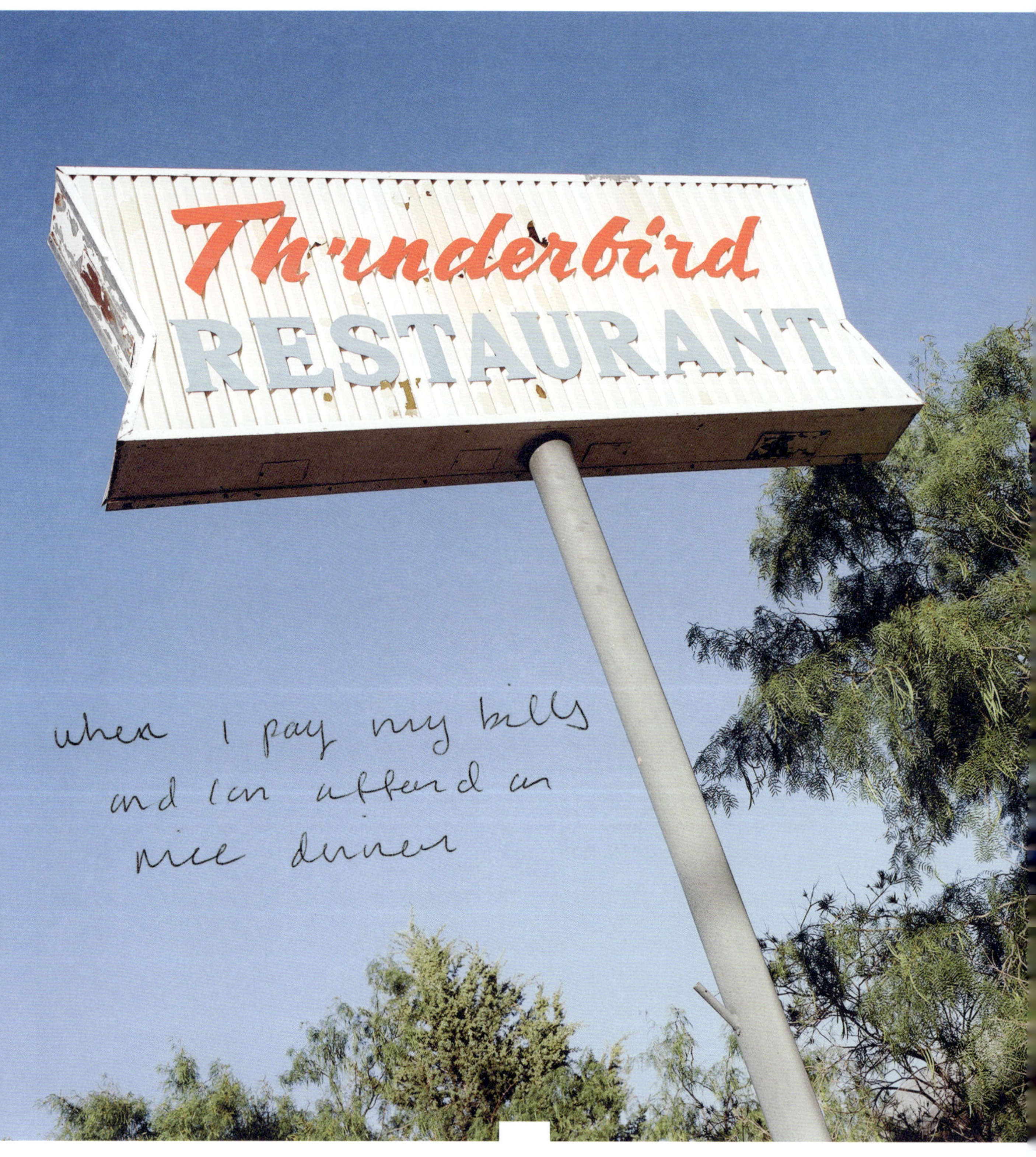
Thunderbird
RESTAURANT
when I pay my bills
and I can afford an
nice dinner

I ^(will) feel free when
when my parents
reach financial freedom♡

When I'm creating music.

Nívi Canela

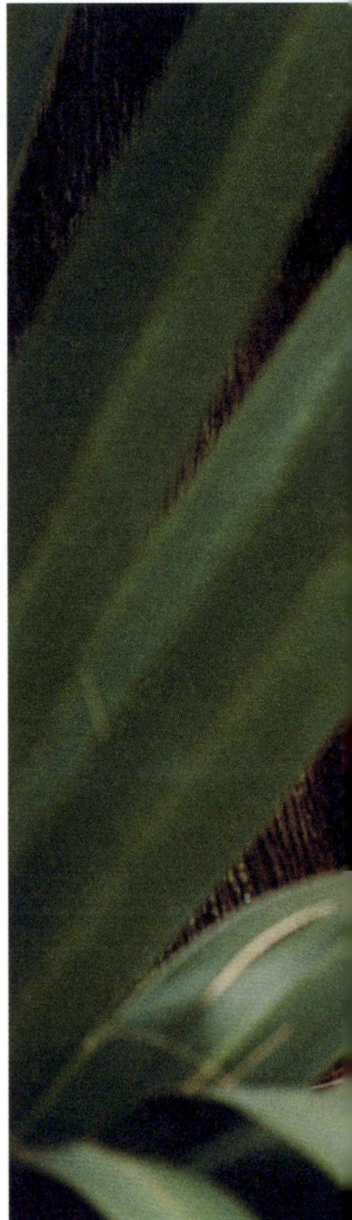

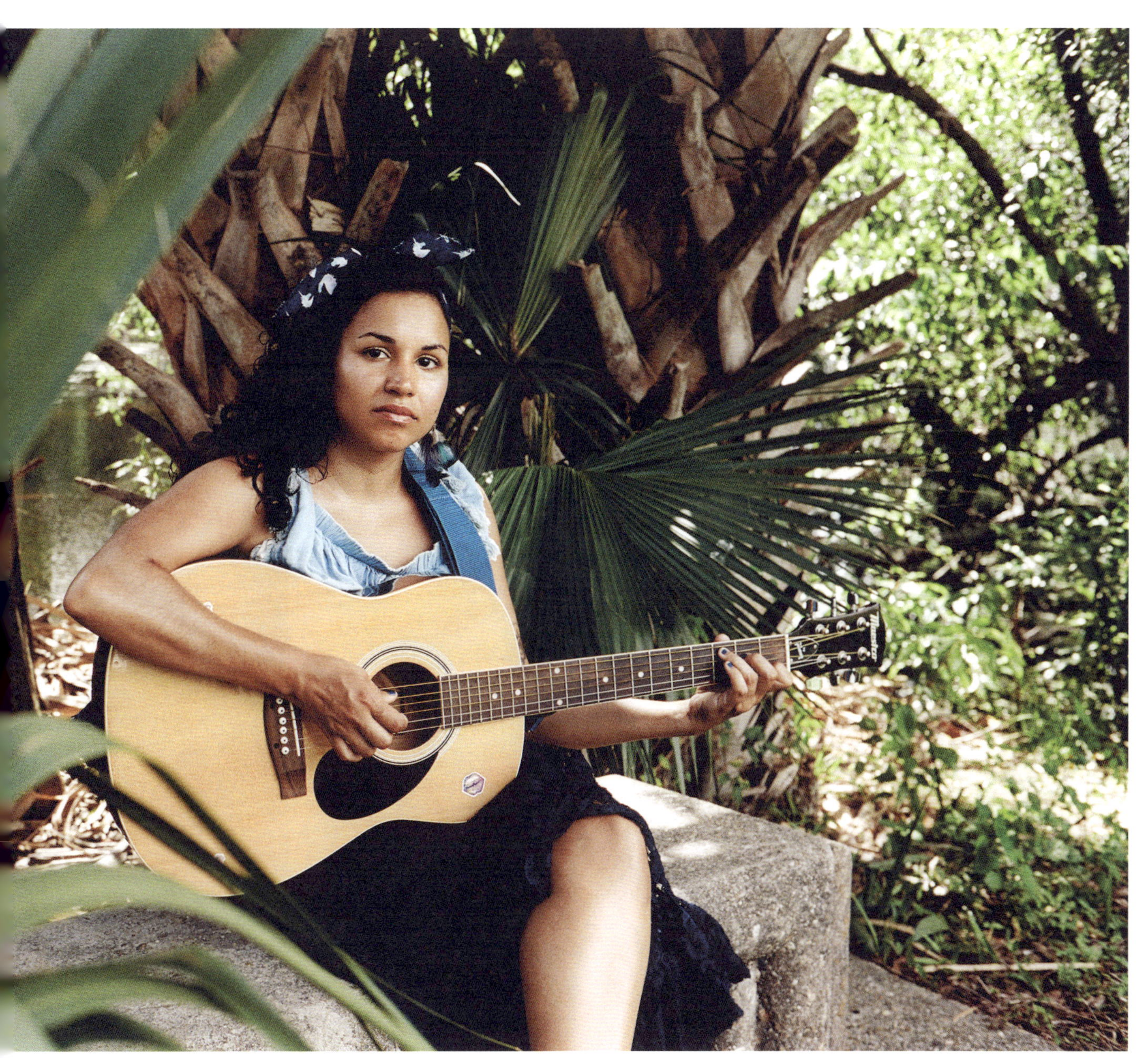

New Orleans, Louisiana · April 2022

Looking to the sky &
Playing my guitar !

playing out doors
day or night
energized by the
audiance,
pluged into
a 100 watt
marshall amp
on 11
—
Moving Air
+ 12 notes
onthescale

RED PRIEST
Love Over Gold

84

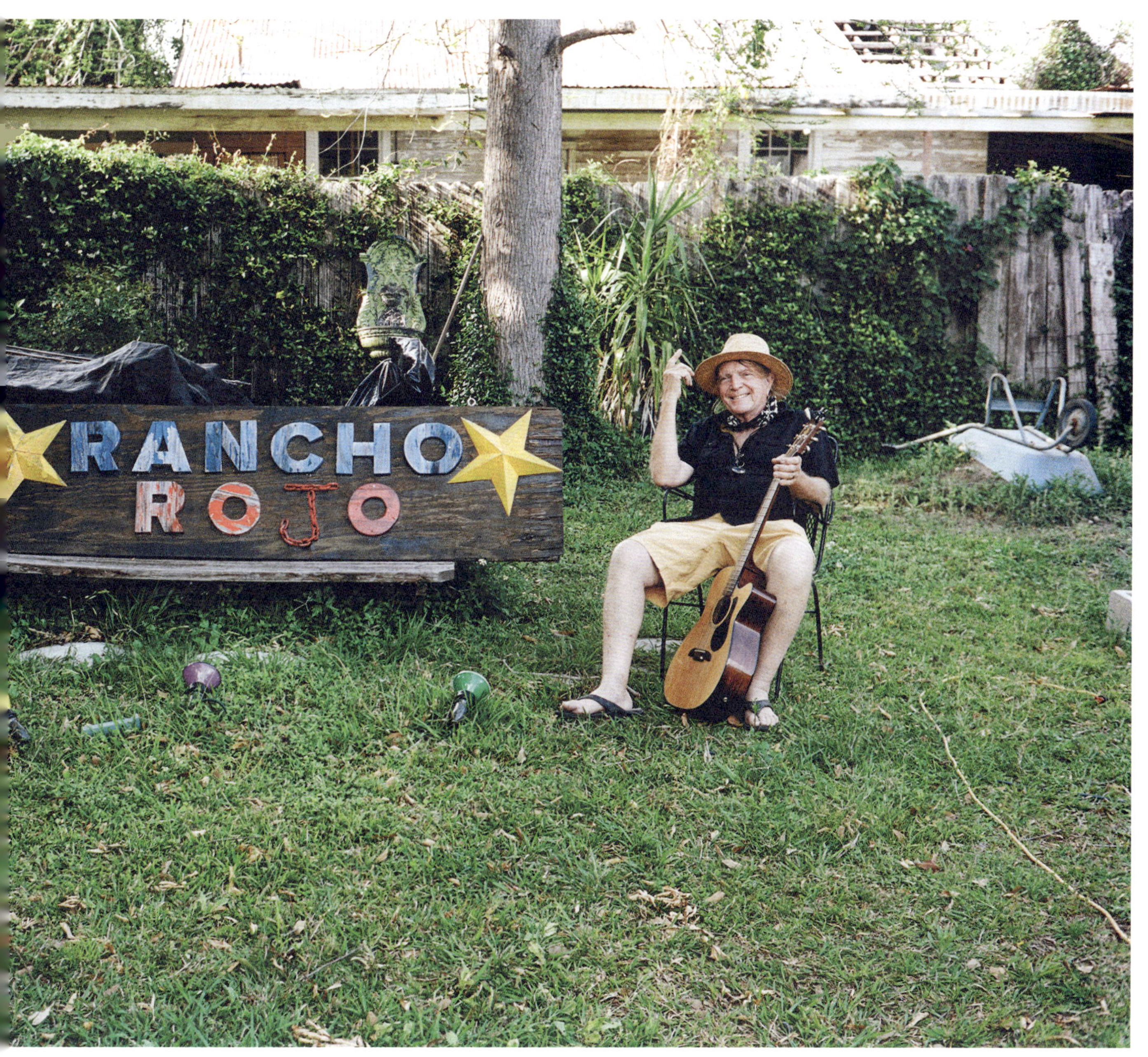

RANCHO
ROJO

When I am galloping a
horse.

Rick Creel

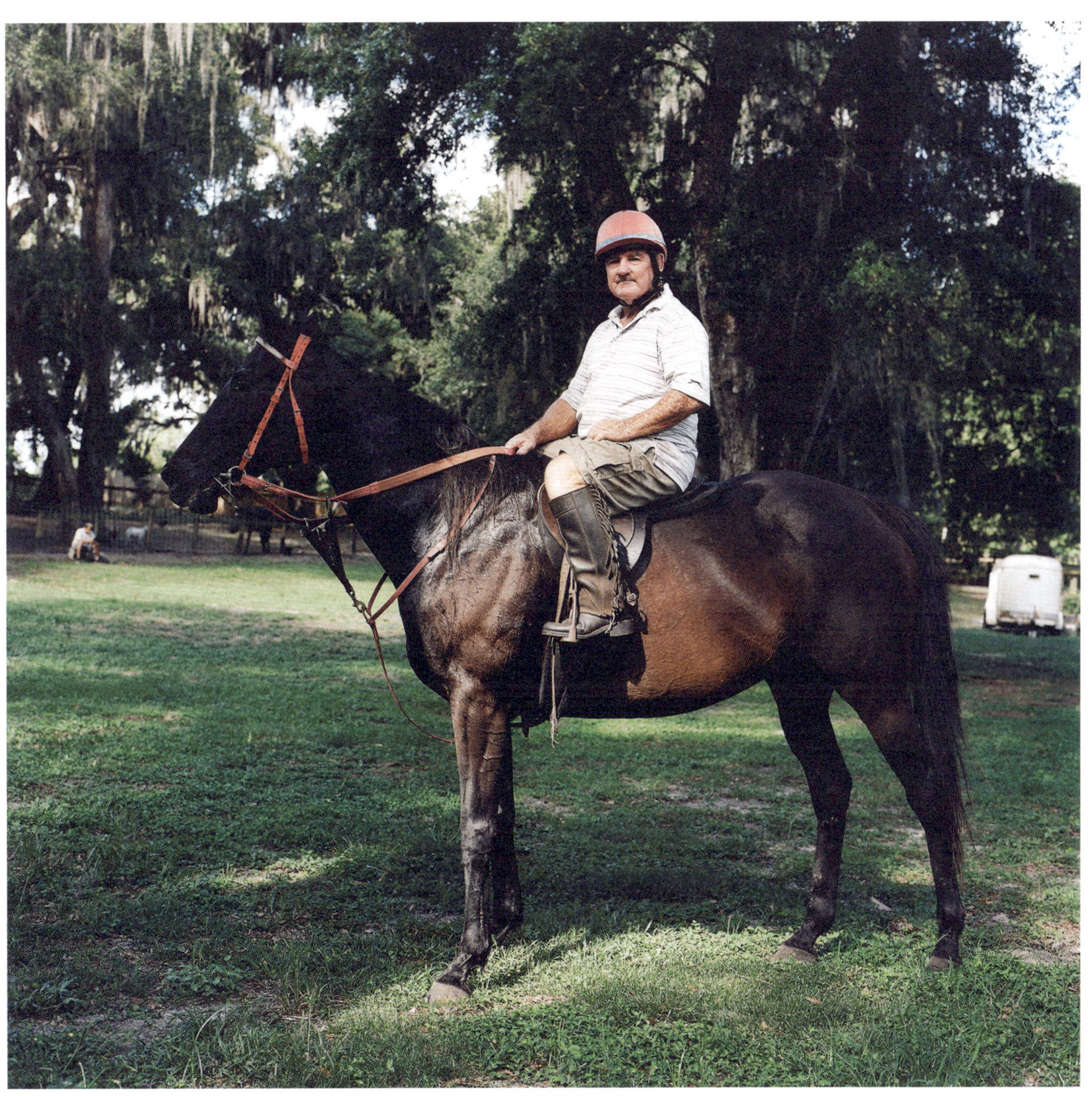

Ocala, Florida · May 2022

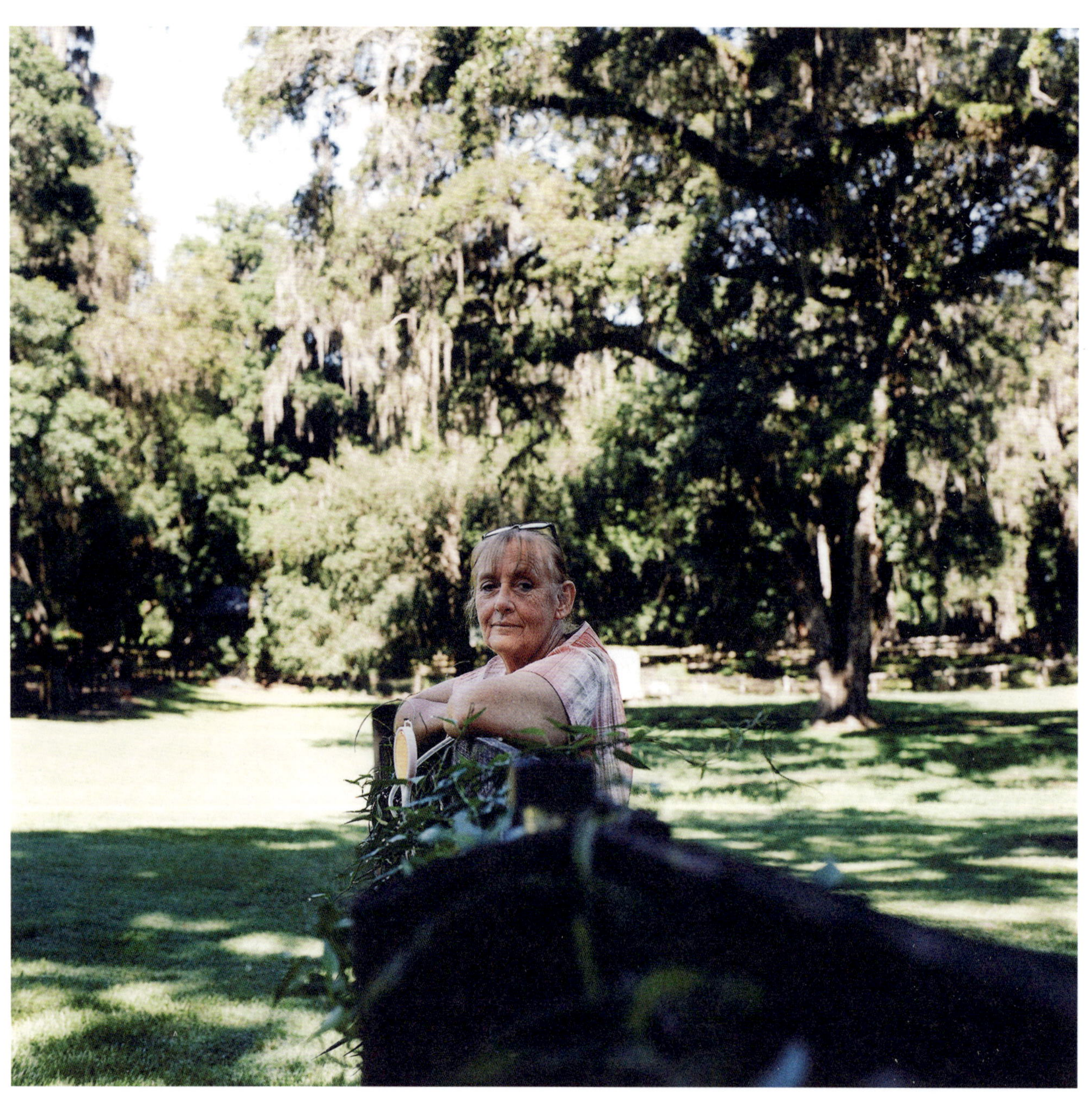

Janice Creel

I feel free when swinging
HIGH on a tree swing

Ocala, Florida · May 2022

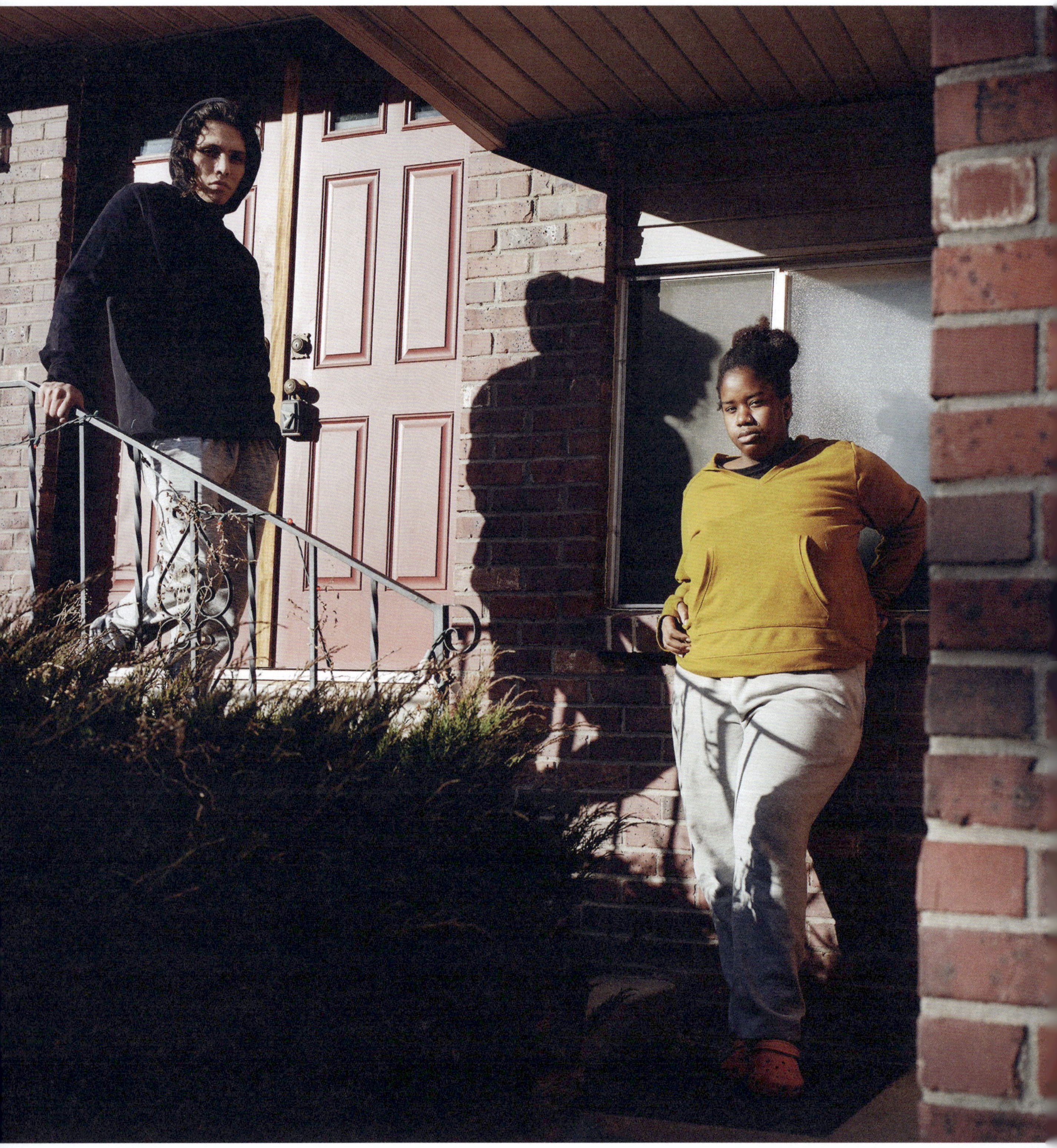

Freedom is the choice to follow rules or not.
The universe is filled with rules some but
we can disobey some we cannot. Hence
freedom is an illusion we use to distract ourselves
from the constraints of day to day life.

Kayla Ricks

Freedom is the state of one being in
control of one's center. And this can be
when you are, happy, sad, disgusted etc.
Ultimately freedom is living the
human experience for better or
worse.

Matthew Plosmith

Denver, Colorado · December 2021

R// Poder disfrutar la vida cada
segundo siendo Yo mismo

R// la libertad de poder vivir plenamente
sin importar que pasara despues.

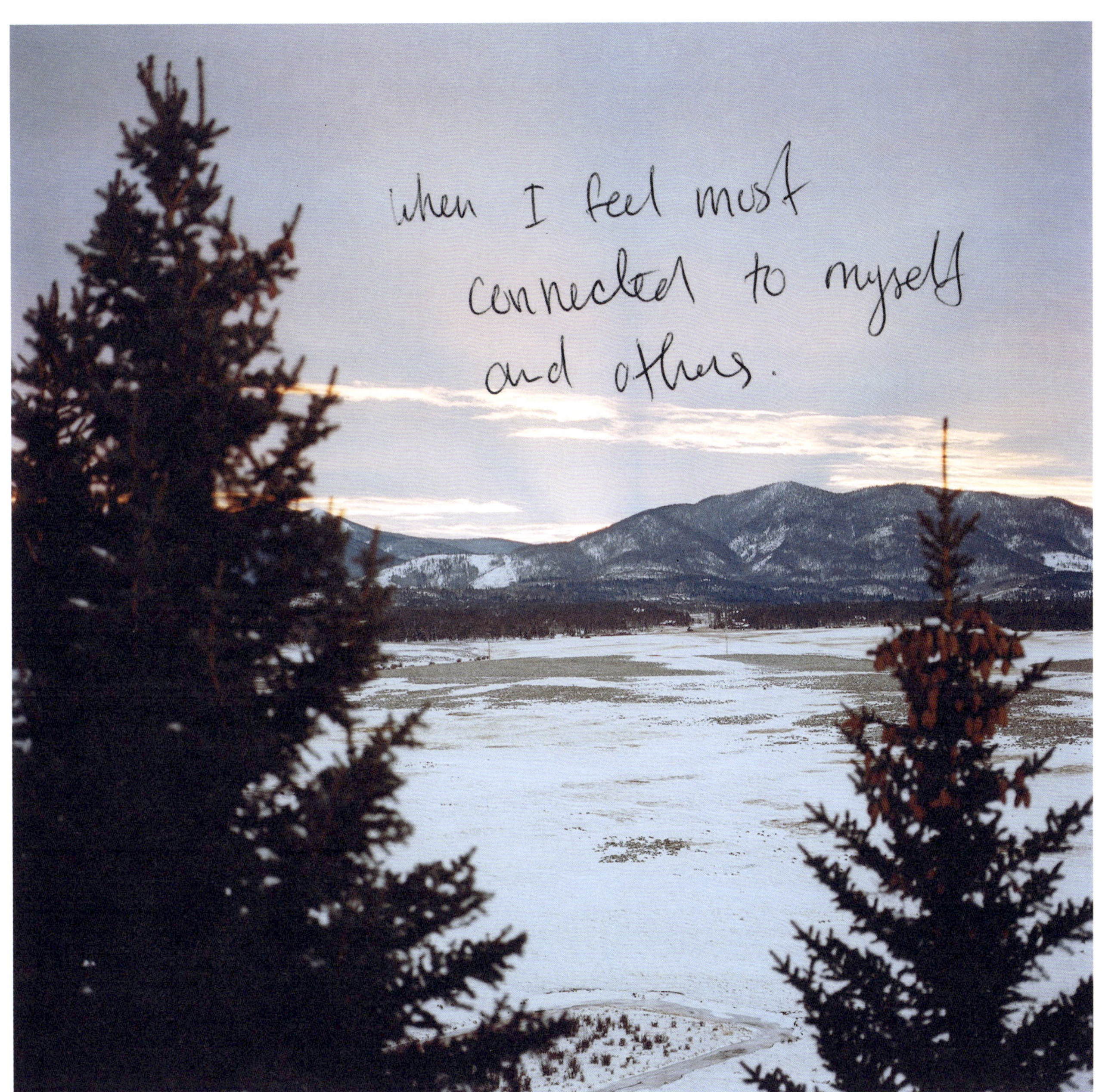

Anonymous

Wenn ich meinen
Lebensunterhalt mit
meinen Hobbies bestreiten
kann

When I can make
a living with what
I like to do
Annie Veenhuis

When I'm doing
what I want
Wesley James Bartlett

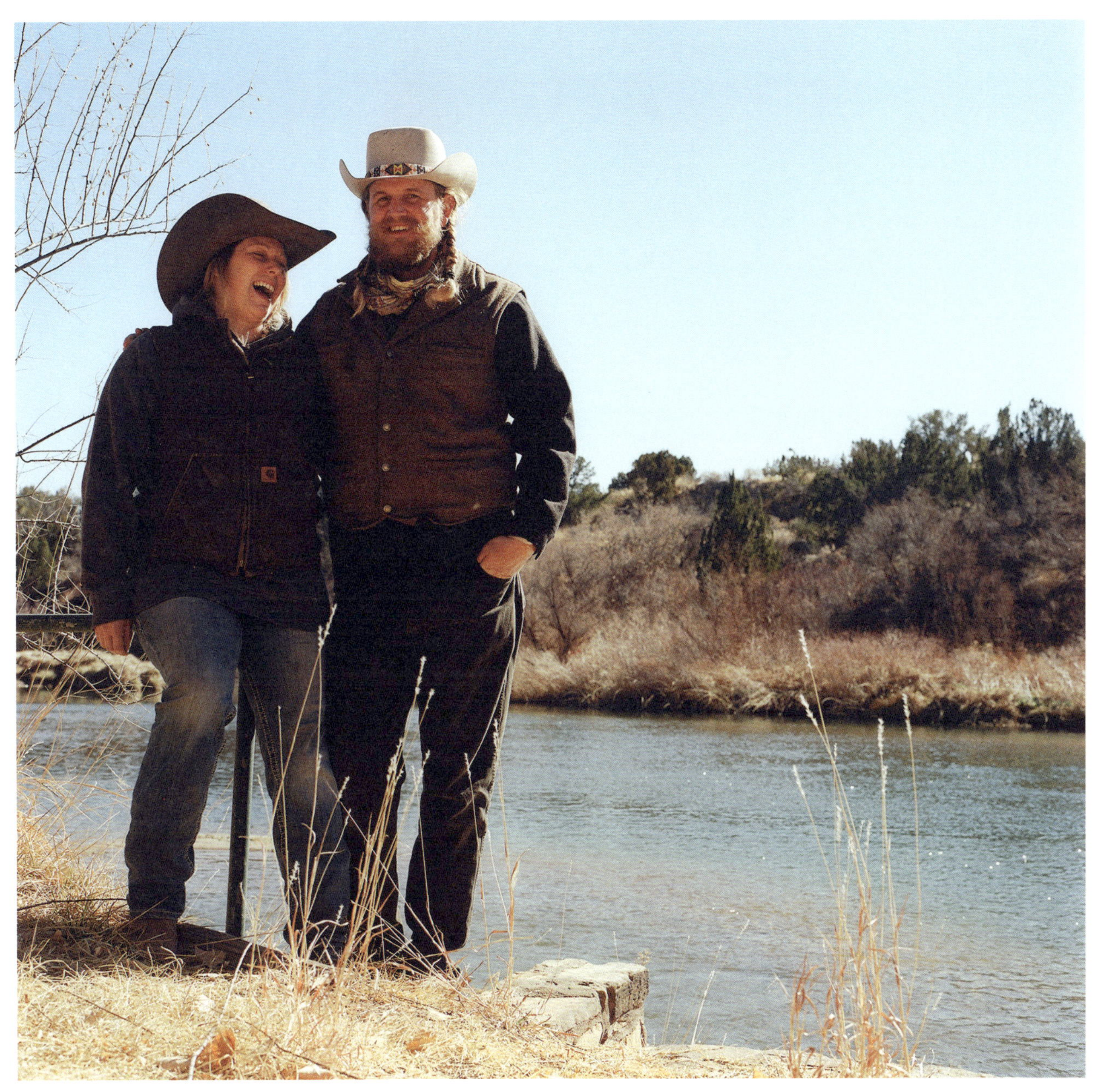

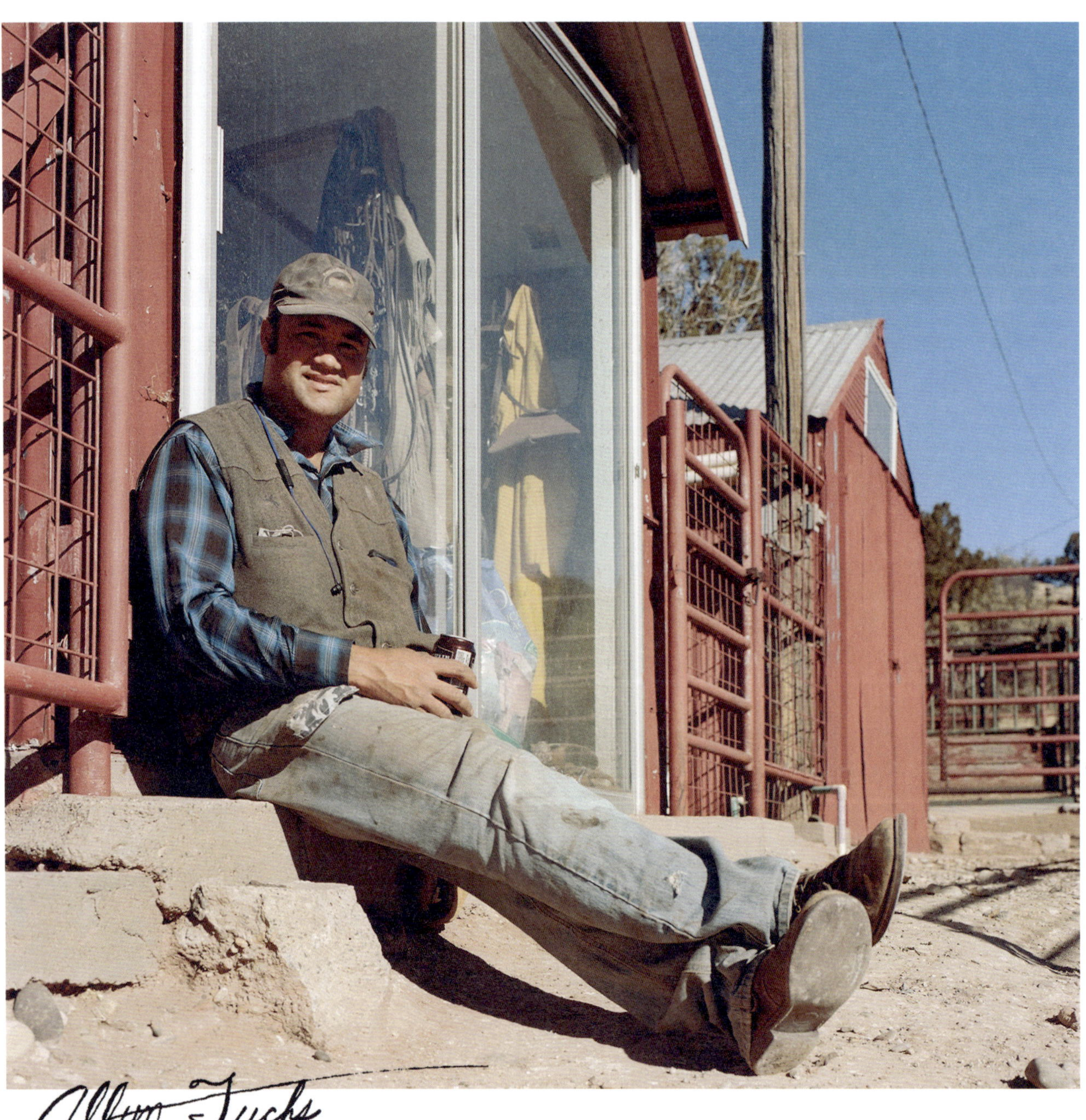
Allyn Fuchs

True freedom is
a state of mind;
therefore, I feel the
most free when
I choose to feel
free.

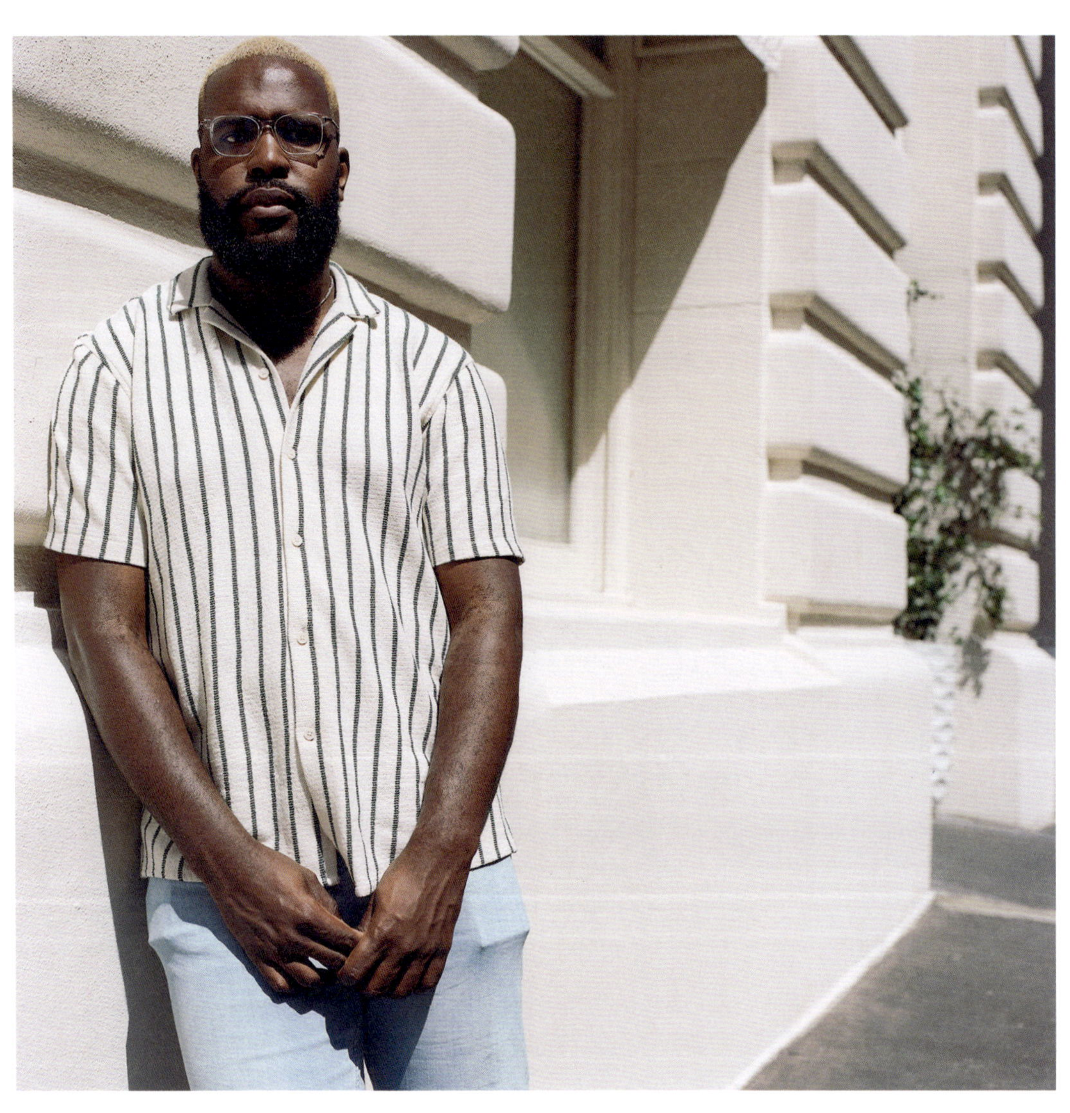

Darryl   St. Patrick
Gladstone

I feel free on the
other side of fear.

I feel the most free when
I am outside the normal constraints
of every day life – When I am
traveling, meeting new people, having
new experiences. I am even more
free when I am prioritizing
myself and that freedom.

I feel free
when I realize
that a lot of my fun
is Mostly Ego.

Marlene Aponte

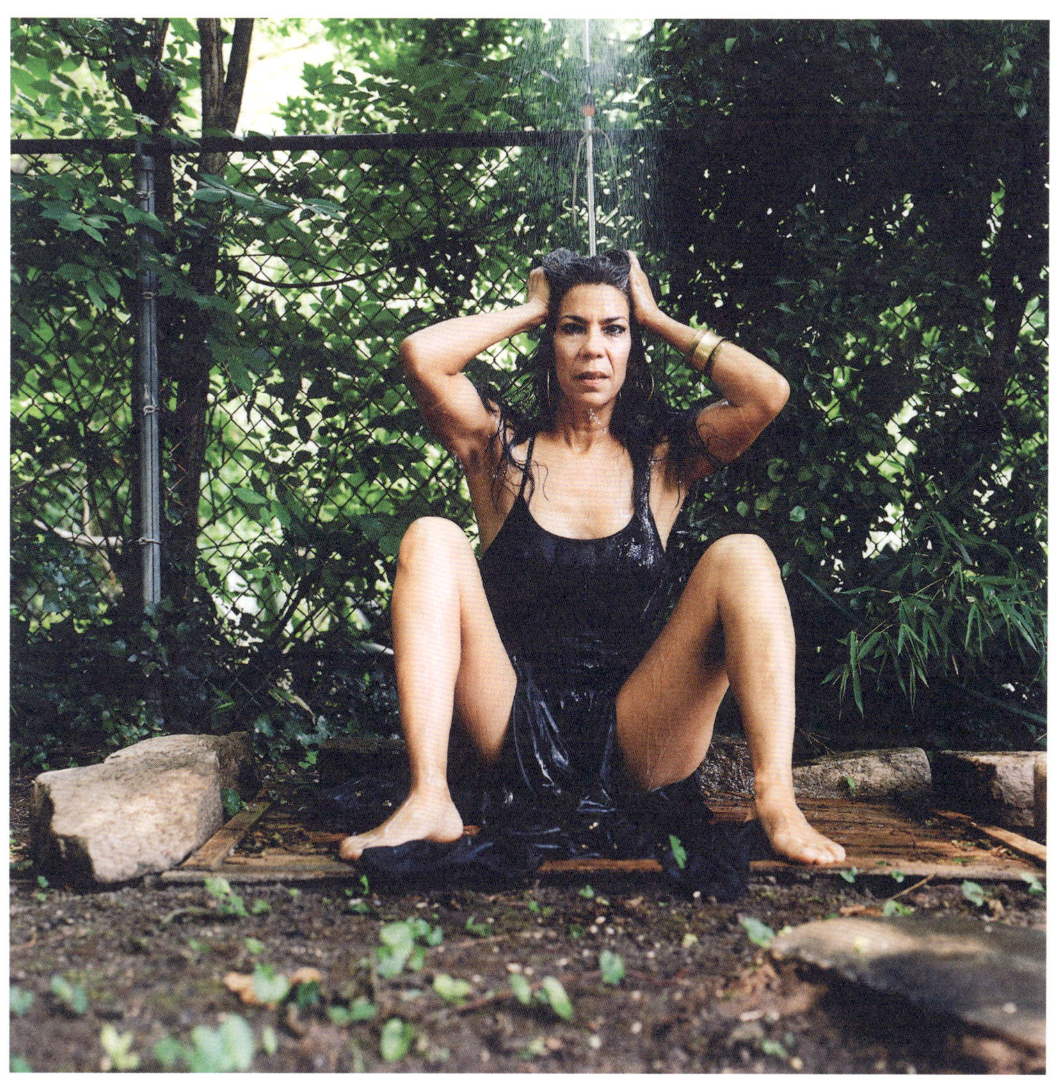

Atlanta, Georgia · June 2022

I feel free in the moments where my life feels like a movie, whether it be a cruise through the fjords in Norway, a hike in Colorado, truck bed surfing through a cattle ranch in Florida, watching sunsets from the rooftops, and many more moments where the world seems to slow & I feel like I can finally breathe again.

Haley Sulich

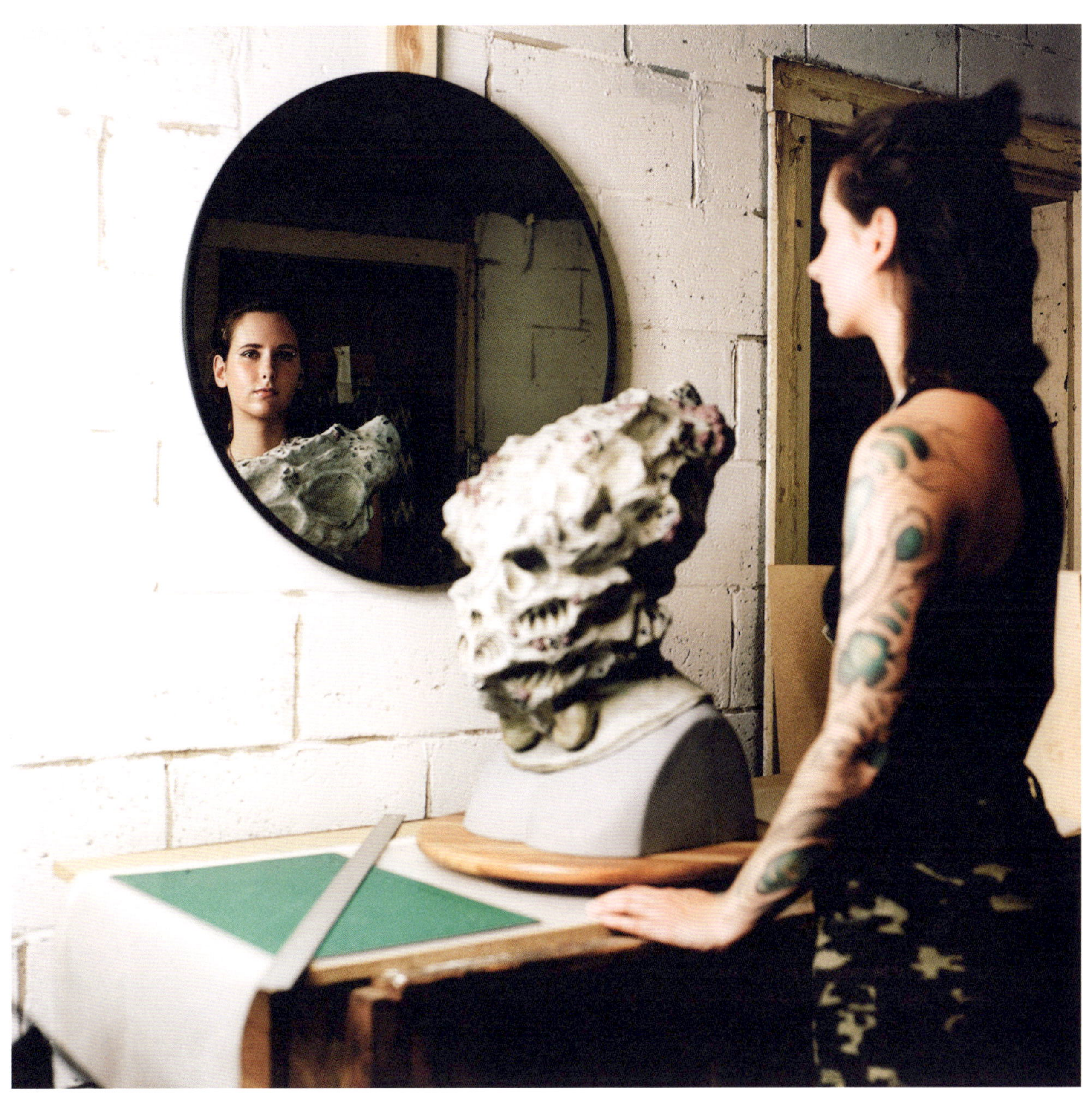

Atlanta, Georgia · June 2022

Freedom is...

- A midday nap with my cat on my chest and my dog at my side.

- a cup of iced coffee perfectly curated to my liking

- a morning poop after said coffee is

- scrubbing out of a successful procedure.

- a patient's first unassisted breath on the ventilator.

- sliding my shoes off after a 12 hour shift

- an opposing view that makes me think

- the ability to change my mind.

I feel free when I can
be alone with my thoughts,
without the need for distraction
from my anxiety and the awful
thoughts that usually come
along with it.

Anonymous

1 When I'm with NATure
alone in The woods
listening To all Gods CreaTors

JusT booT Helping oThers
when I CAn and doing The
righT THing mAkes all The
Difference in life

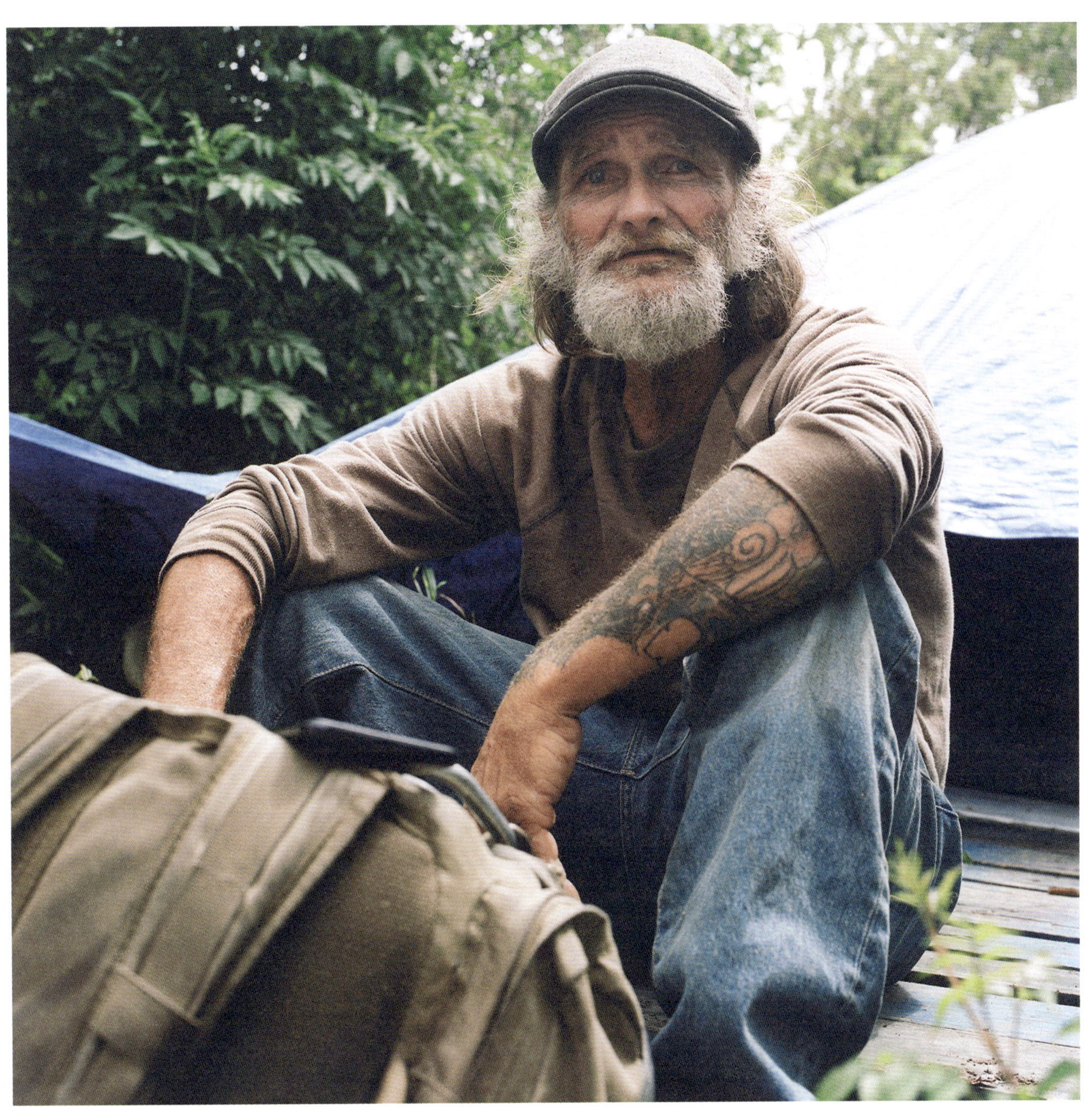

Jerry Lambert SR

I feel most free screaming
my face off at a concert or
at home in my undies having
a concert of my own with
a hair brush microphone.

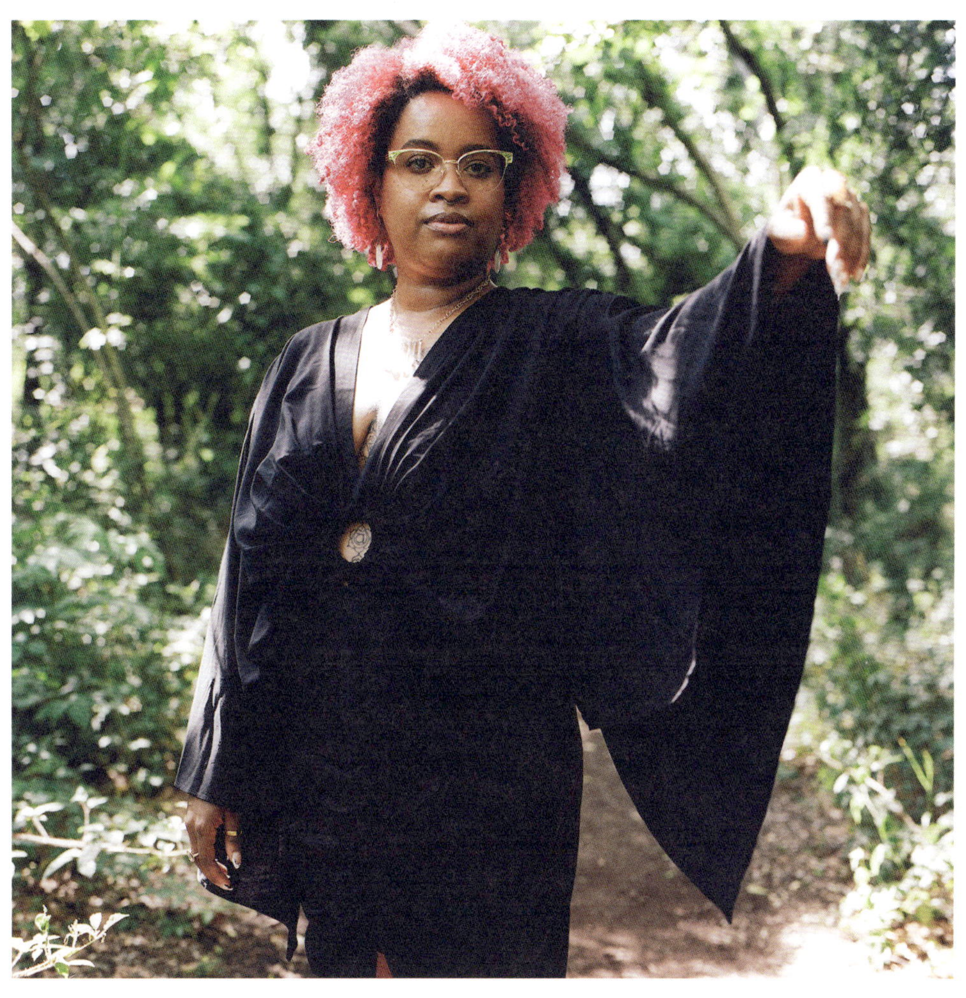

TAMARA SOUBLET

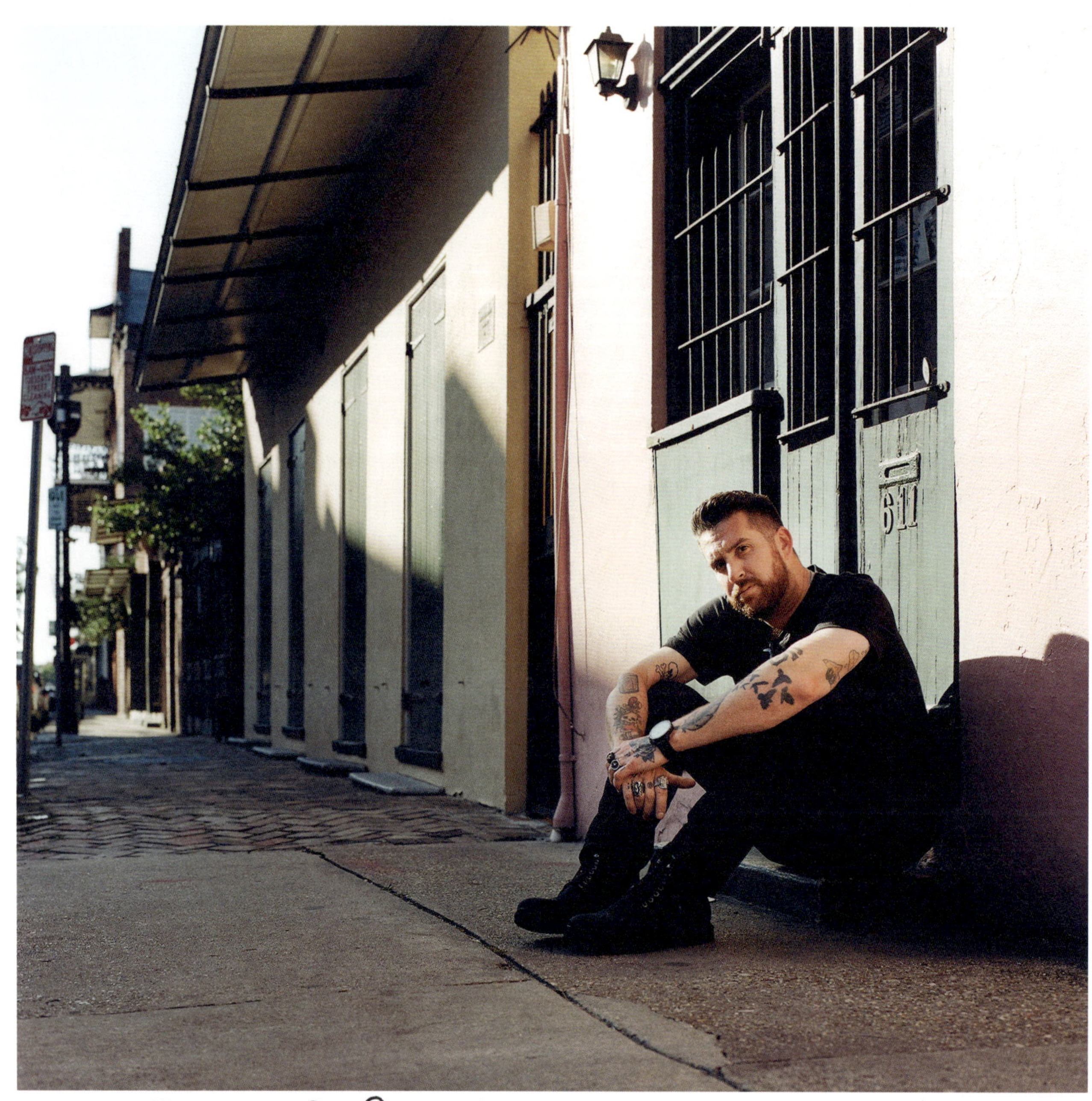

Jack Raymond Stewart

I feel most free when creating
honestly, uninhibited, making
something from nothing.
Freedom, for me, is great food
shared around and with great
People, without a moment of guilt.

I feel most free when
I'm able to express who I
am, and know I'm accepted
exactly as I am —
flaws and all.

New Orleans, Louisiana · April 2022

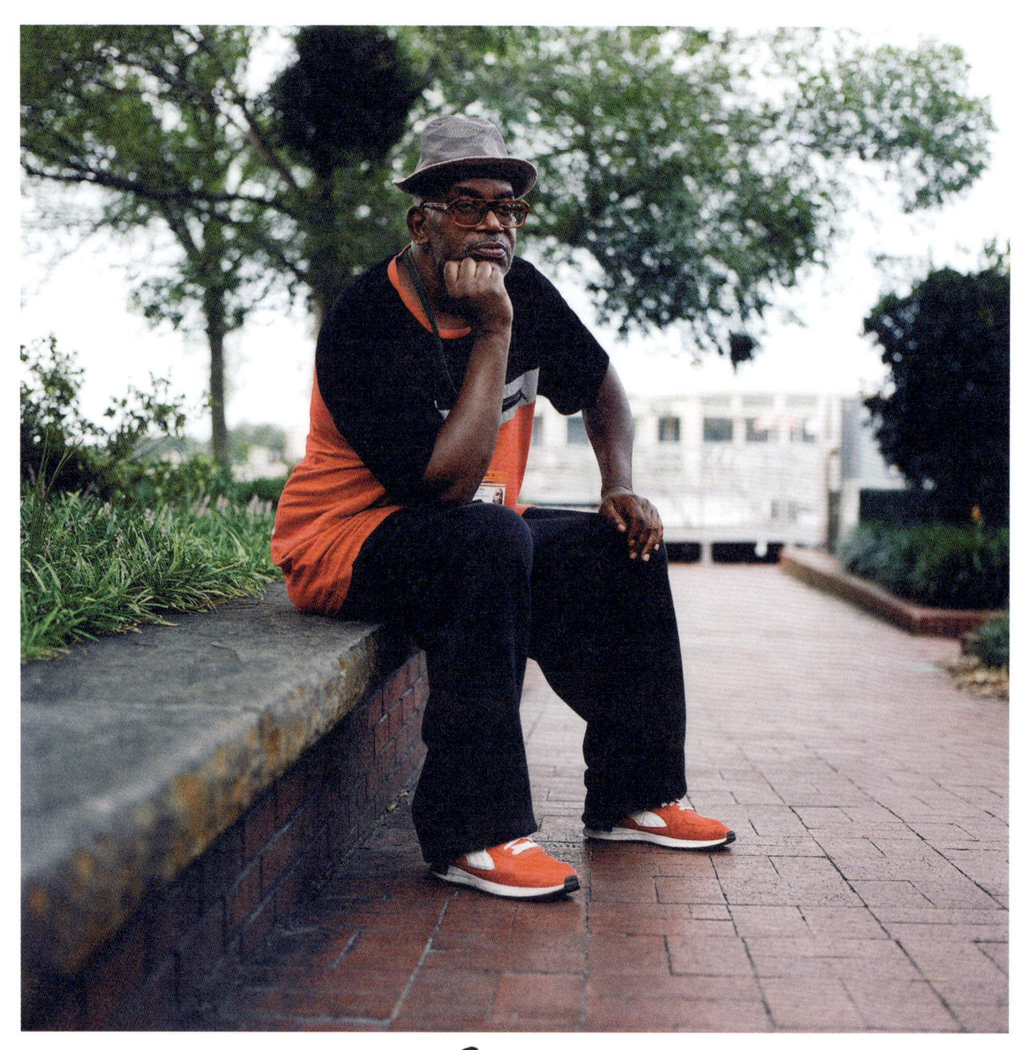

Ricky on the River

I Feel Free only in my sleep
and when I sleep thats when I be
free to breathe toss and turn
free to laugh free to learn
free from the past future bright
but only in my sleep

Savannah, Georgia · June 2022

I am Free when Im surronded by Nature. The animals, trees and esPecially the Atmosphere, its My happy Place.

Mike Cano

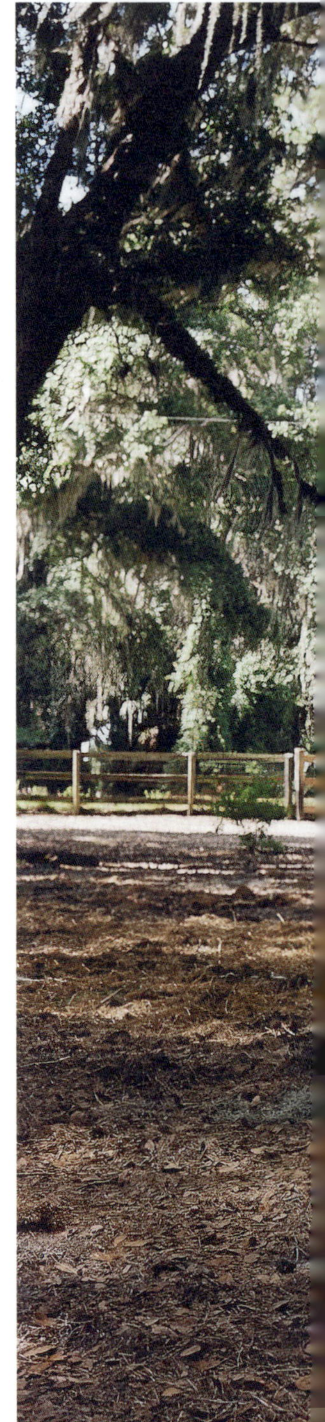

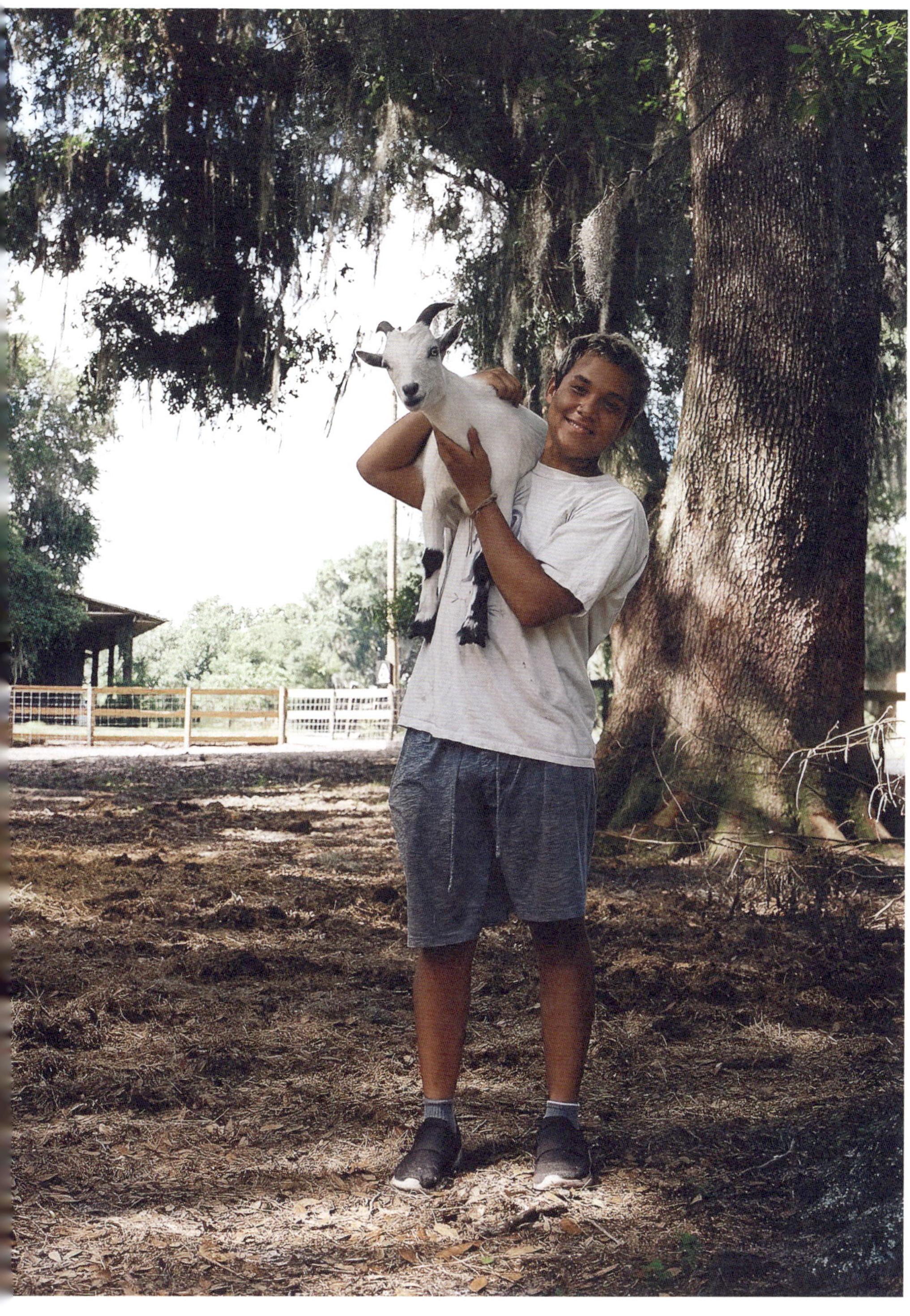

Ocala, Florida · May 2022

WEEKENDS, WHEN IM IN NATURE,
WITH FRIENDS FAMILY THAT ACCEPT
ME FOR ME.

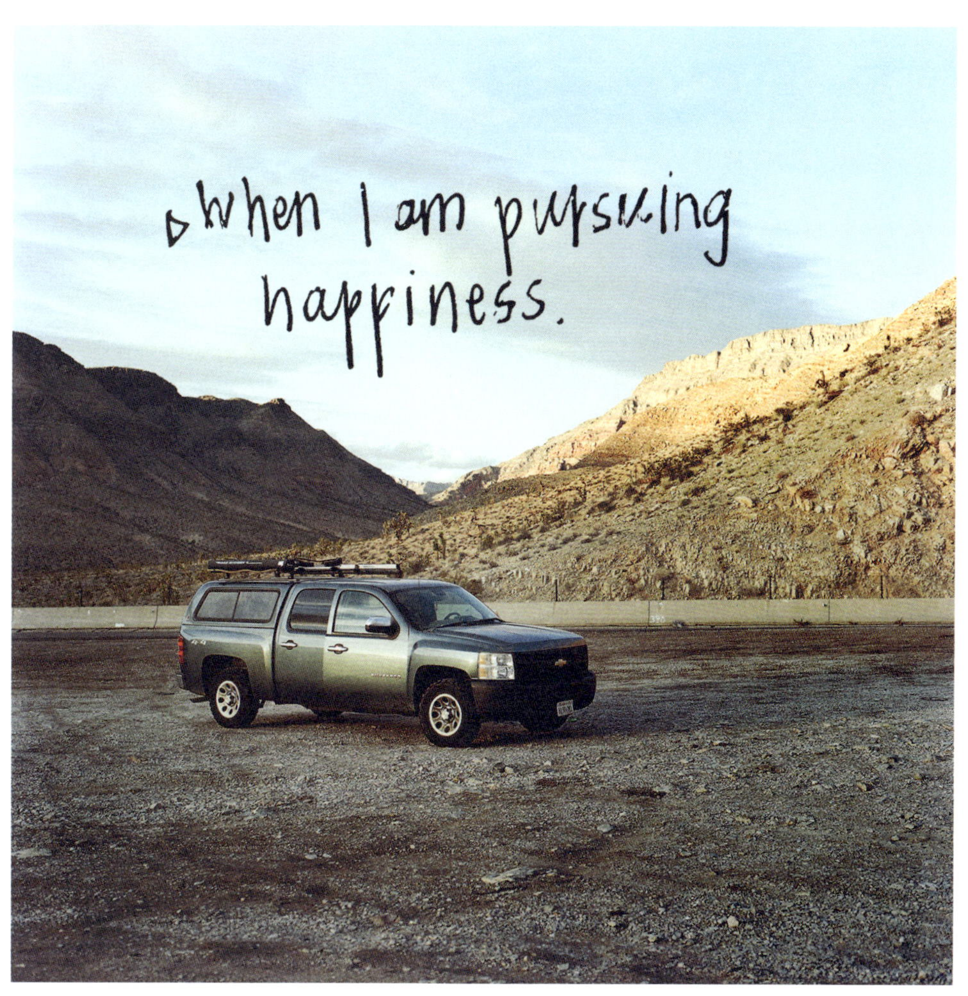

when I am pursuing happiness.

Past: using substances to escape reality.

Now: genuine connection with people & experiencing the world w/ fresh eyes every day.

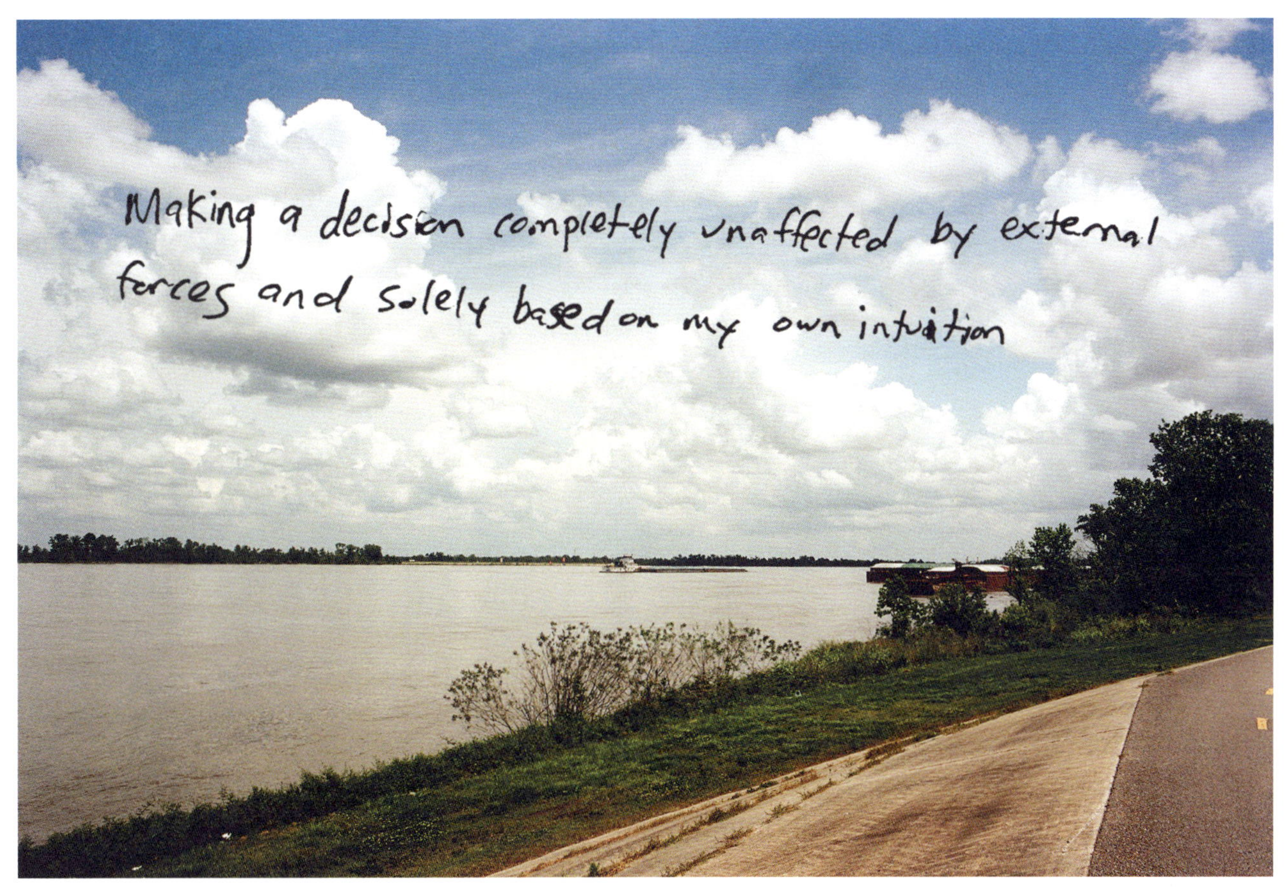
Making a decision completely unaffected by external forces and solely based on my own intuition

MR Ralph Feel Free
All the time. At 86
I Feel Good.

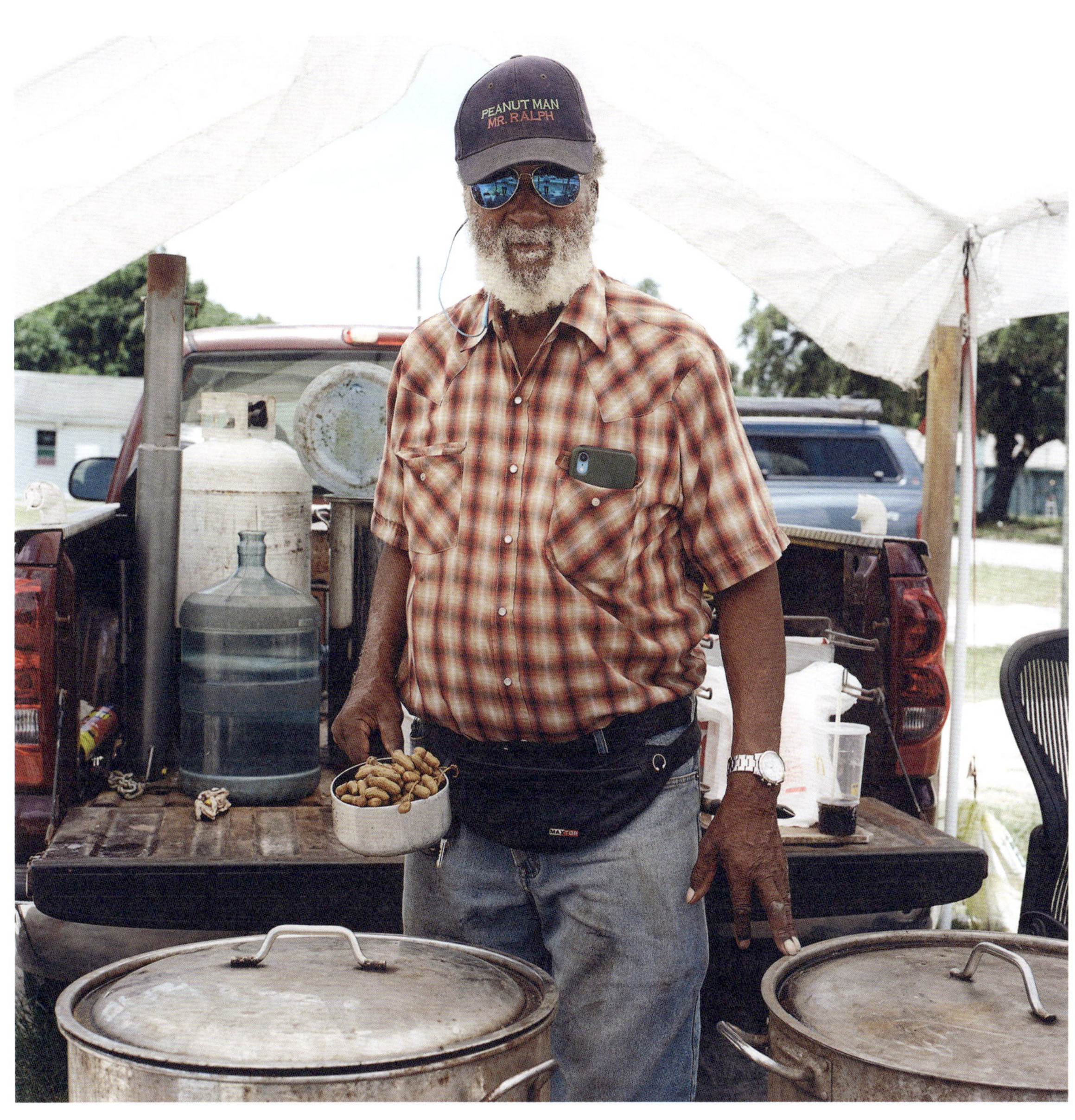

Ralph peanut man #1

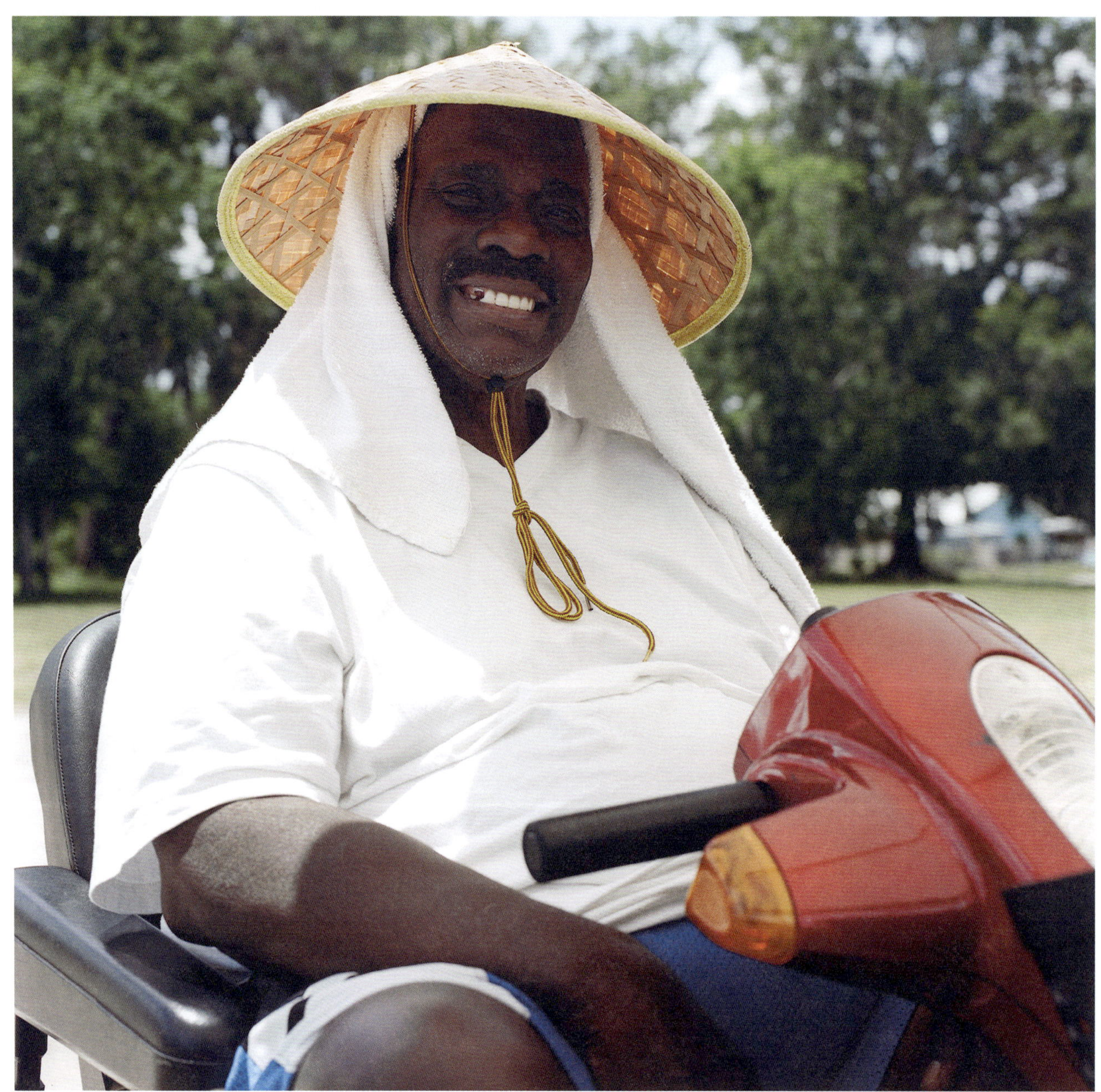

Freddie Garmon
I AM Peanut man #2

When i Fell Free
I coue To work in the wood
Land claving. Nothing to Distrube
Me

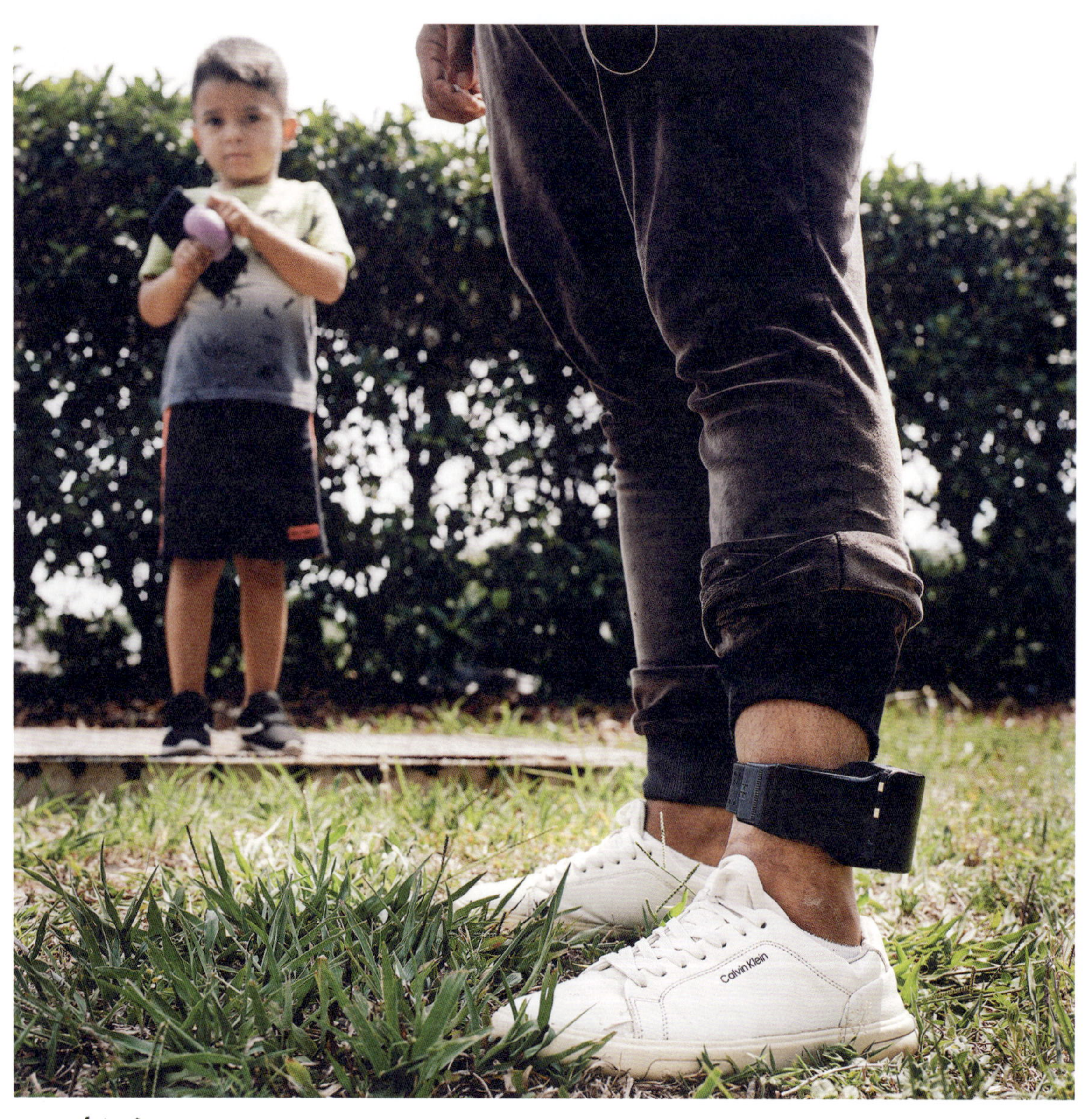

VA-ROG-AMERICA-AJUTATIM
·SA·ĔIU·LIBER·VA-MULTUMESC
GOD·BLESS

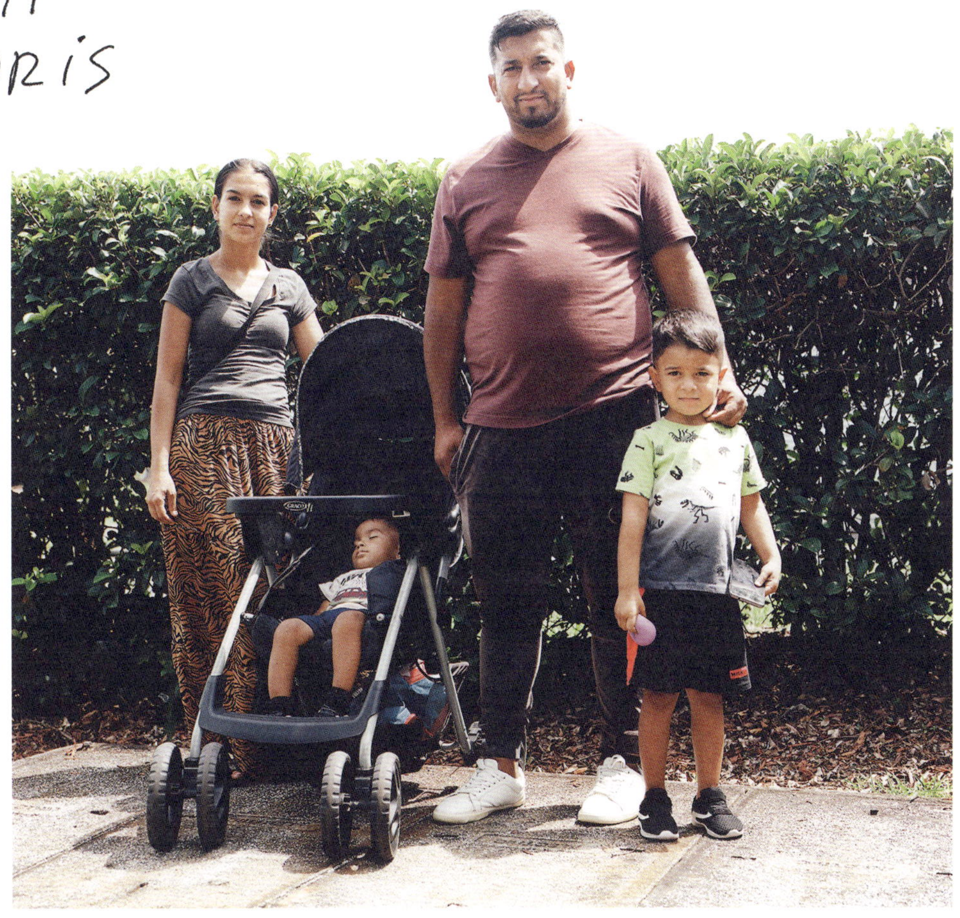

Ocala, Florida · May 2022

Deep in my soul
    in a place seldom seen
where I visit in times when
my life is serene
Sometimes quite by chance
though I'm sure it exists
the doorway's concealed in life's swamps
and its mists

Deliverance I find there with the vision
    to see
the keys to the shackles that life's put
    on me
I'll linger awhile and inevitably find
The lock most secure is the one
    on my mind

        Thought Conquest.   Patrick Beadle 2022

Abiquiu, New Mexico • July 2022

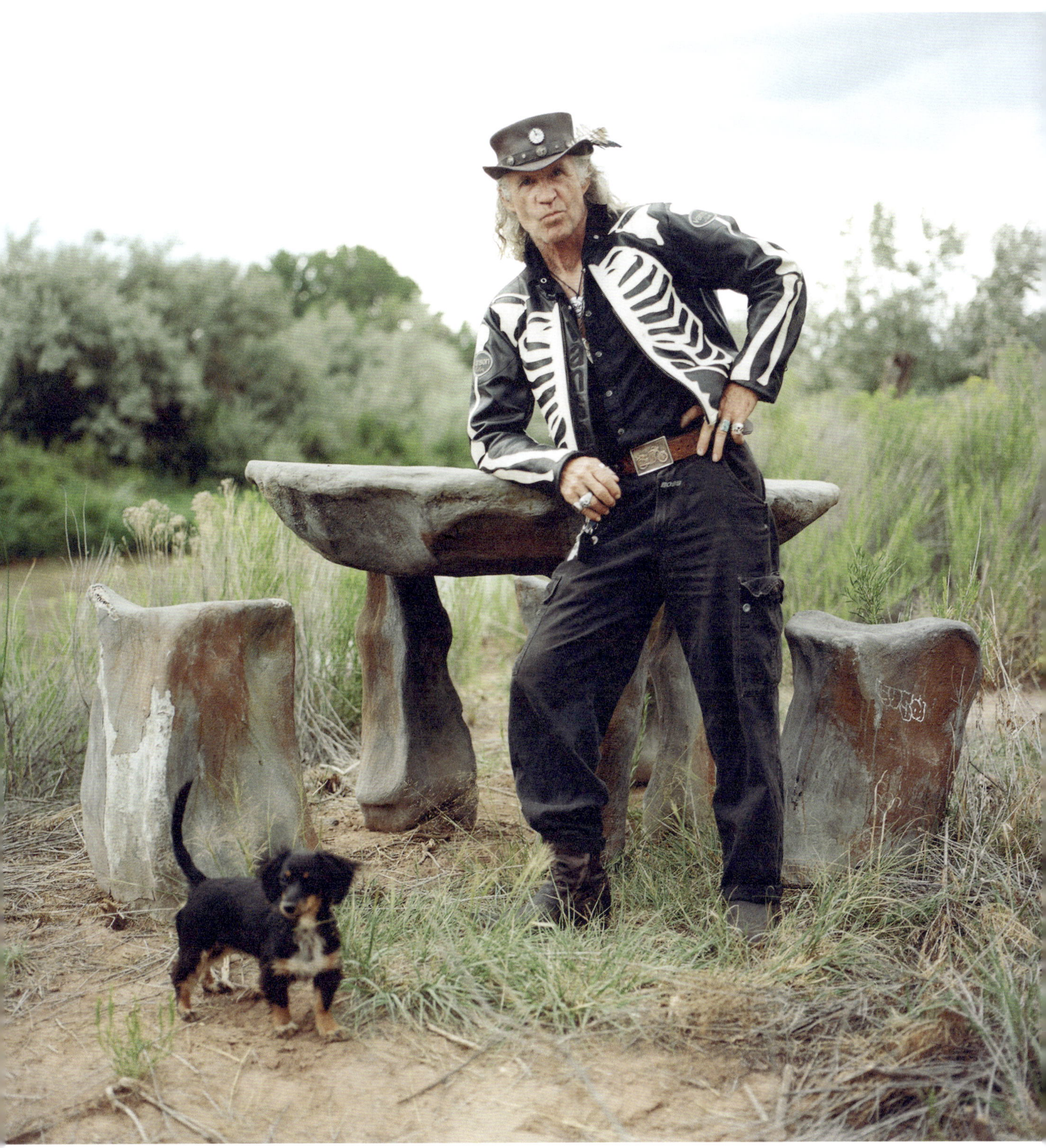

I FEEL FREE WHEN
I HAVE A TRUE
CONNECTION WITH
ANOTHER PERSON

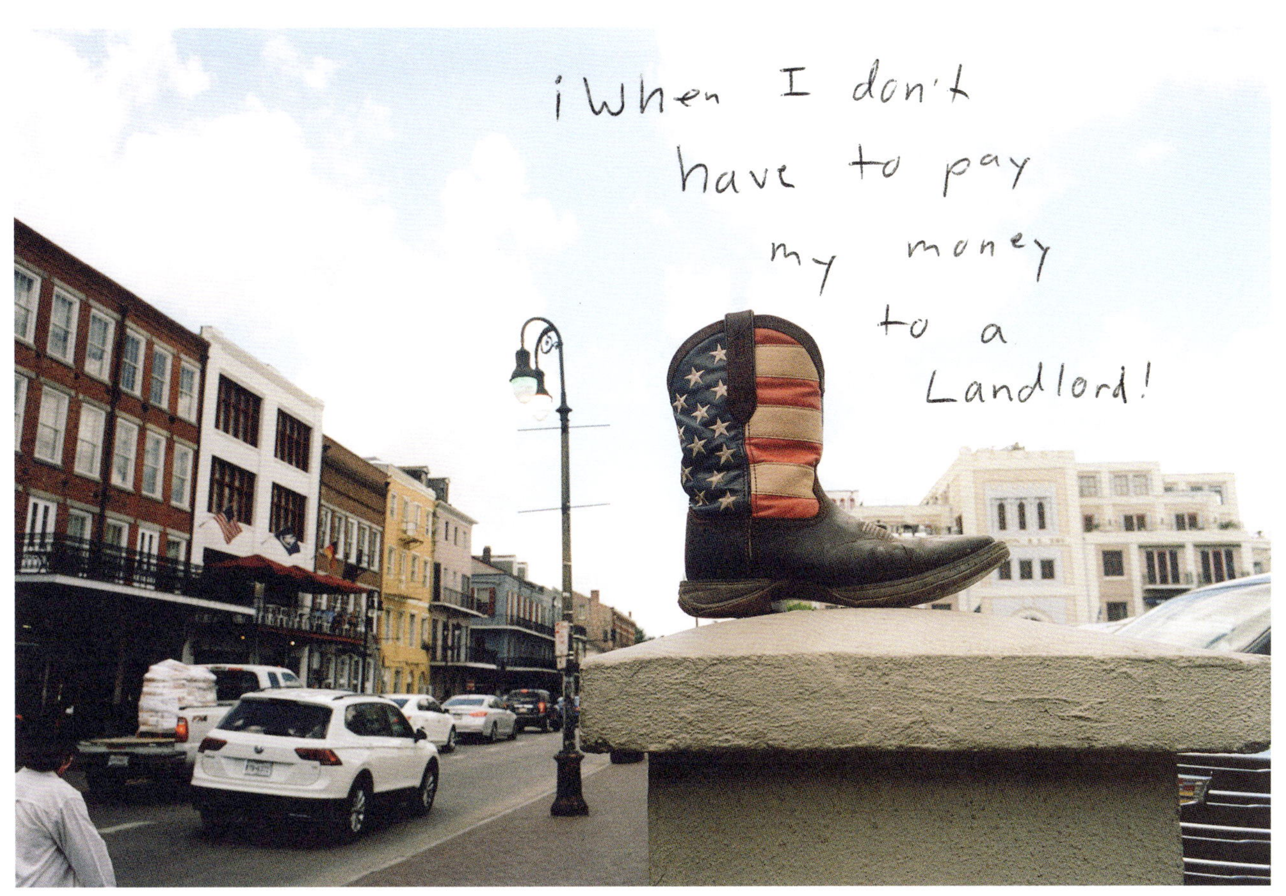

Anonymous

I feel most free when I am truly living life on my own terms, without worrying about how other people perceive me. I experience a great sense of freedom when dancing, traveling, and connecting authentically with other uniquely beautiful human beings.

BRYANT MICHAEL HUETHER

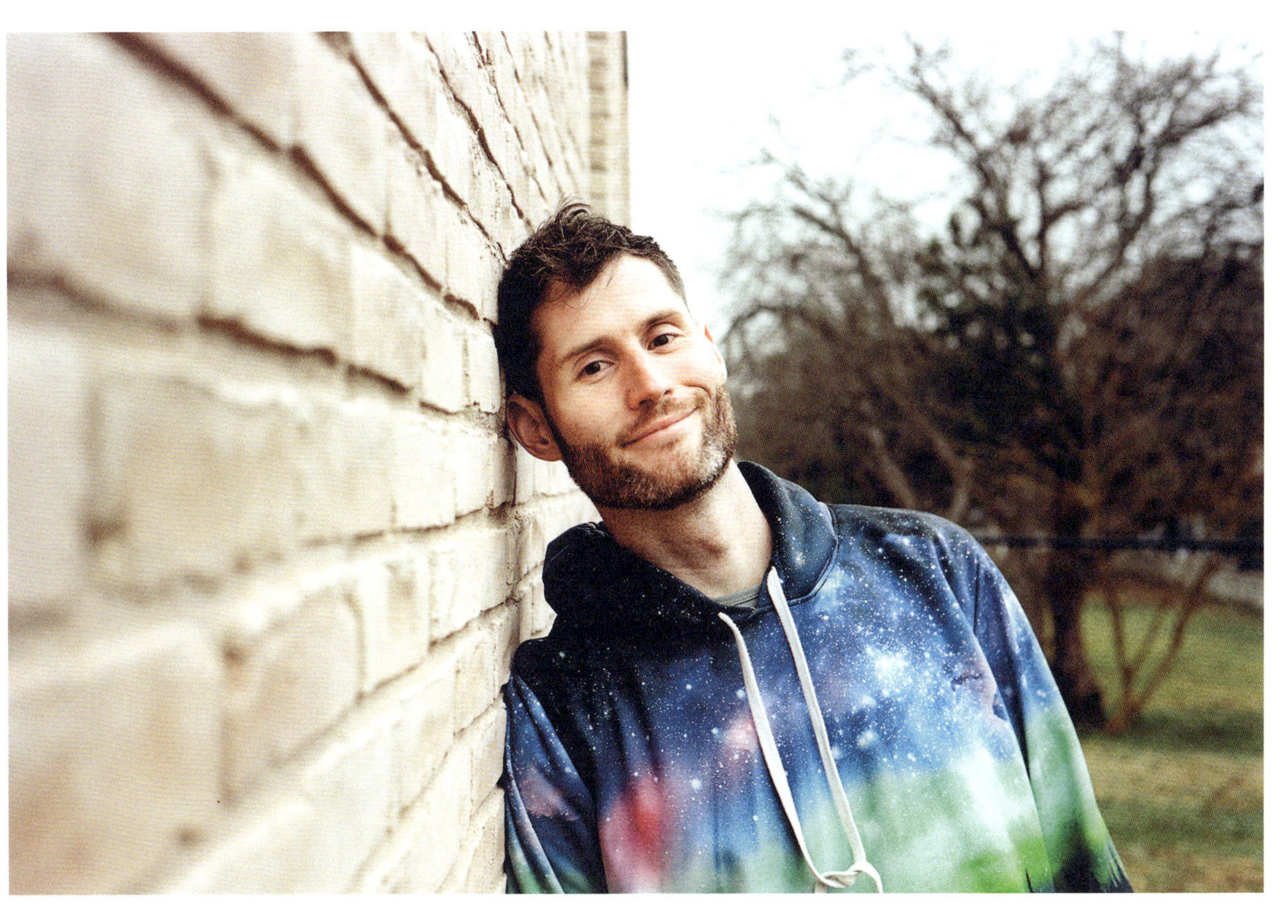

I feel free when I feel the resonance
of truth in my body. I feel it on
occasion when I read it, hear it spoken,
or when it flows through my own voice
in spoken word or song or a perfected
form of movement. The overwhelming
sense that I have when I feel free
is that I am connected to something
greater than myself and that I have
become a pure vessel of truth moving thru
me.

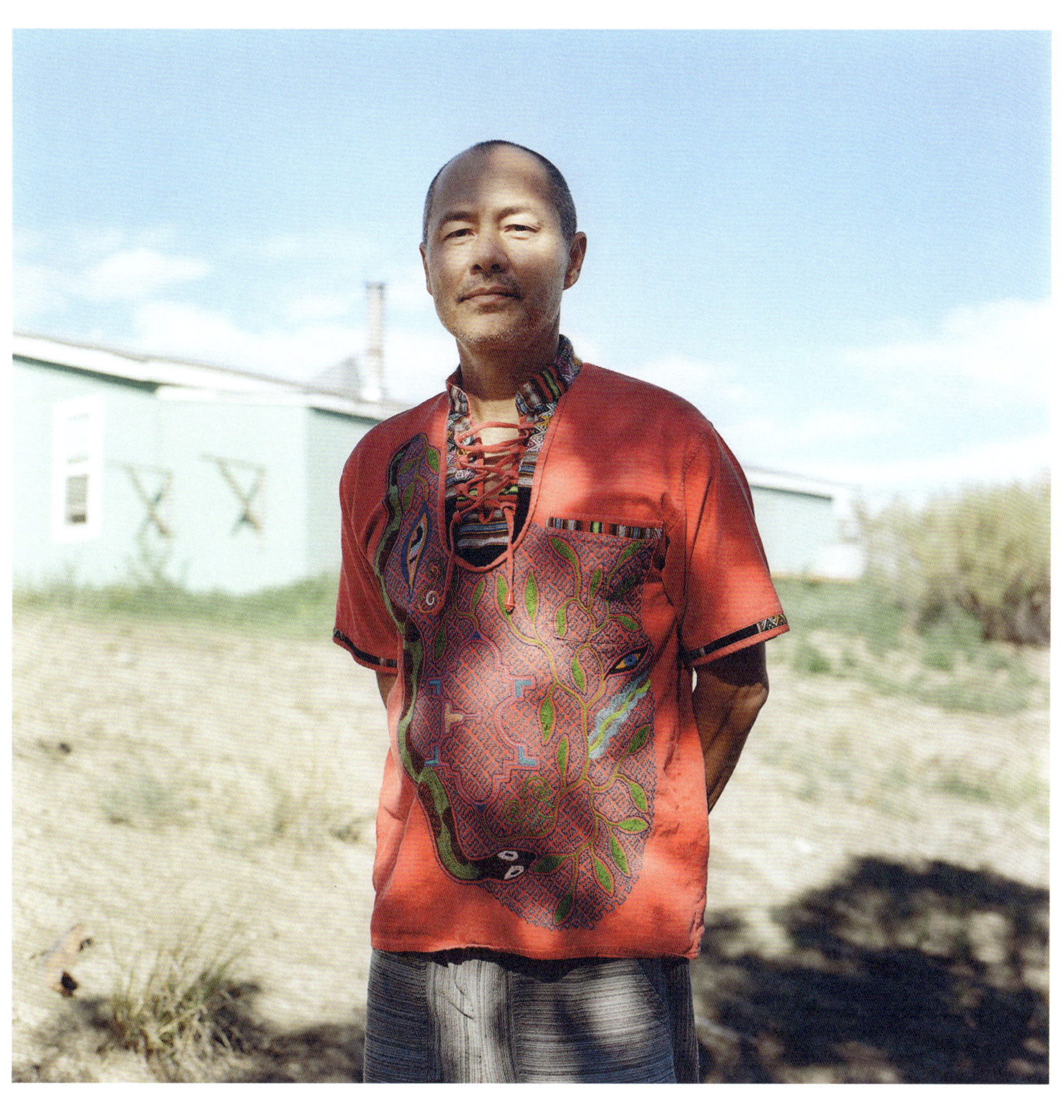

ALEX STICKLER

Durango, Colorado · January 2022

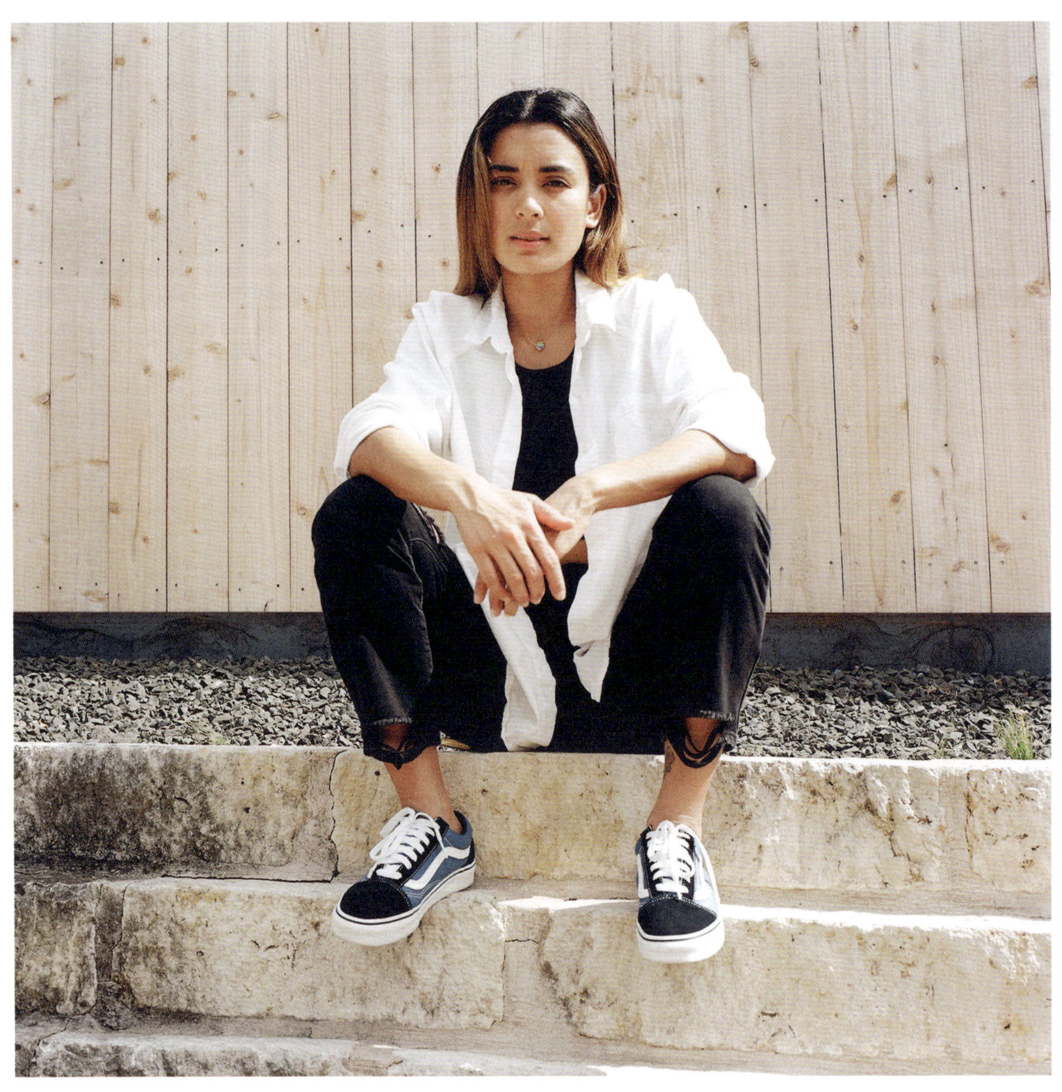

Michelle

when I'm not in my mind...

I feel free when I'm surrounded by GREEN not concrete; when I get to indulge in natures gifts; when I smell the trees, flowers and just the scent of the earth. ♡

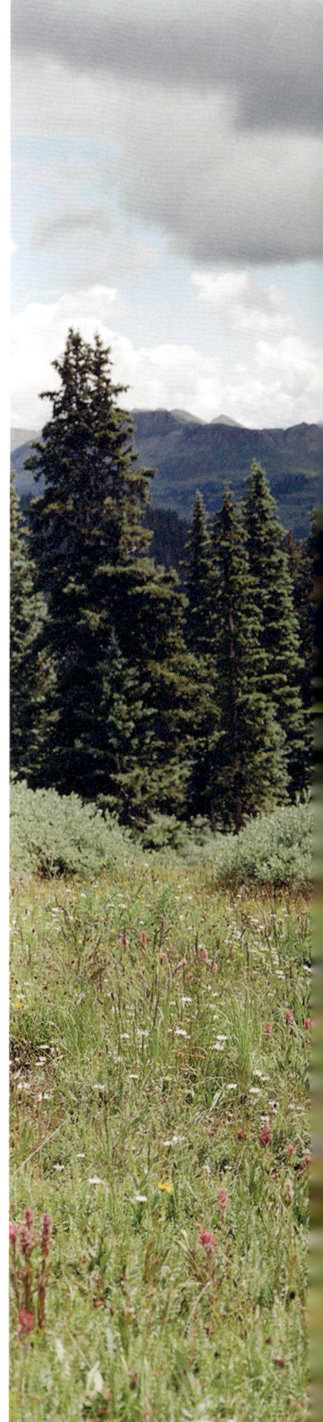

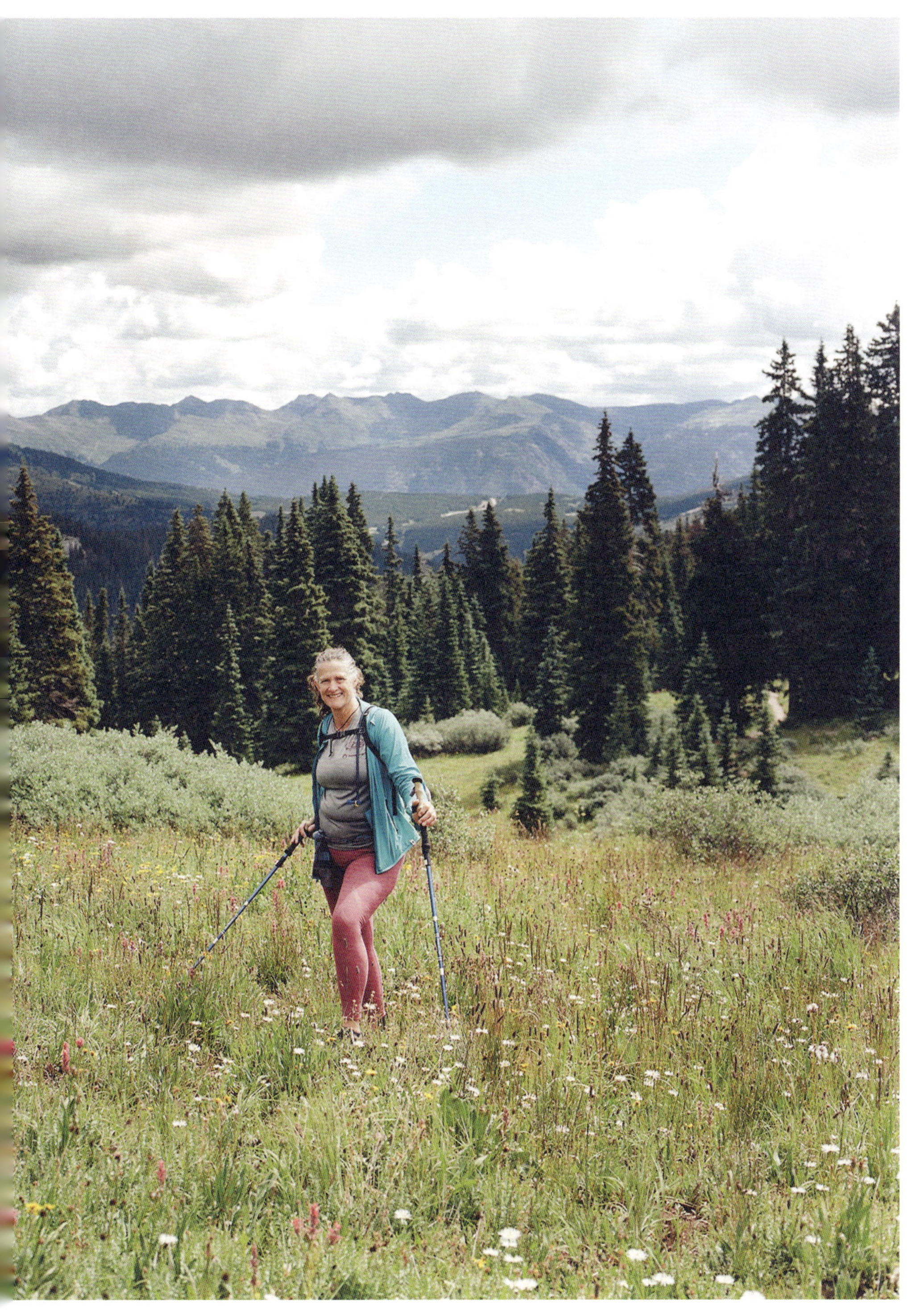

Durango, Colorado · August 2022

*1 feel happy and free when I'm myself in everything I do.

* ~~I'm~~ feel that I'm alive when I see carefully the place where I live. Also when I practice surf and soccer, and when I make smiles in other people.

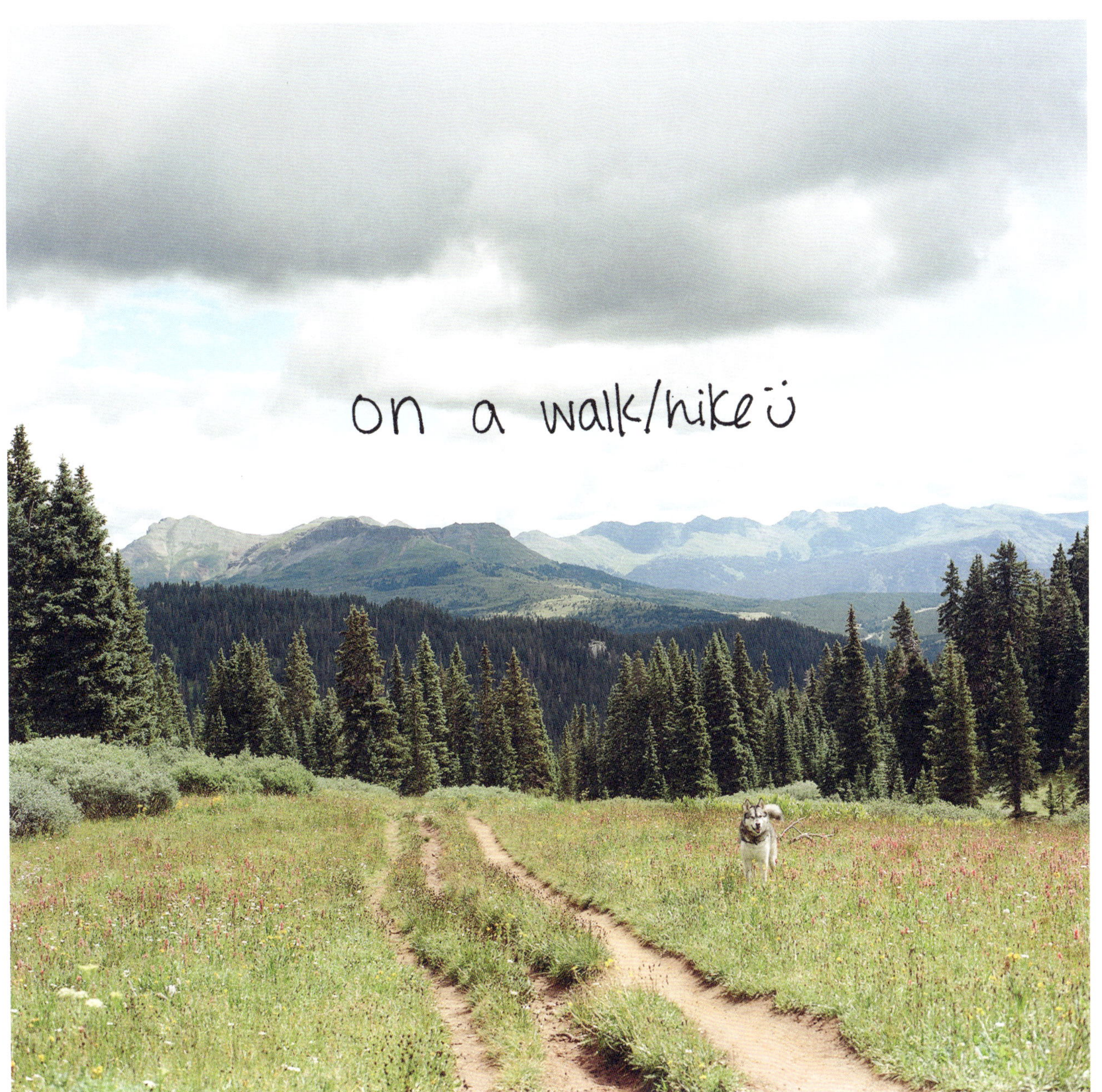

Anonymous

When I am
Surrounded by
plants and flowers
while sitting down.

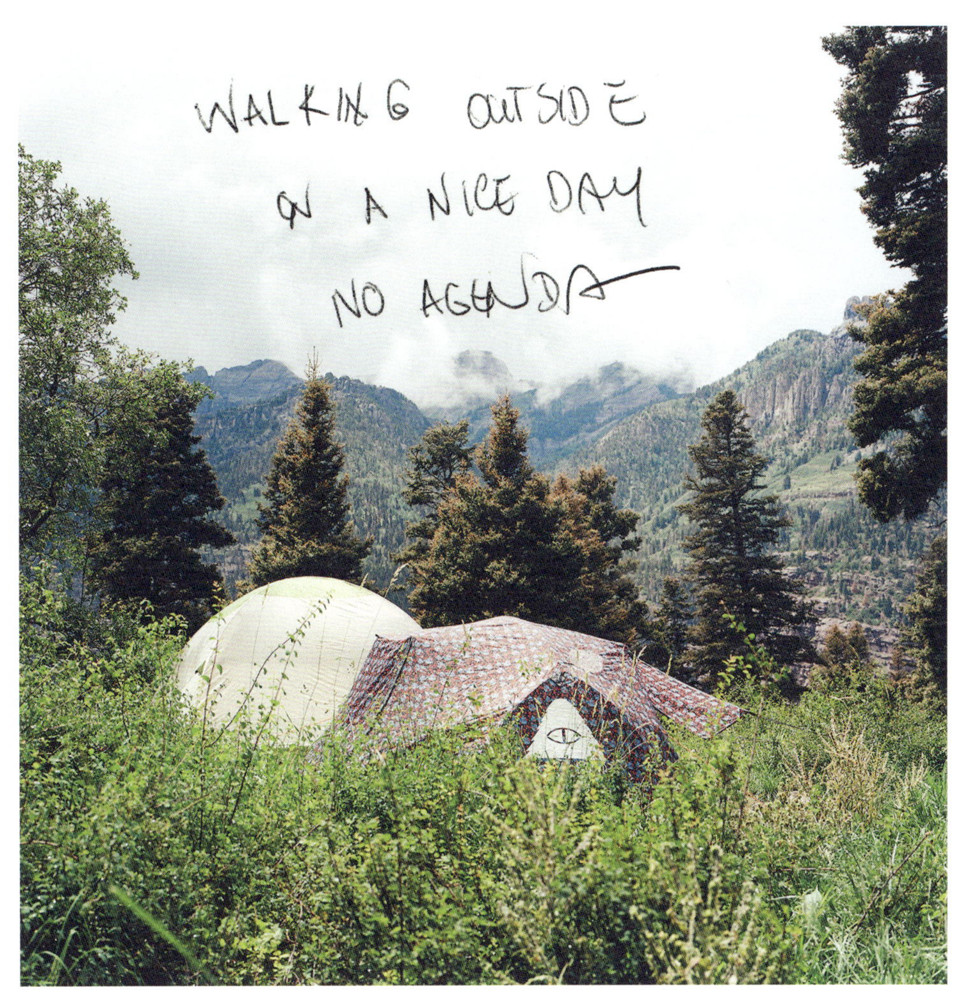

Anonymous

VICKI | LA VIX

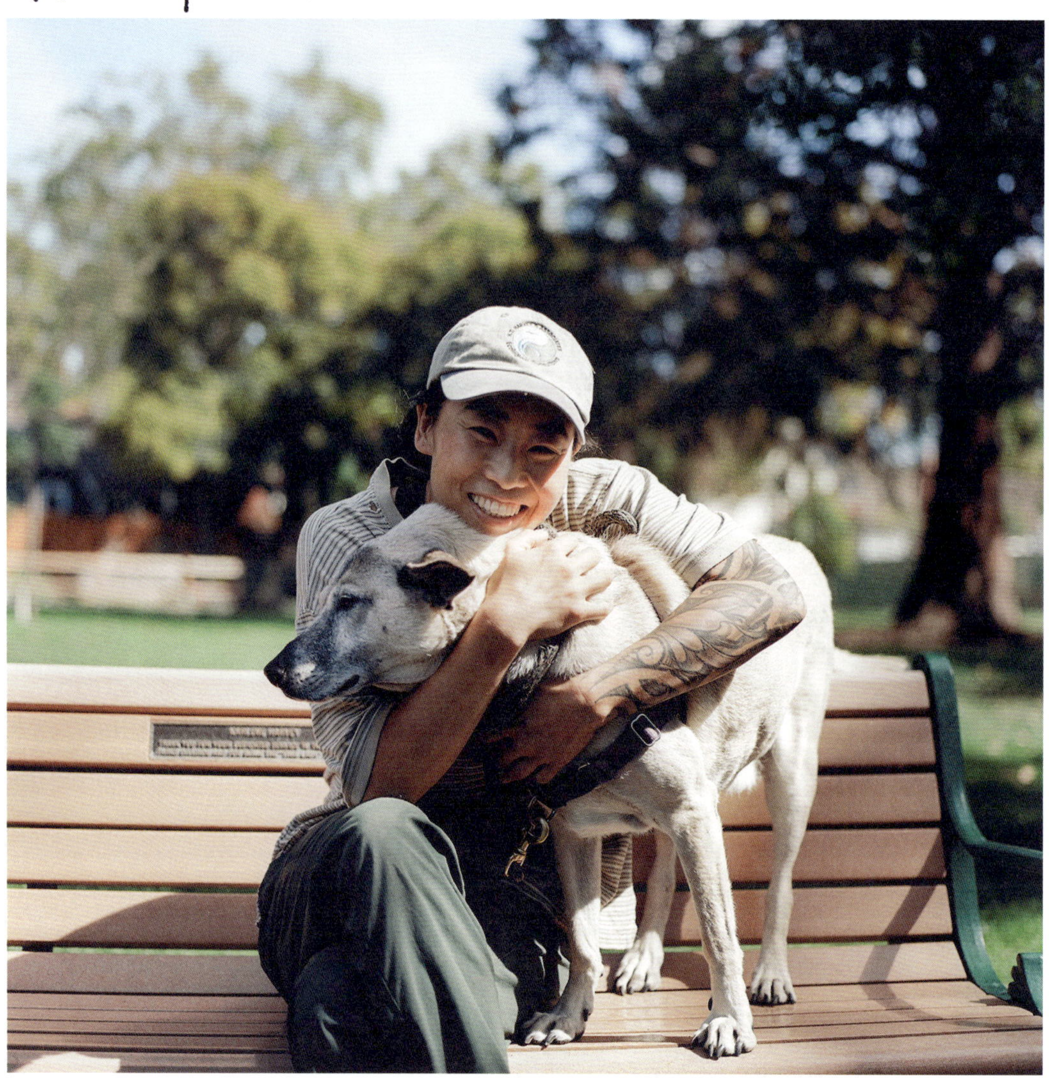

I feel free when I am in the presence
of loved ones, laughing together, experiencing
the joy of life.

Burlingame, California · October 2022

When do I feel Free?

I feel most free when I am alone in nature.
Up in the Mountains, no distractions, no obligations,
no sounds - other than the Perfection of
Mother Nature. Untouched, Pristine water. No signs
of human Contamination (trash). Grounded, Bare
feet connected to Earth. I feel most Free
when I am in Nature, because I am Nature. —Tim

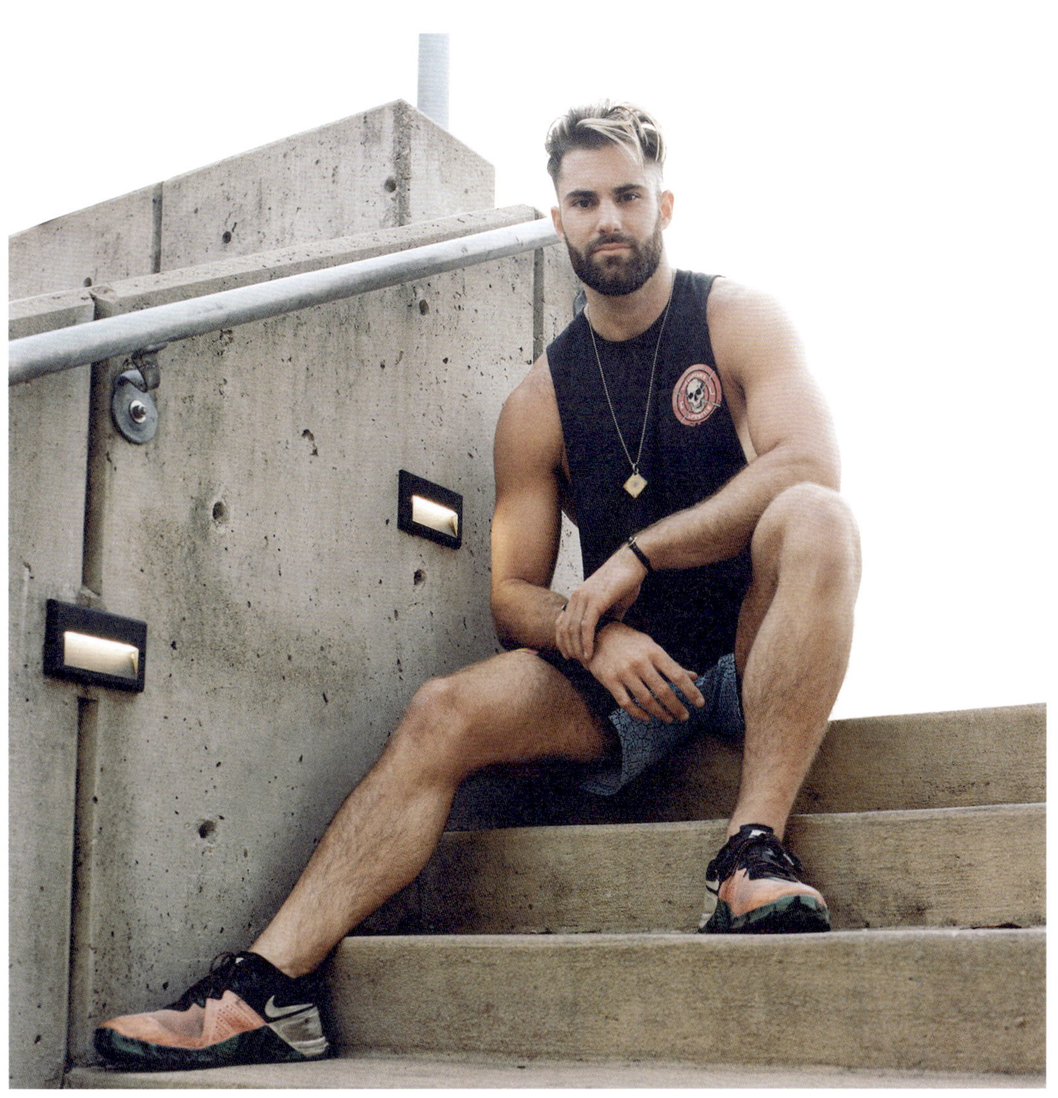

Taylor Morgan

Erica Rhinehart

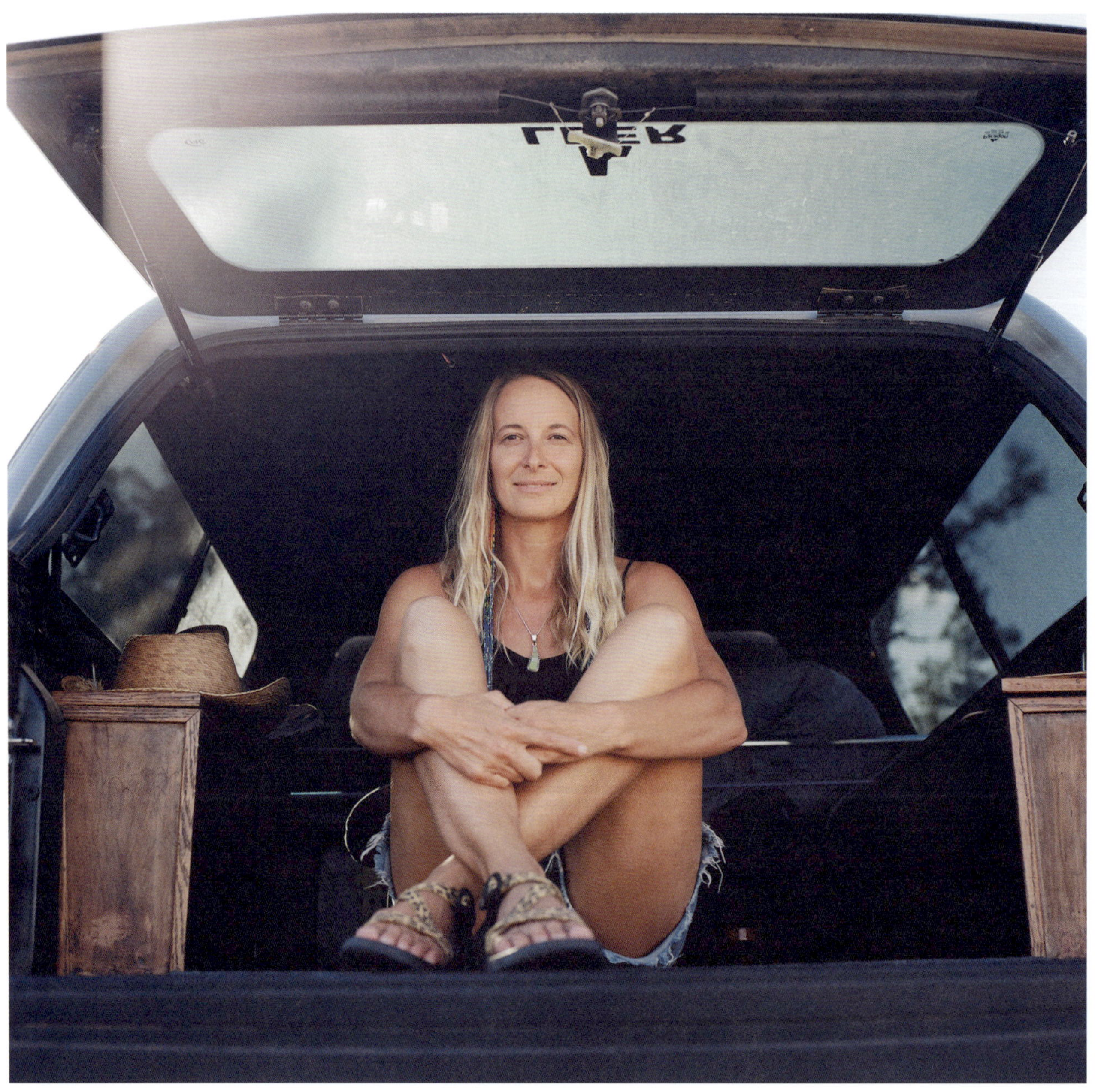

My true freedom is in making
Love to the world — wildly, without
restrain:
Listening to the Dream of the Earth
surrendering to the power of Earth's
dreaming to shape & transform me. And
Spending my days making the Earth's
Dream visible to others.

I feel free when I am
in a state of consciousness
of no resistance. When I
am in a flow state. It happens
when I am meditating, when
I am chanting and when
I am effortlessly offering
my gifts to the world.

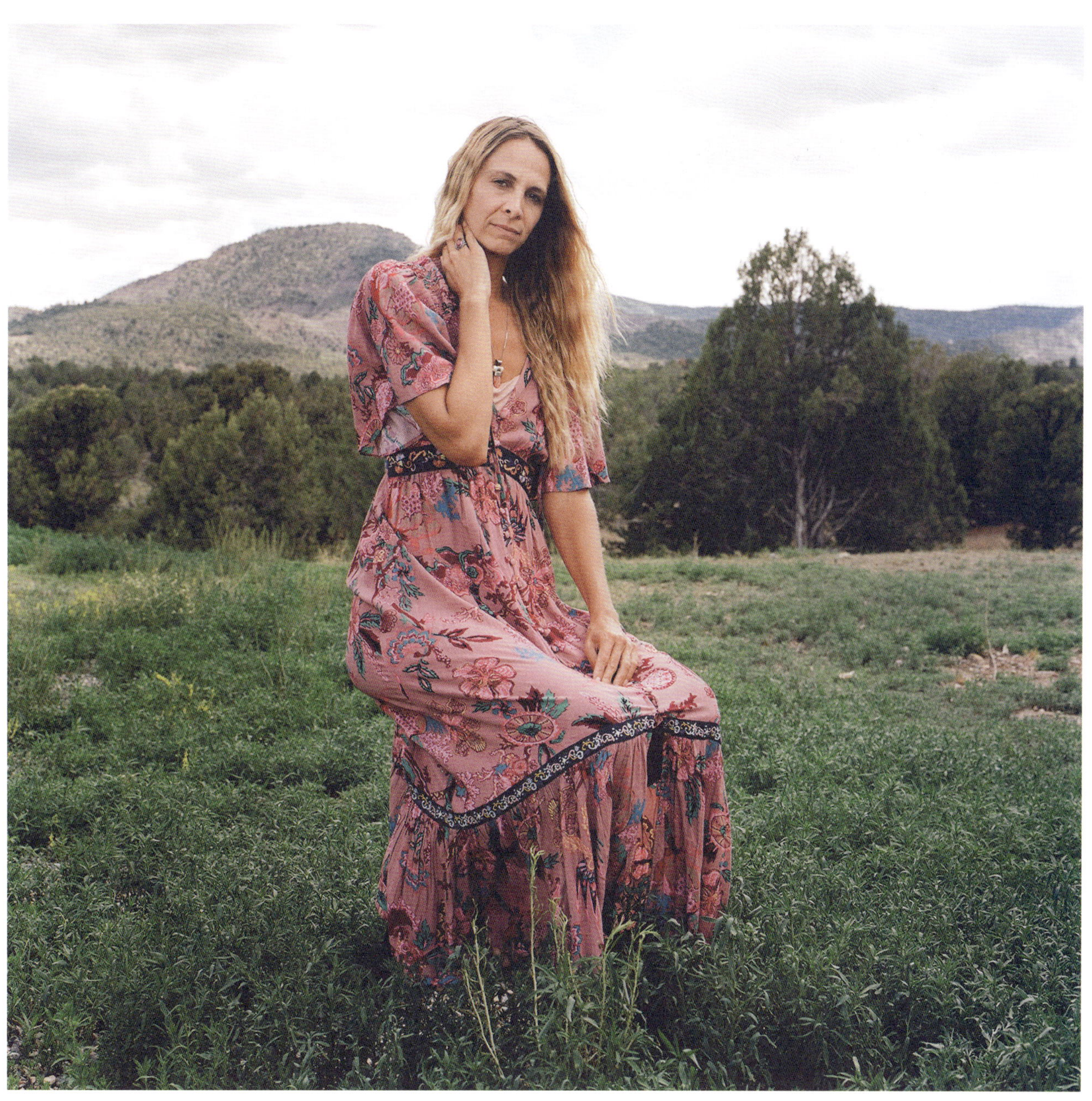

Krista Rhinehart

149

I feel free when
~~[crossed out]~~ I'm engaging
in the world the way
I want to. restricted
in the way I want it
to be.

the ability to
choose.

Power in boundaries.
Believing in myself.
Honest expression.

New Orleans, Louisiana • April 2022

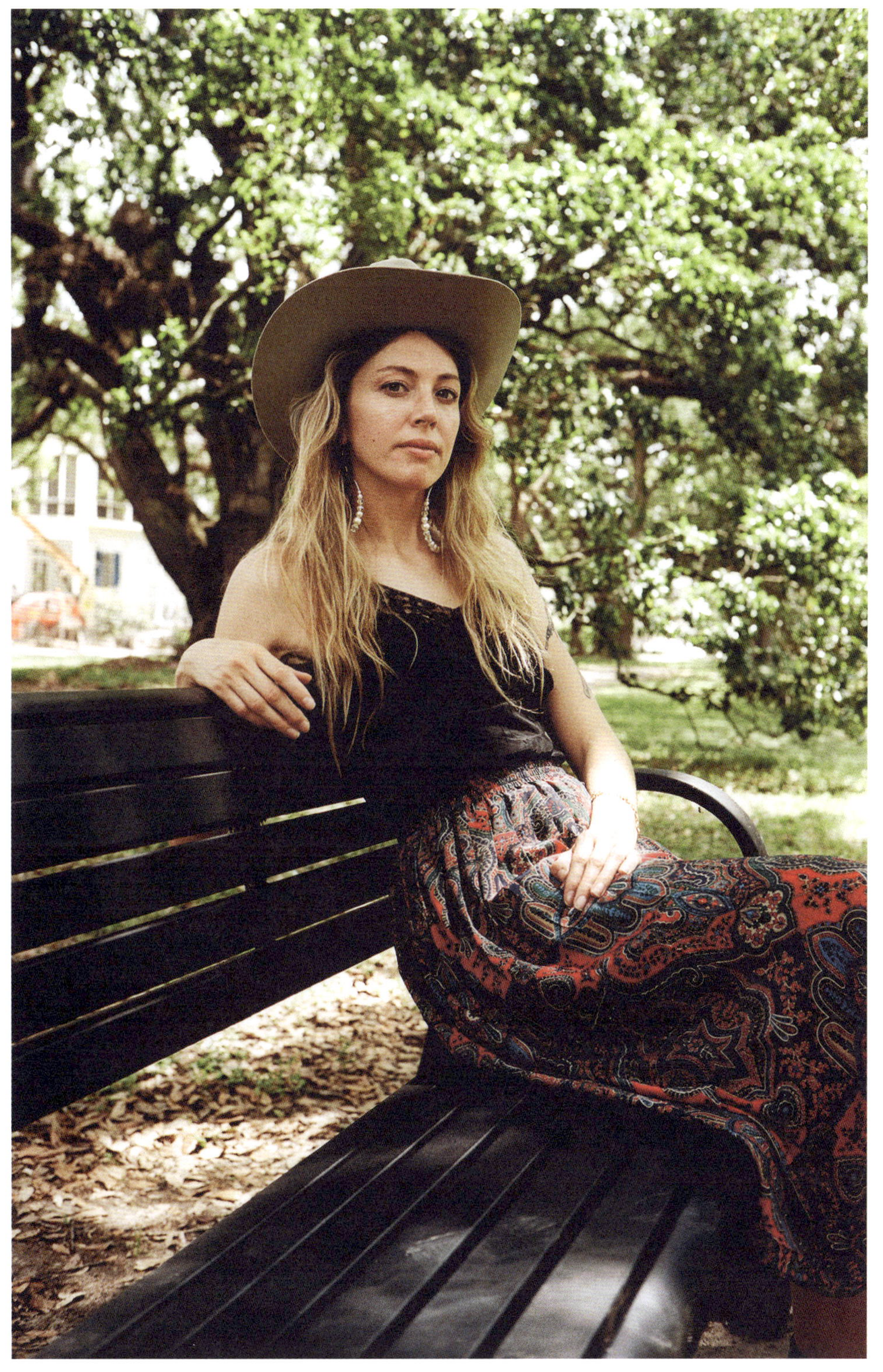

Marilyn
McDougall

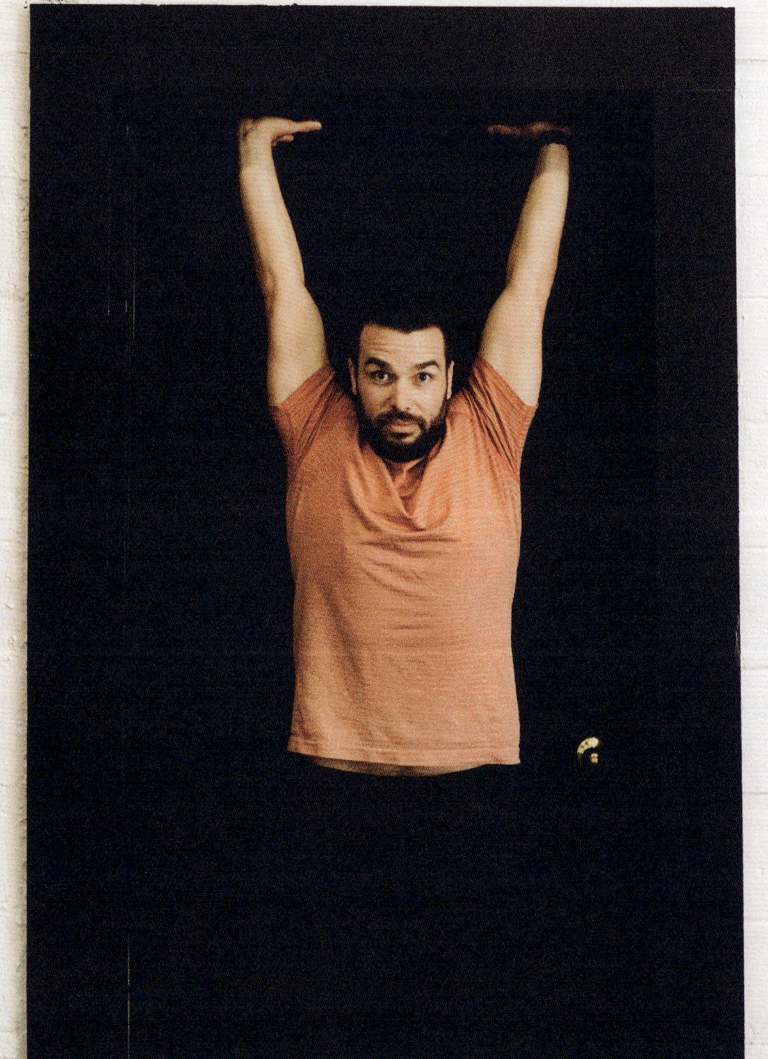

Travis
Goyeneche

I feel free when
Playing sports

- Play
- sport
- freedom
- competion
- connection

freedom creates the choice

when its not in my
control

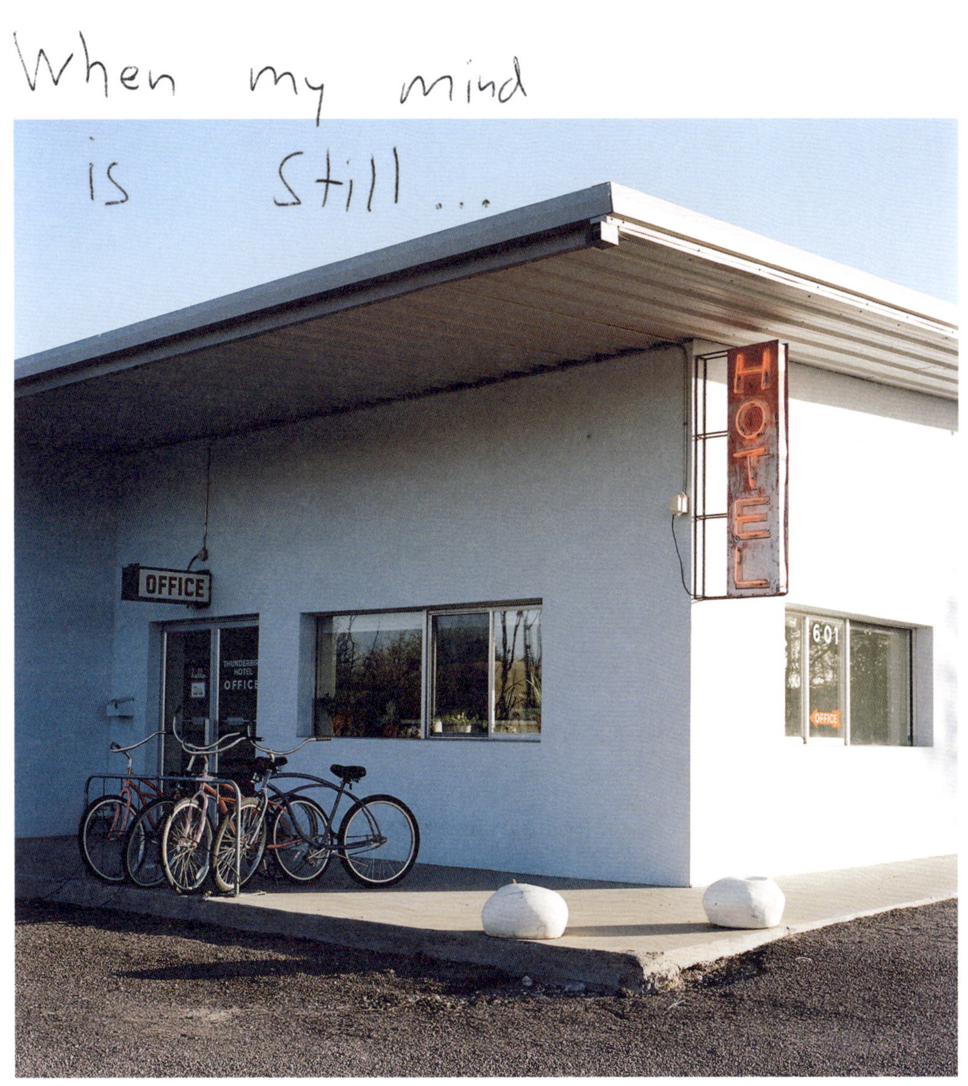

Anonymous

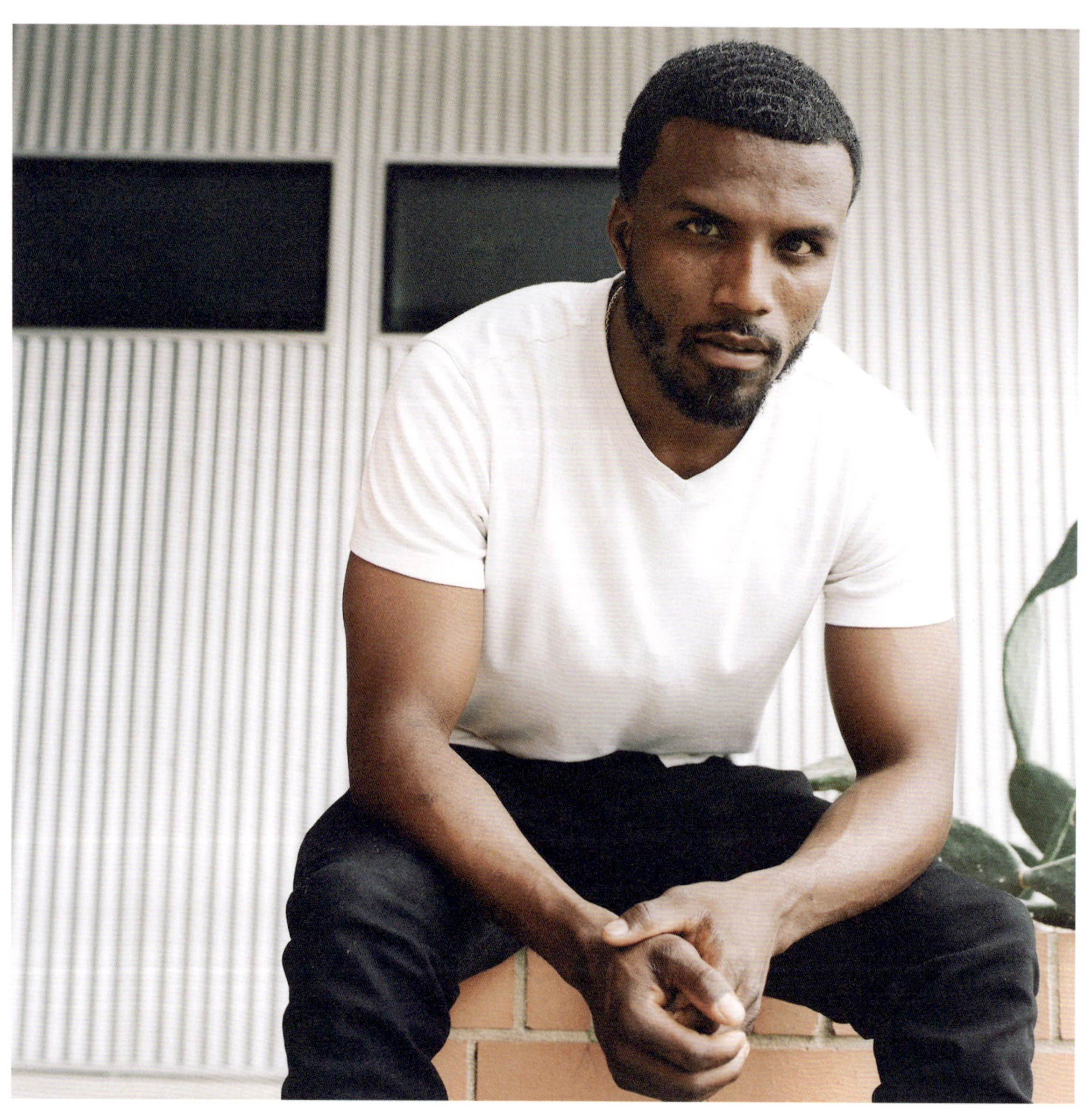

LAMAR BOWMAN JR.

I FELT FREE WHEN INCARCERATED! 13 months
I WANTED TO BE FREE SO BAD IT TOOK ME GOING
TO Jail.
FREE TO TAKE opportunities I didn't or would
EVER Know they Existed.
FREE From thoughts of money, cars, ~~women~~ sex
Women, Drugs.

I FEEL FREE WHEN I Believe in myself!

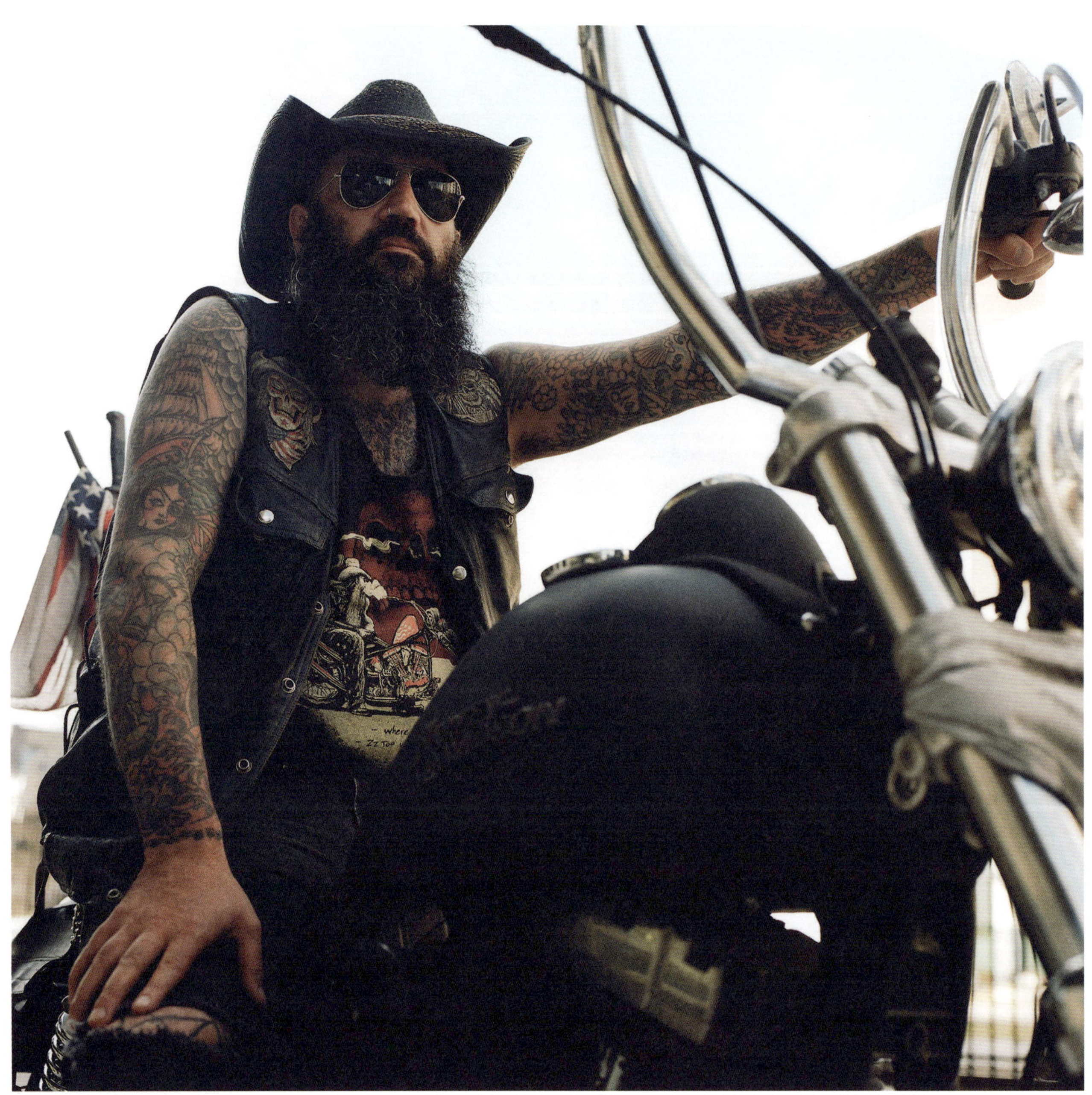

Being Happy
Enjoying Living
Keeping Good Company
Self worth
Hobbys
Cooking and Eating Good

Richie Pearce

Driving w/ the
windows down

* At the White Horse!
  - free at the piano
  - free to smoke

  - dancing w/ my
  honey

  free to have
  exceellent
  conversation!

Ross Tillman Puryear

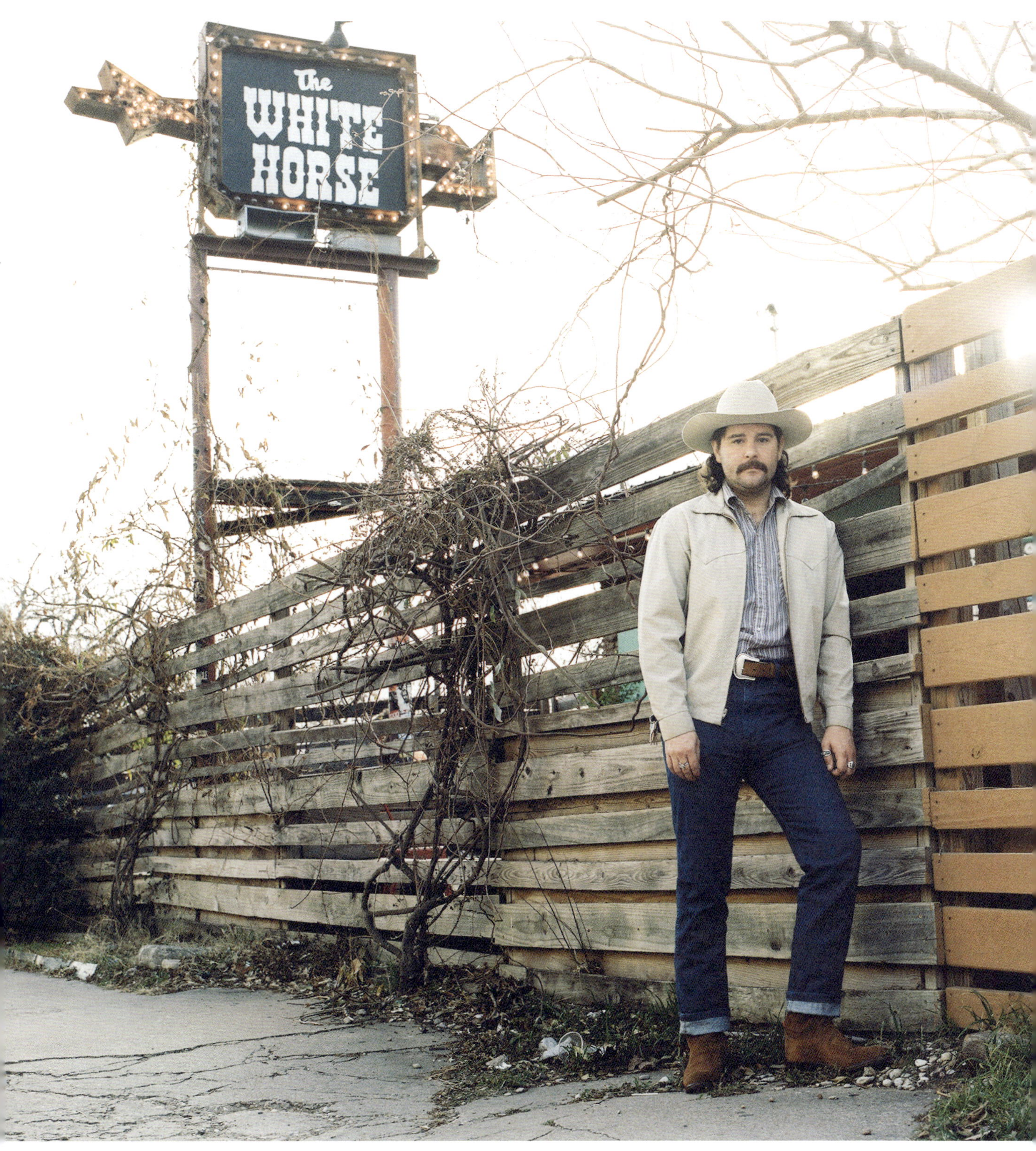
The
WHITE
HORSE

I reckon freedom can mean a lot of things
& can be defined on many levels...
For me — from a soul-level perspective —
Nature is where I find freedom.
open roads, open skies, open fields,
thick forests, blues & greens, browns &
tans. Trees rustling in the wind, birds
chirping, rivers flowing, waves crashing.
That calm that settles the soul & makes
you feel connected to yourself & GOD — nature.

Jessica Rockwell

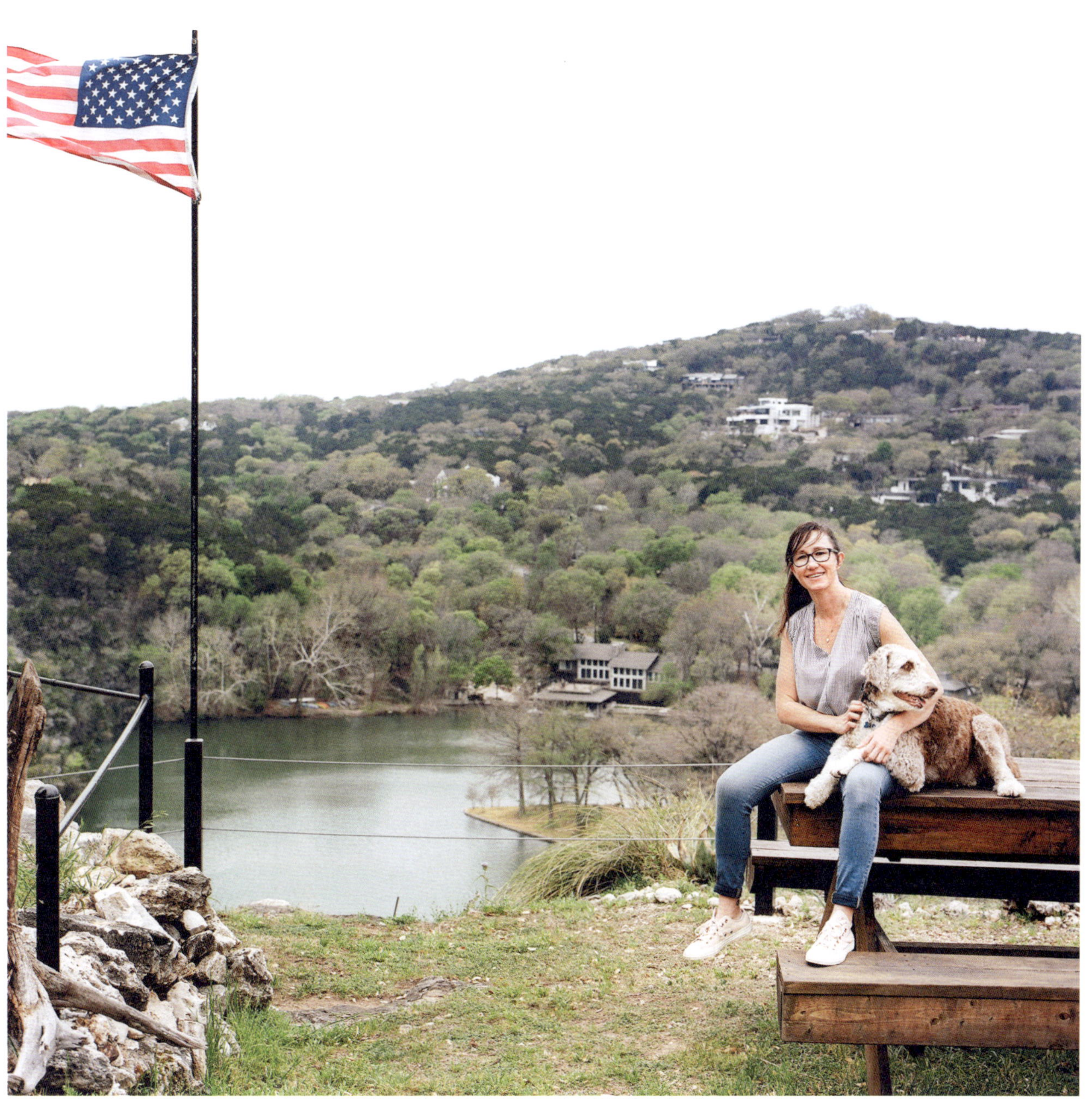

Austin, Texas · March 2022

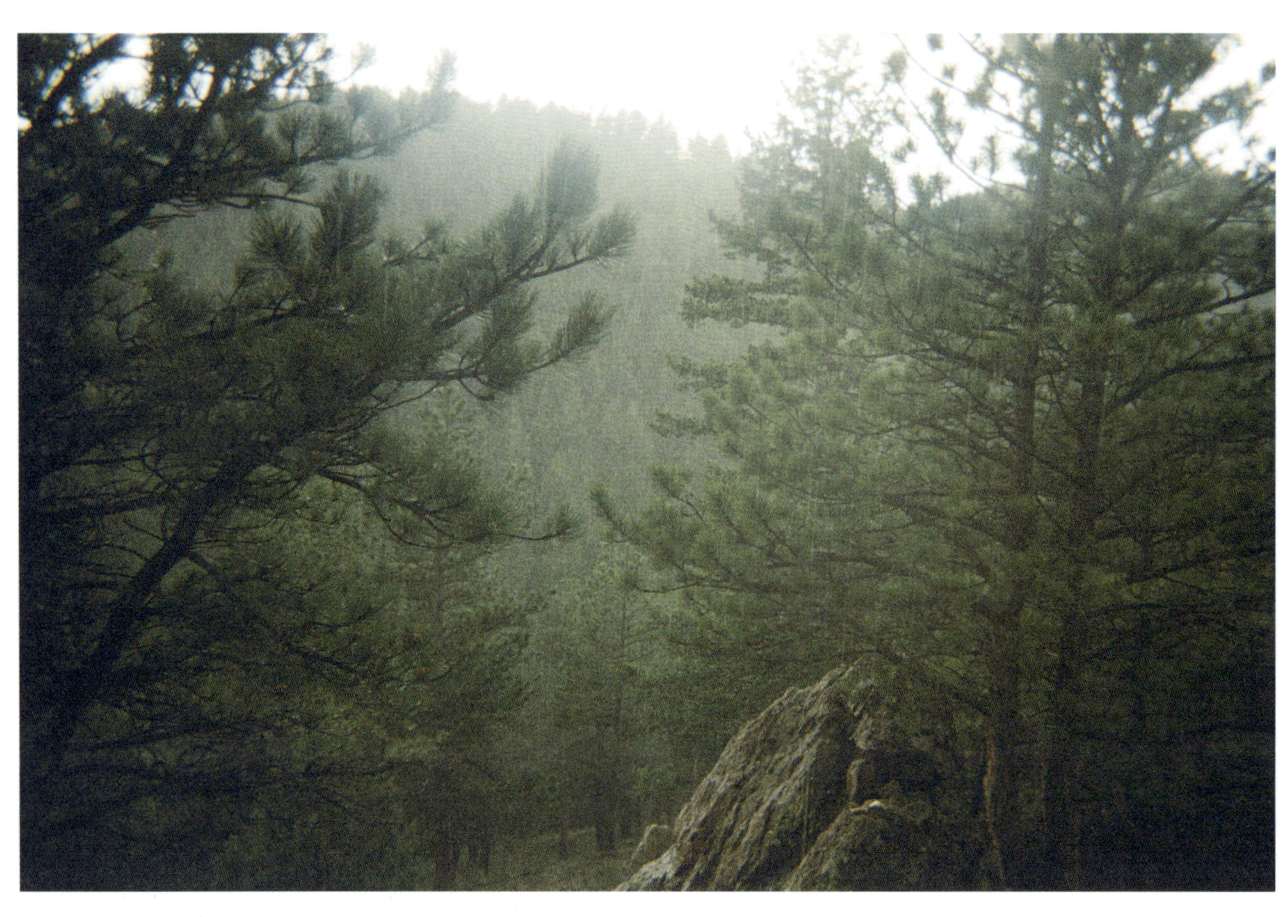

when I am in
nature with my
loved ones

WHEN I HAVE NOTHING LEFT TO LOSE.

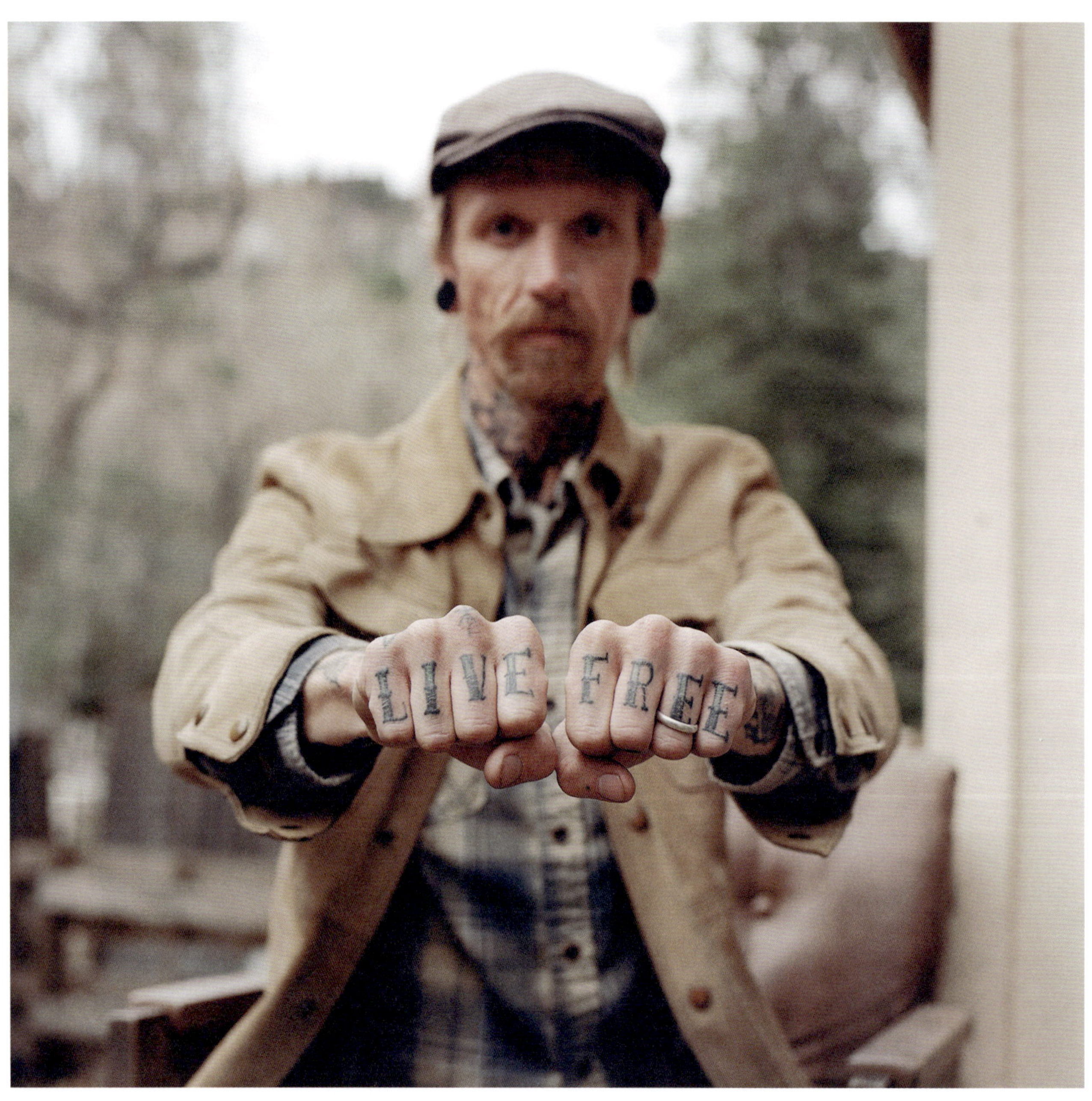

TYLER JONES

I FELT FREE
WHEN I CHOSE
TO BE FREE

I feel free when I'm in the sunshine,
spending undistracted time with
the people I love.

I feel free here at Zilker Park with
my pup winnie who reminds me
the beauty in being present.

Reilly McNerney

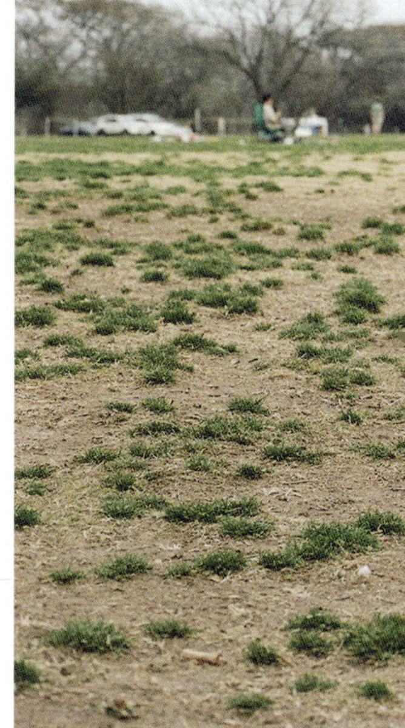

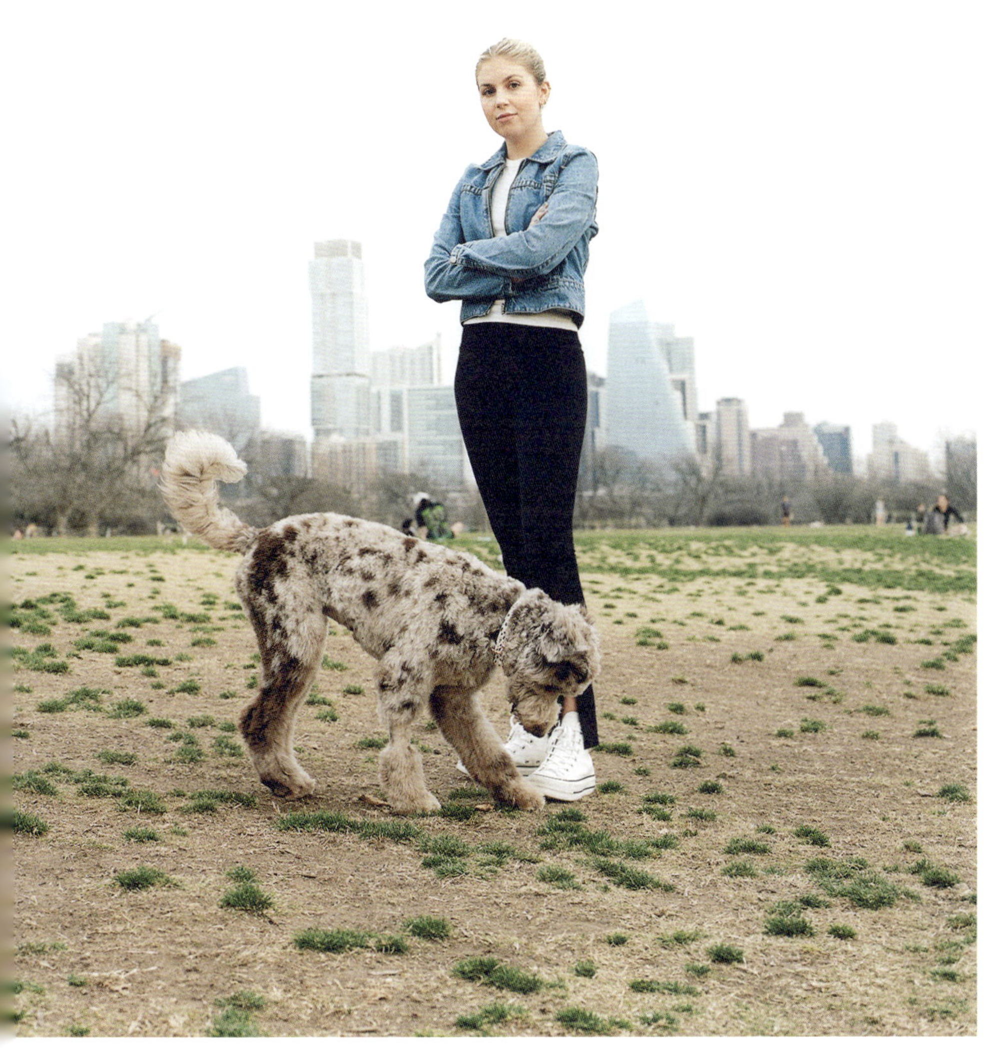

Austin, Texas · March 2022

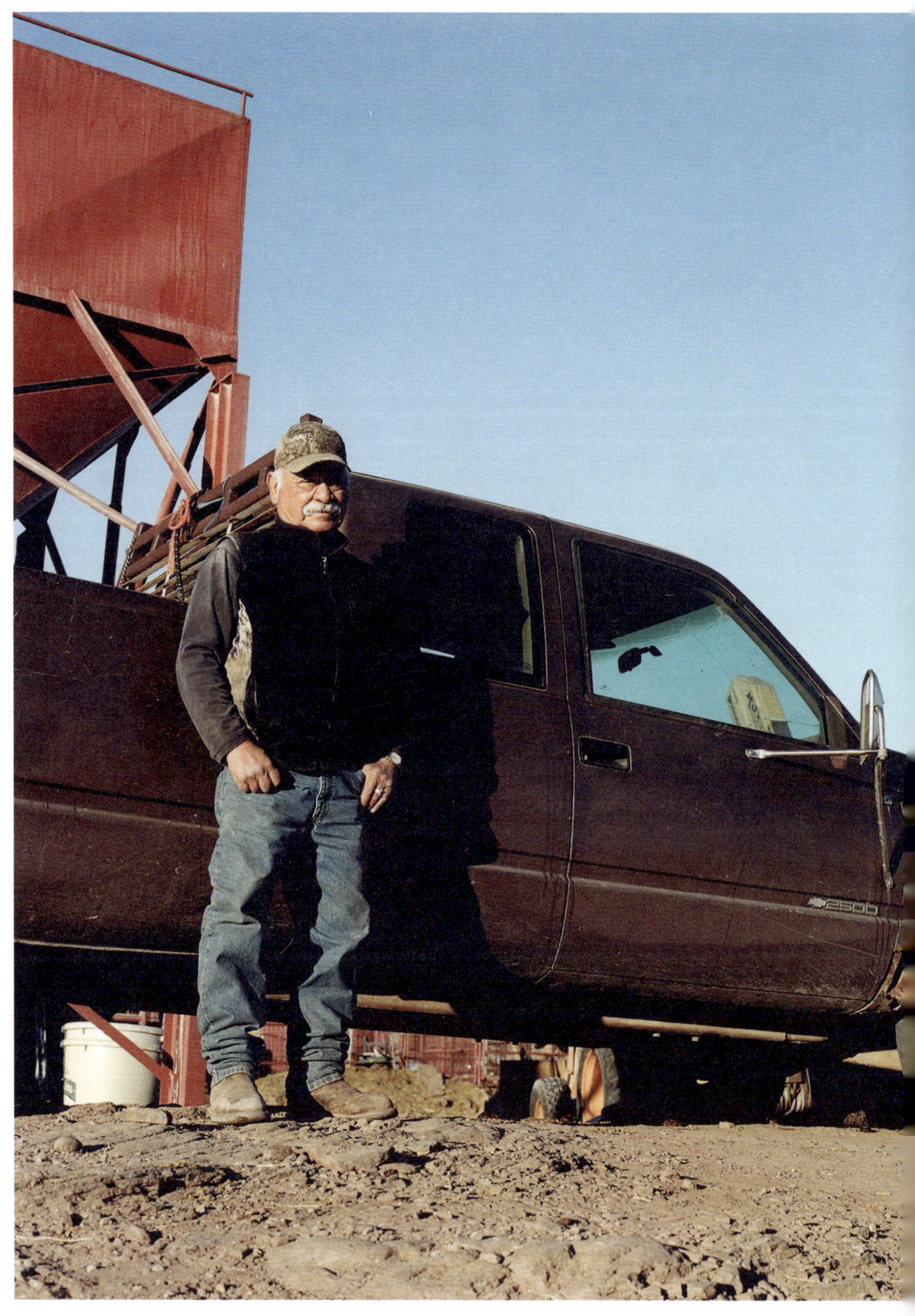

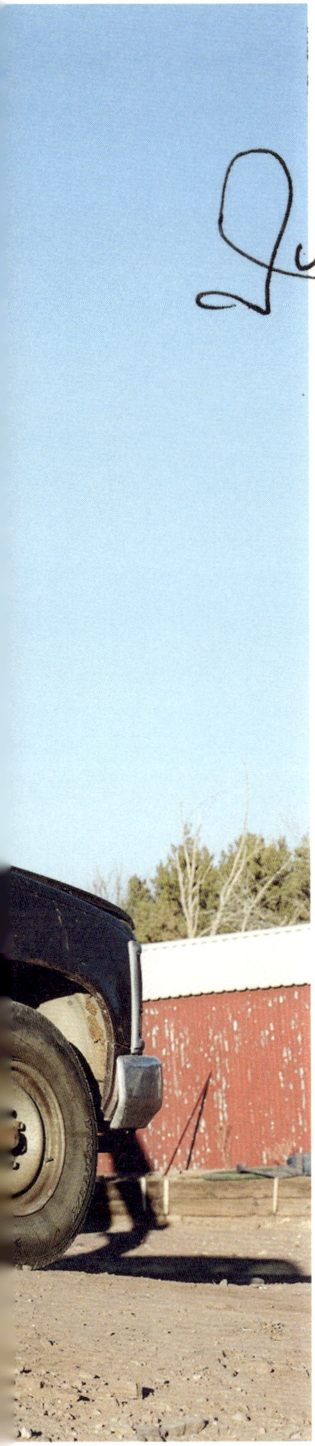

Juan Macias

cuando estoy en
el Rancho

I feel free when I release constraining thoughts through meditation, writing, creating, allowing the present moment to be without judgement

I feel free when I perceive I'm in control (ie - when I am driving to a destination vs. flying.)

I feel free when I am spending my time as I choose to spend it

Stacy Ann Thrash

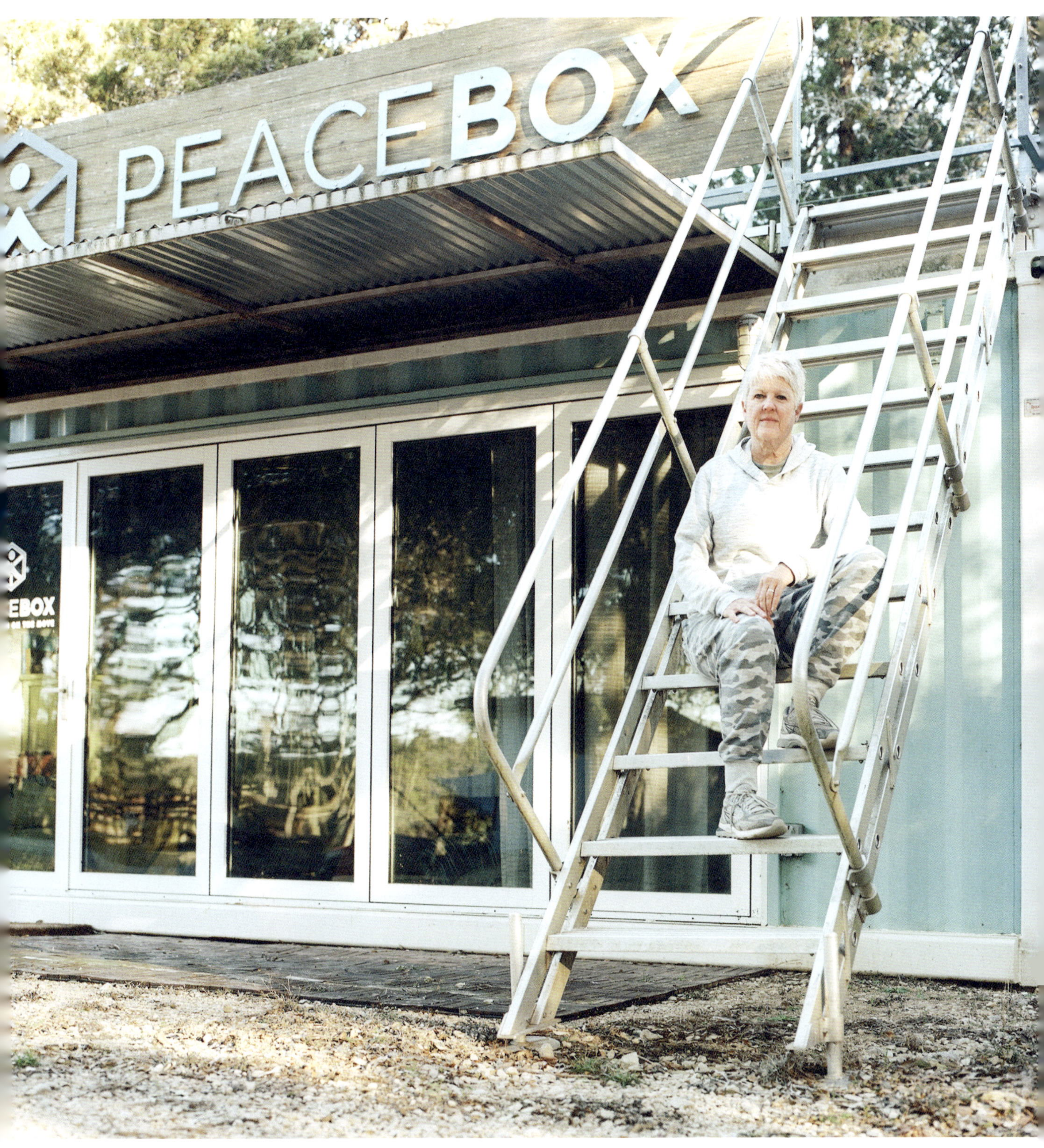

PEACEBOX
EBOX

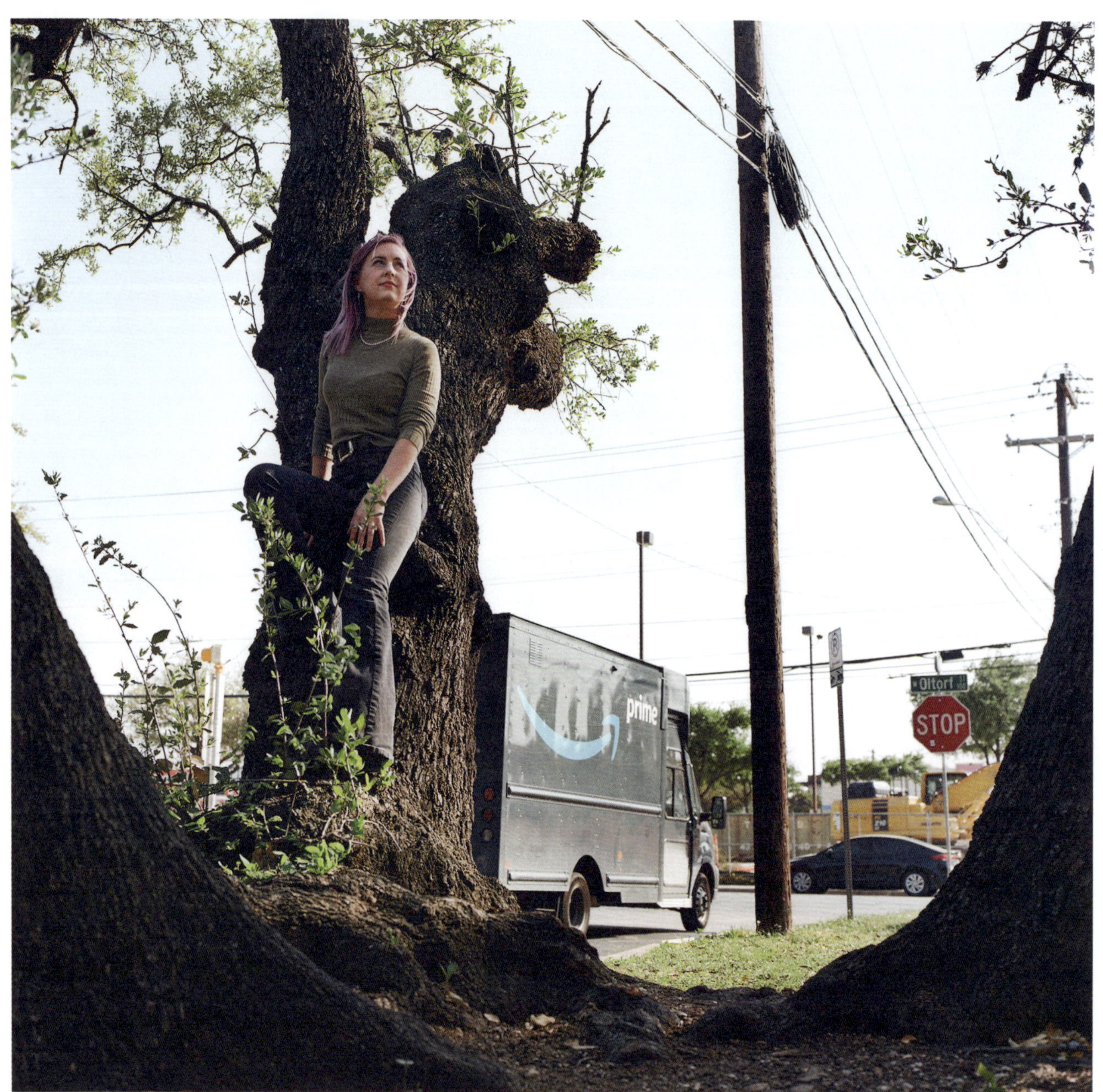
prime
Oltorf
STOP

When I'm @ the beach
after a couple of
drinks, listening to the birds, ocean
wind against my skin,
no phone just myself
relaxing w/ mother
nature
@ my
feet.

Samantha Anne

Austin, Texas · April 2022

I feel most free,
when I can take a nice
walk on the beach...
I feel most free, when
I meet new people...

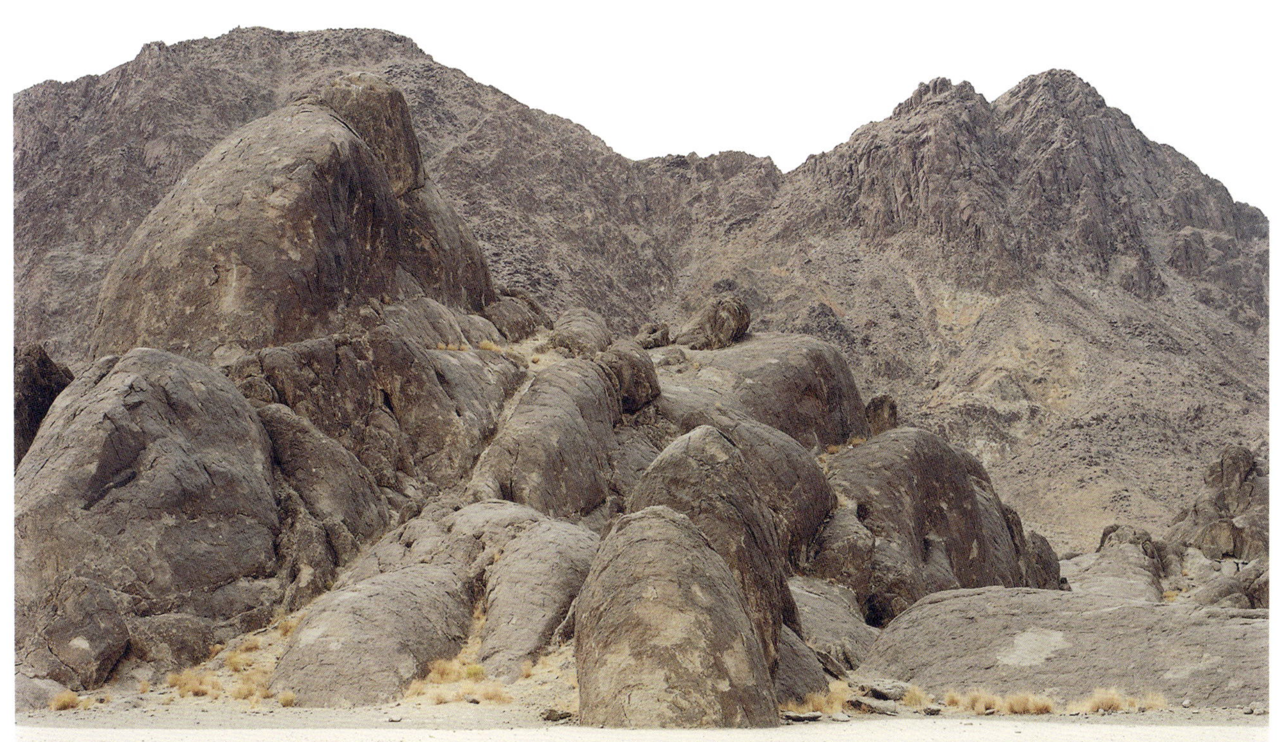

when we need to rely on
the natural world around
us for information

Anonymous

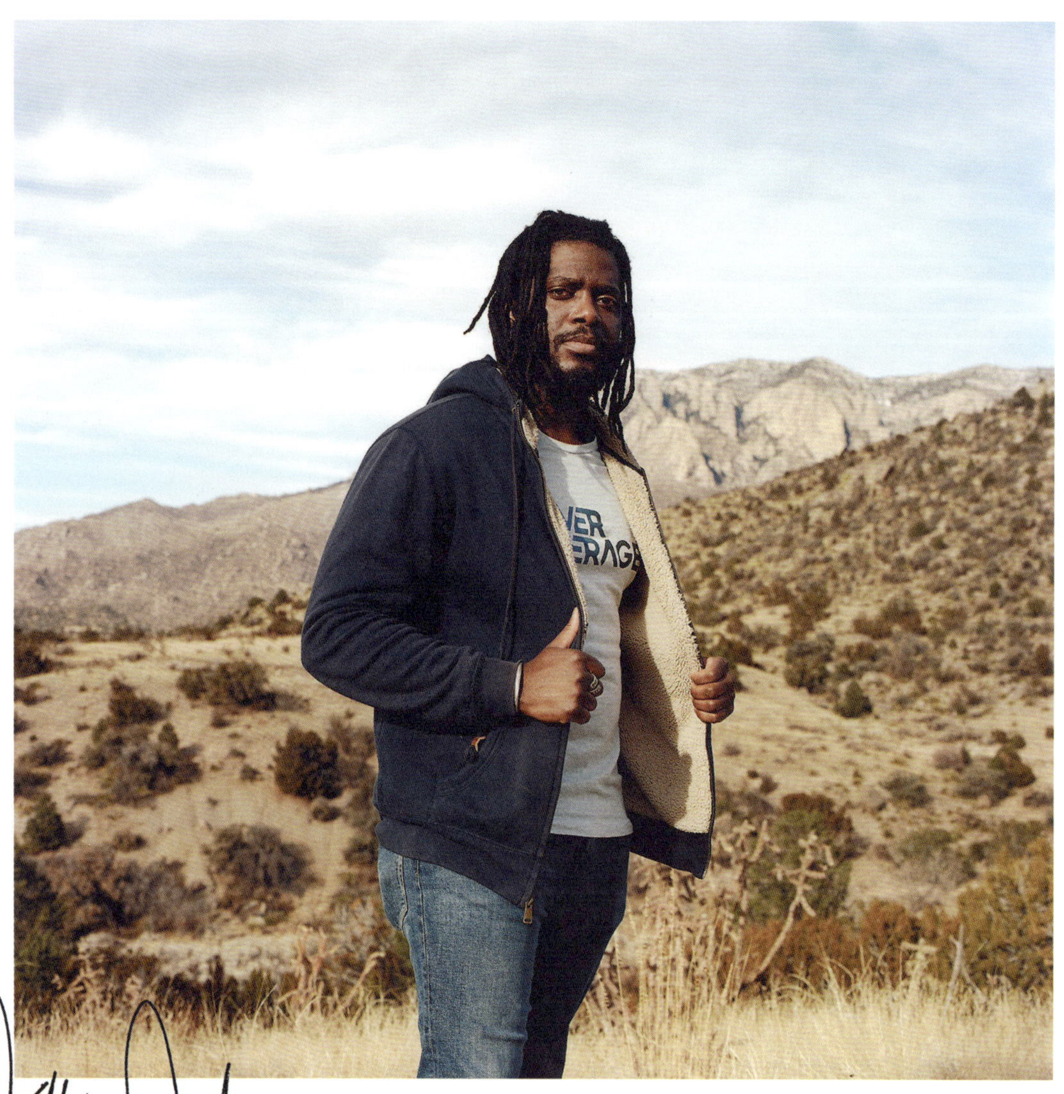

I feel free when the choices and decisions of my life are my own. When I have the liberty to rule over my environment and do as I will to achieve, accomplish, produce, create, and become anything my mind can conceive without restriction or limitation.

I feel free when I am creating,
cultivating, or styling something beautiful
and unique as well as original. I find
most of my inspiration in nature.

— Devin Bajoie

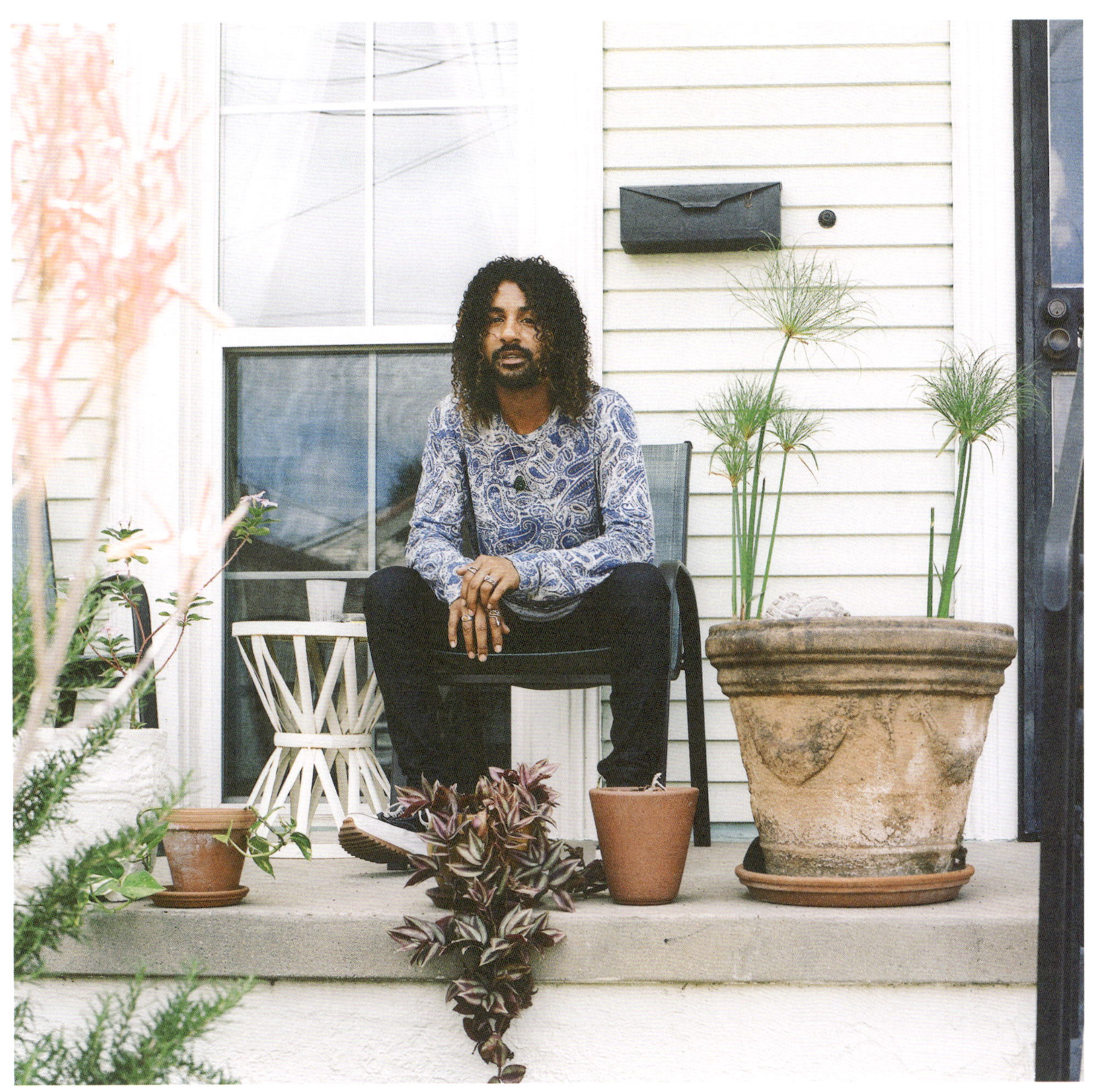

New Orleans, Louisiana · April 2022

Freedom feels like singing
loudly in the car on the way
to a long nature hike
where our dogs can explore
fresh flowers and pine trees and sunshine

Freedom feels like sand
between my toes
at the beach where we read books
and become closer as partners
seashell hunting

Freedom feels like love
in that first sip of morning coffee
pancake smiley faces
eating and dreaming next to a warm fire
safe at home in the spaces we share

— Christina Clark

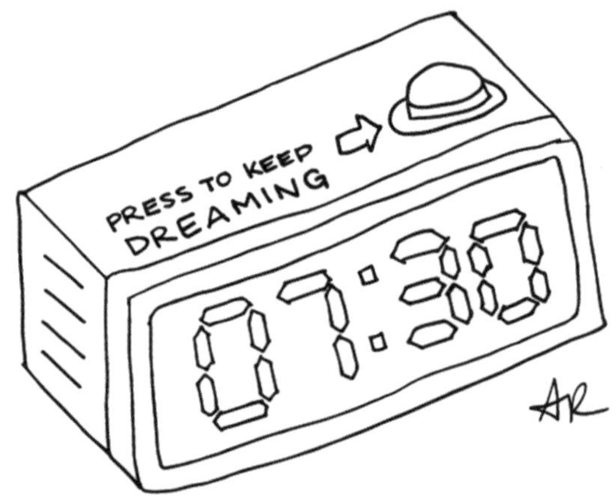

I FEEL THE MOST FREE WHEN
TIME HAS NO CONSTRAINTS AND
MY DREAMS HAVE NO BOUNDARIES.
I AM FREE WHEN MY HEAD IS
IN THE CLOUDS AND MY HEART
IS PRESENT.

— ABBY REDICK

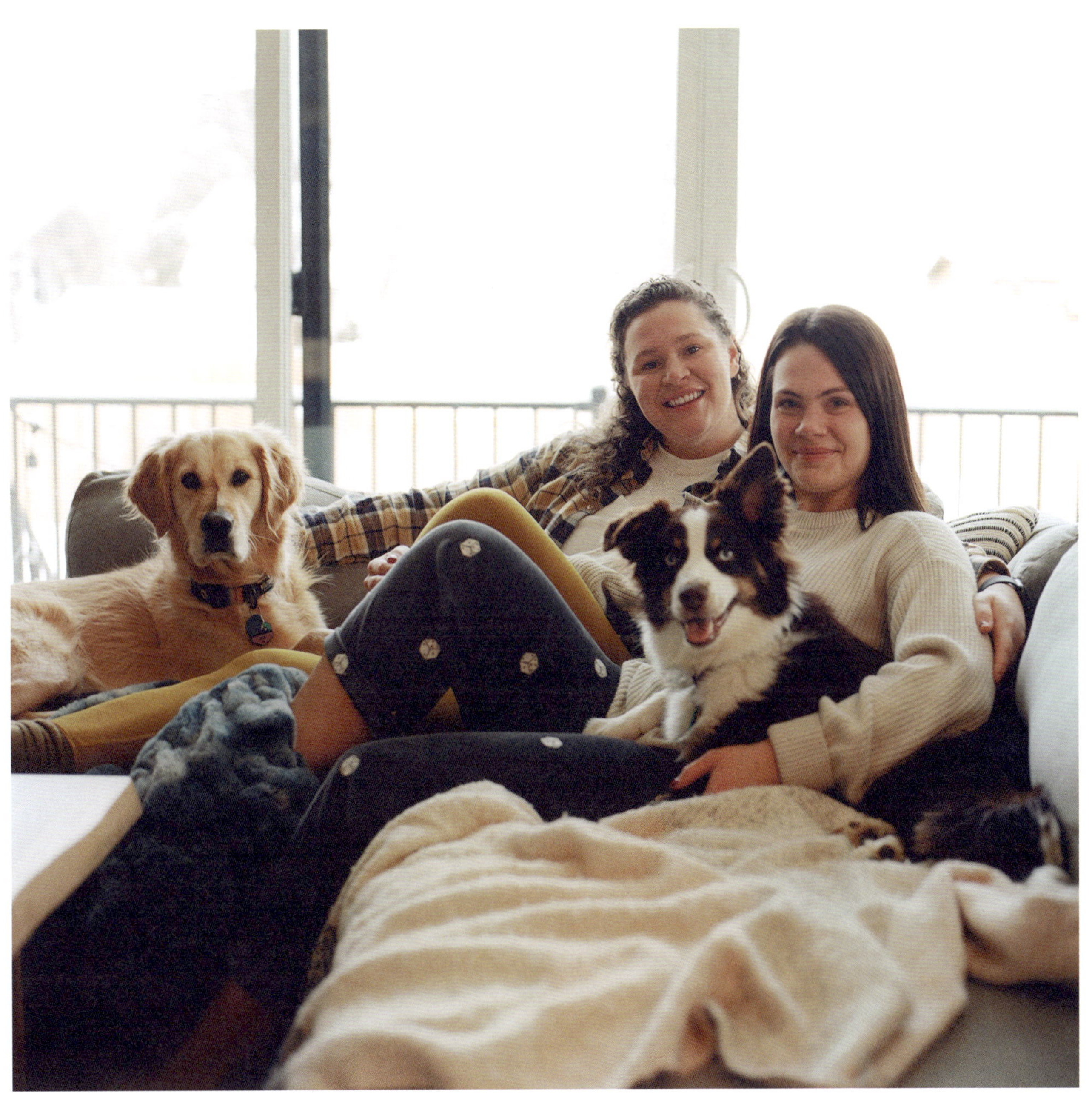

Denver, Colorado · January 2022

Me siento libre cuando
libero mi espíritu y
así poder moverme a
otras dimensiones.

I feel free when I work
my spirit and I am
capable of moving to
other dimensions.

Madame Clarita

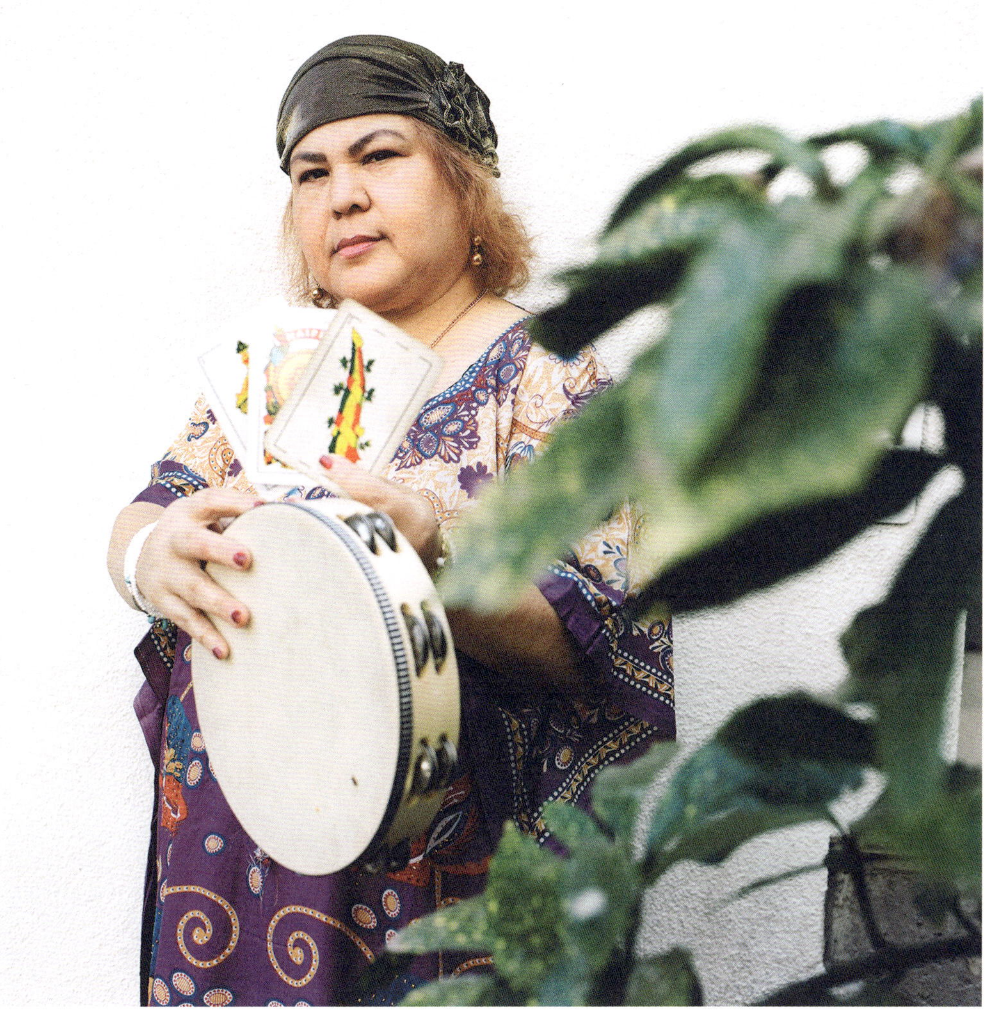

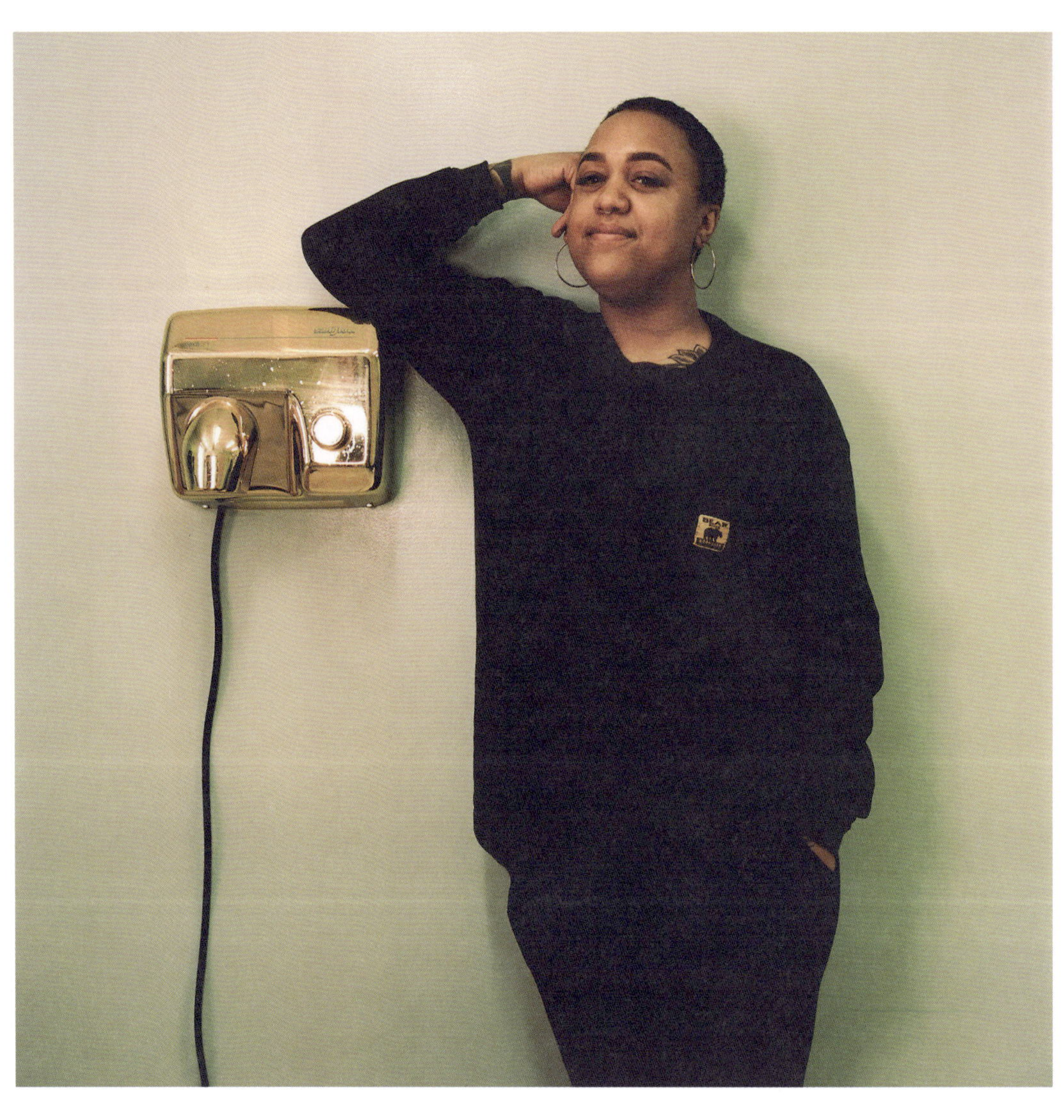

Taelor Gilbert

I feel free when I'm spending time outside in nature. Hiking or spending time in water. I feel like I can be my natural self, free of judgement and totally uninhibited.

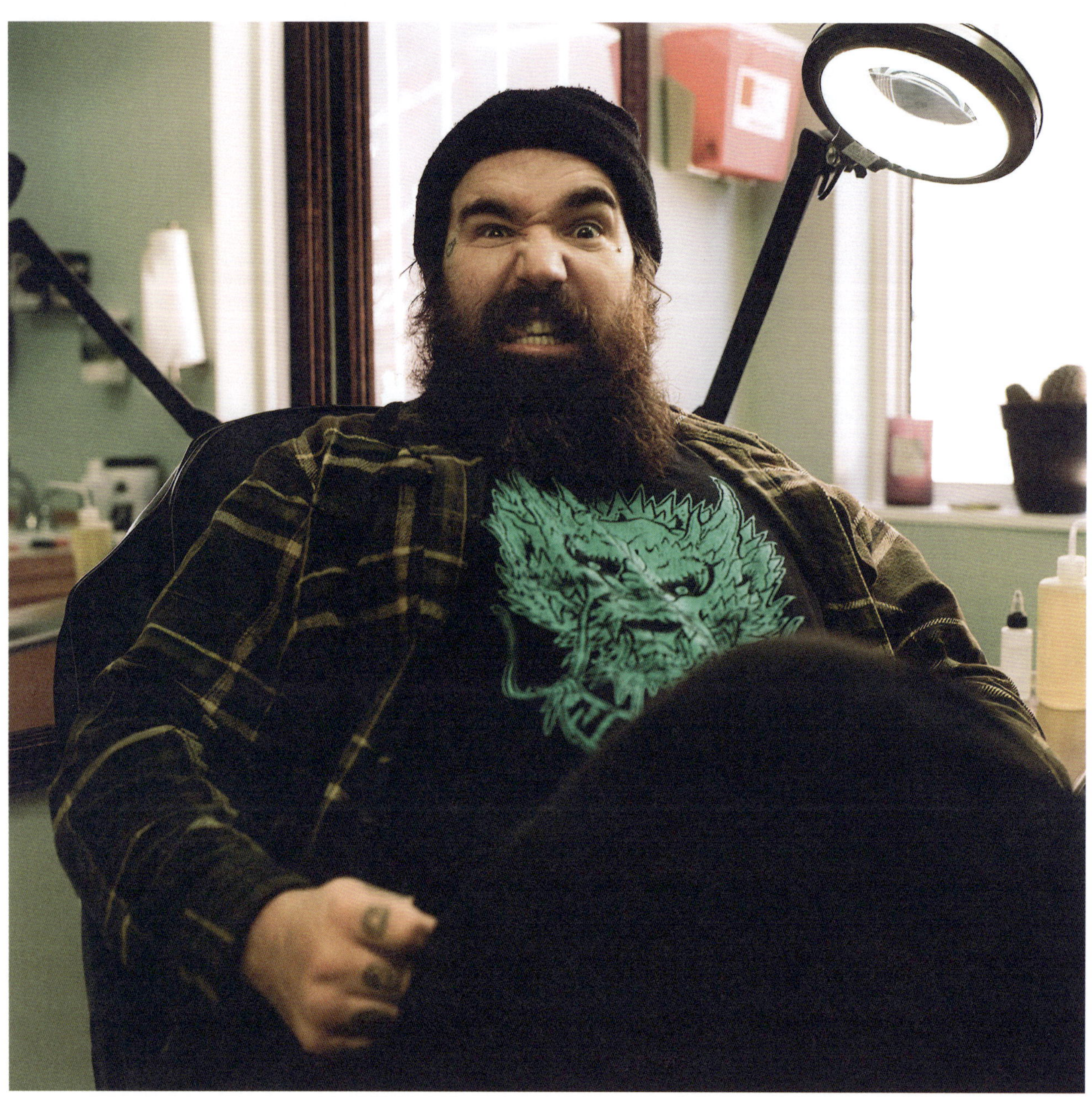

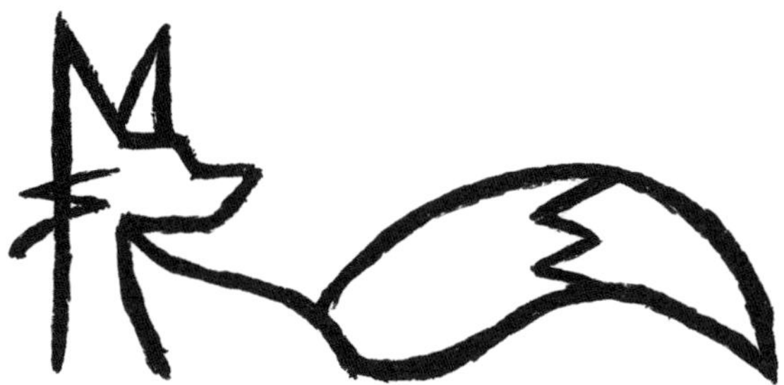

Santa Fe, New Mexico · January 2022

. I feel free when I am leading

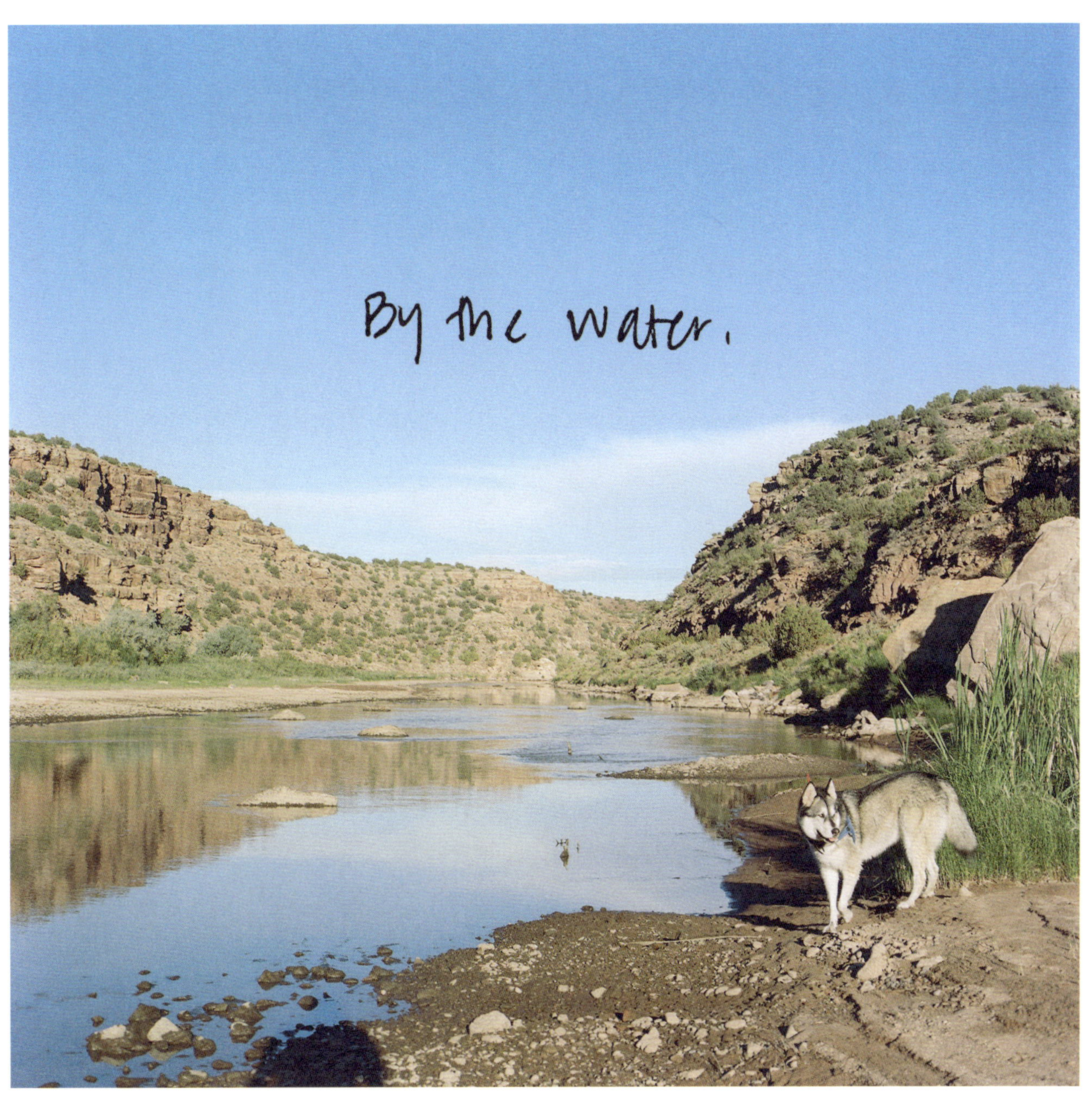

Anonymous

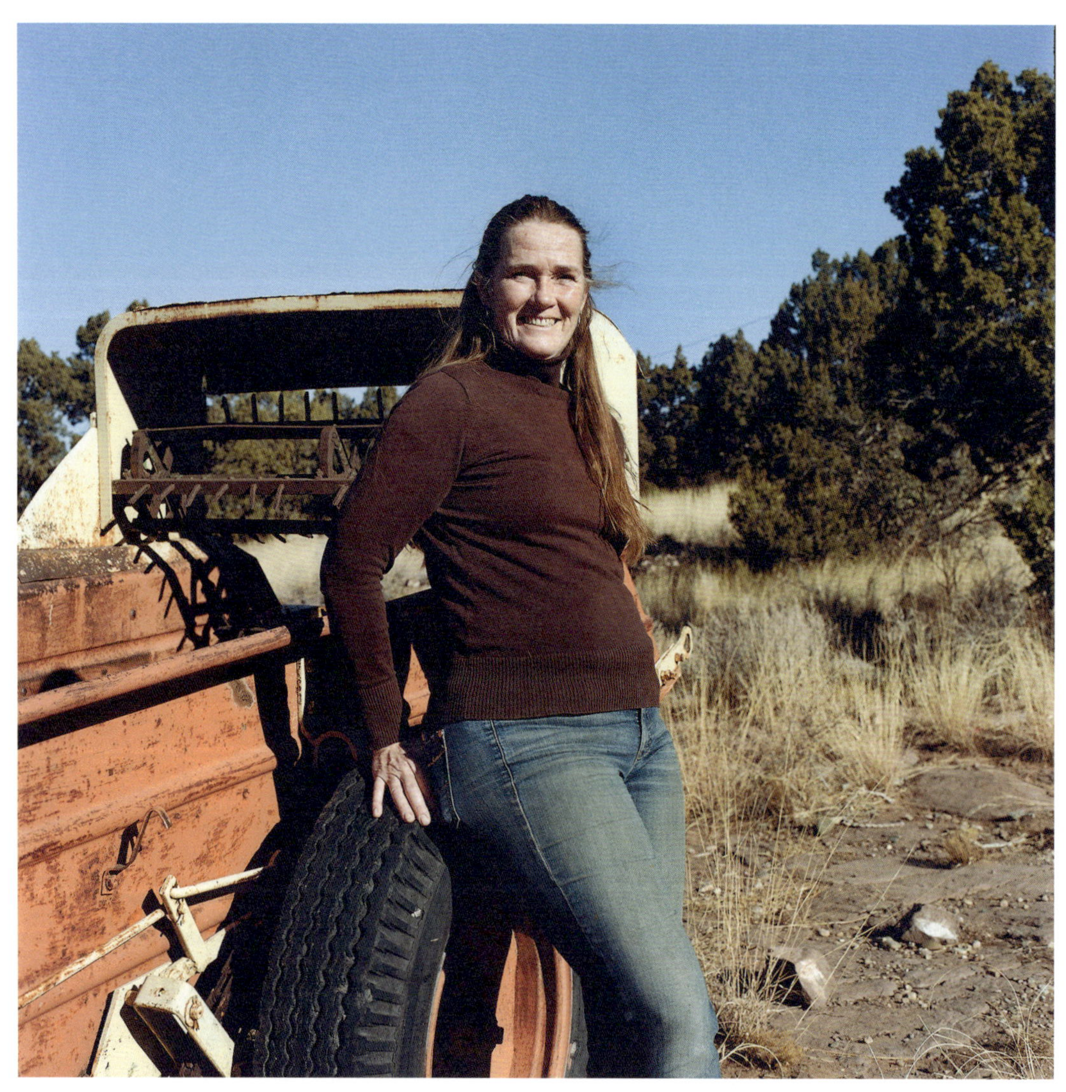

Claudia

Ich empfinde Freiheit,
Wenn ich ~~auf~~ in endlos
Scheinenden Weiten
reite.

Ich empfinde
Freiheit, wenn
ich mich in
überwältigender
Natur befinde, allein
oder mit Tieren.
Sei es zu Pferd, um
Rinder in einer großen
Weide zu suchen, oder
wenn ich auf dem
Meer segle, oder
wenn ich beim
Snowboarden auf
einem Berg stehe ☺

Andrea

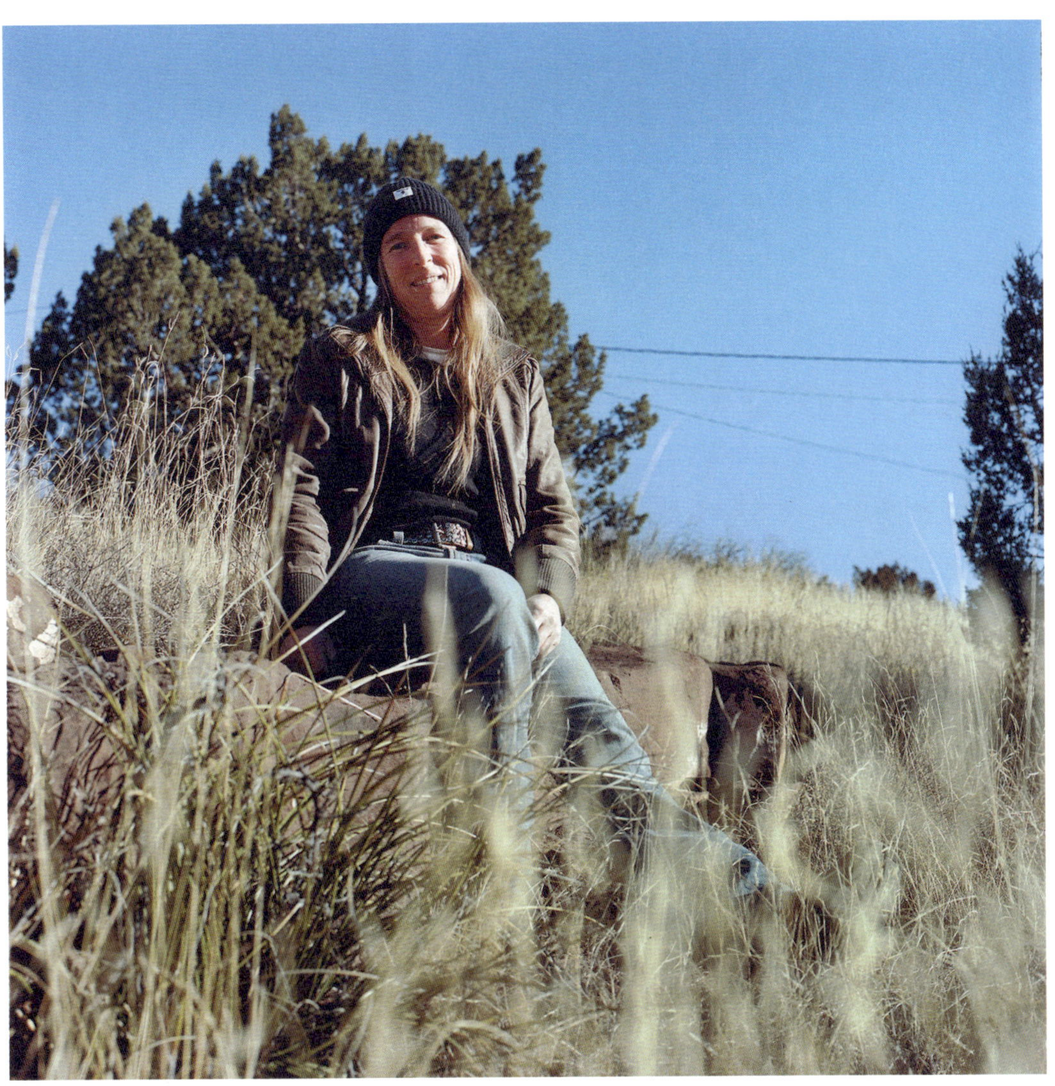

Santa Rosa, New Mexico · January 2022

I feel most
Free when
I'm Dancing! ♡

Alexandria Rae Soliz

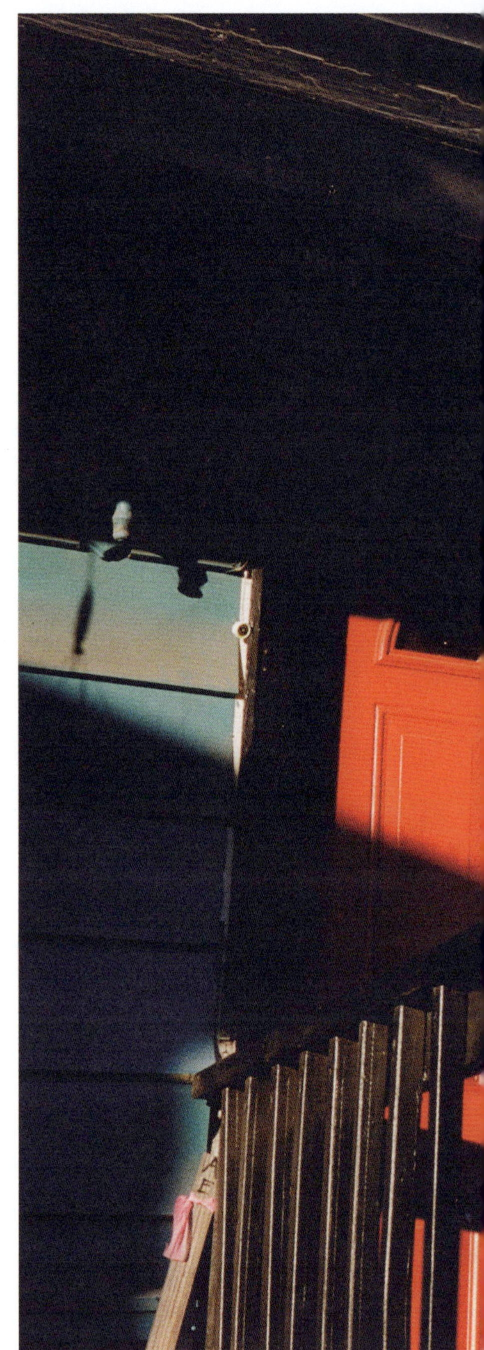

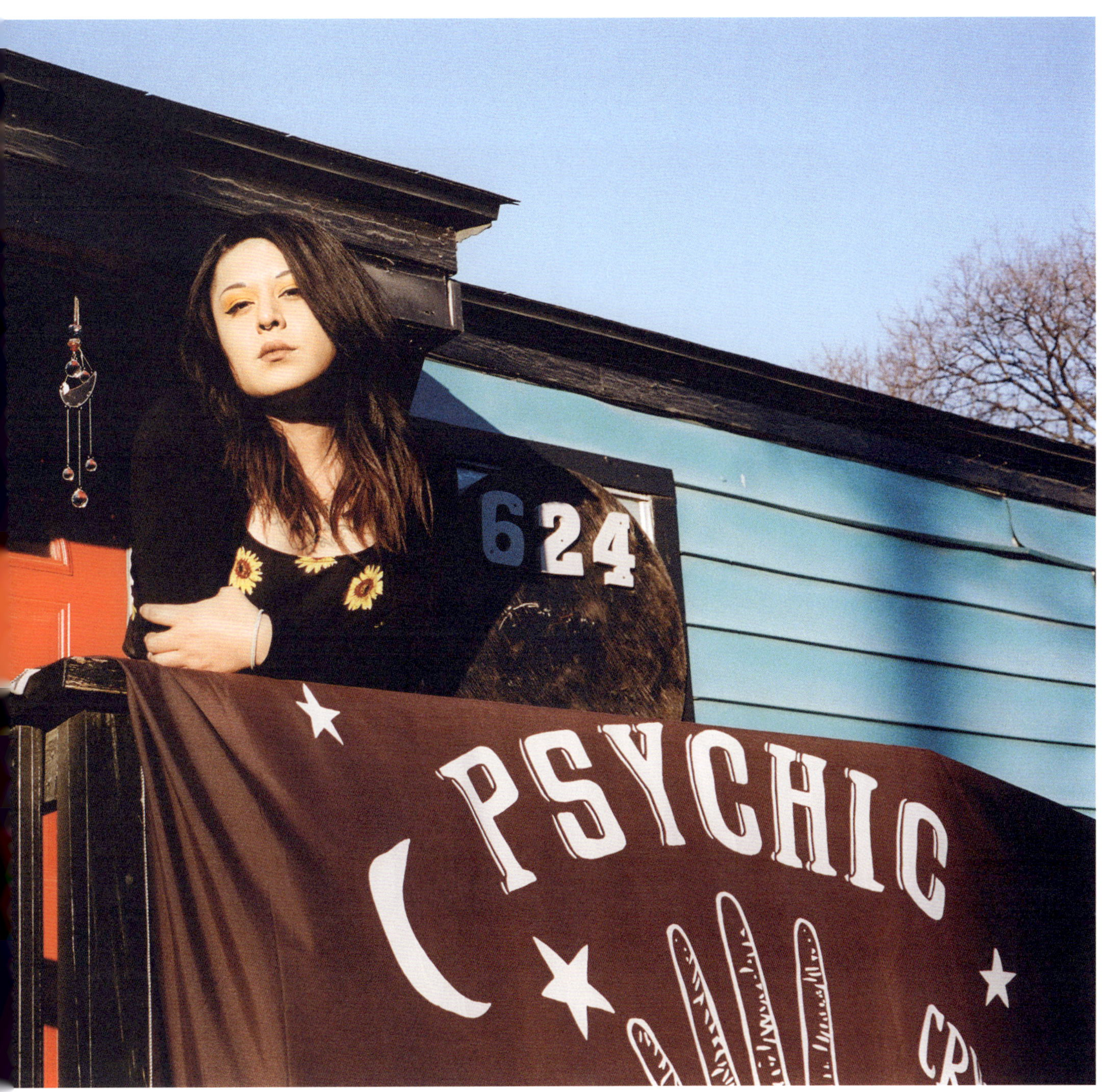

Austin, Texas • February 2022

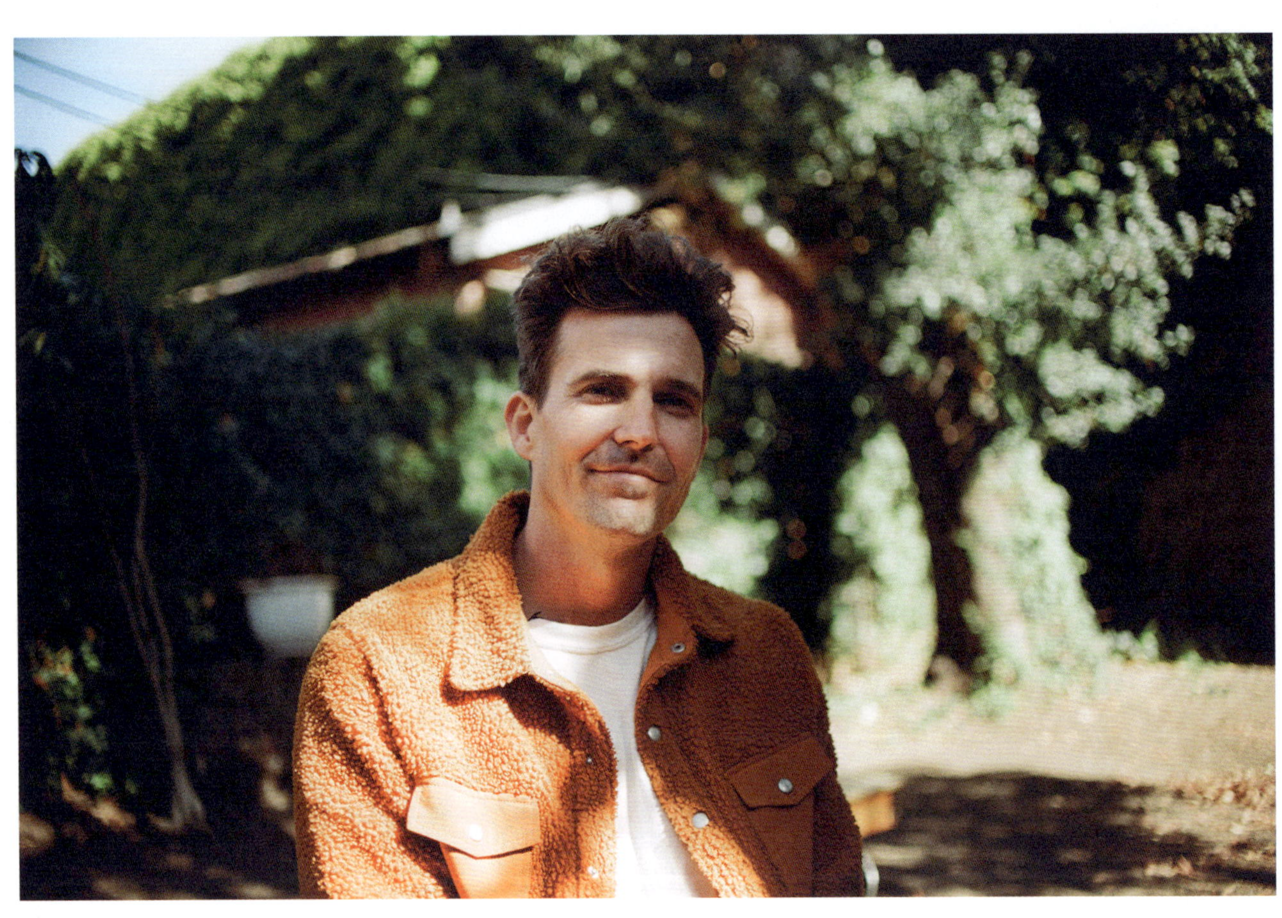
Carl Padi

I feel free when
I take full ownership
of my life and pause
to appreciate it all.

Burlingame, California · October 2022

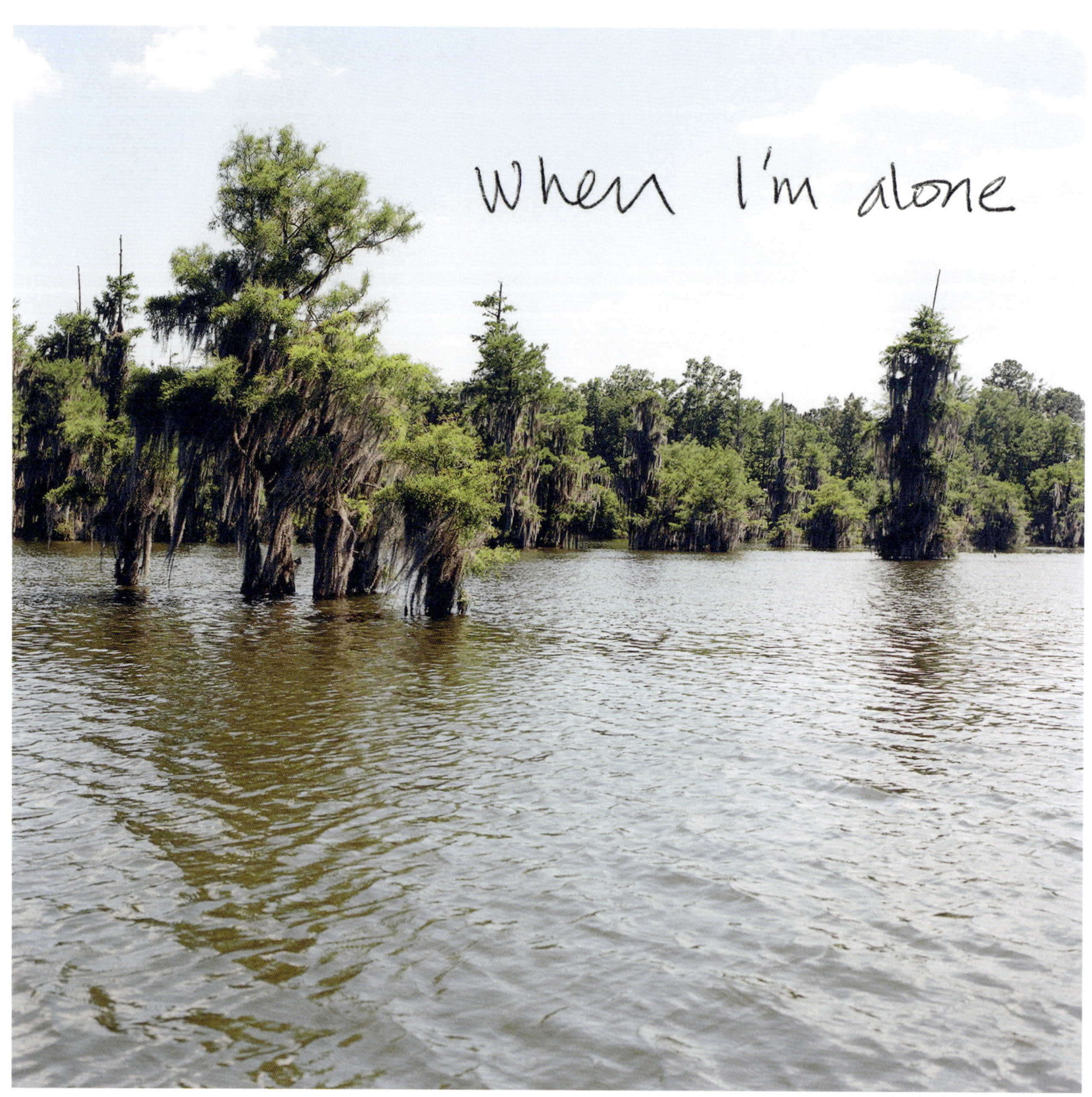
when I'm alone

when my phone
on 'Do Not Disturb'

Anonymous

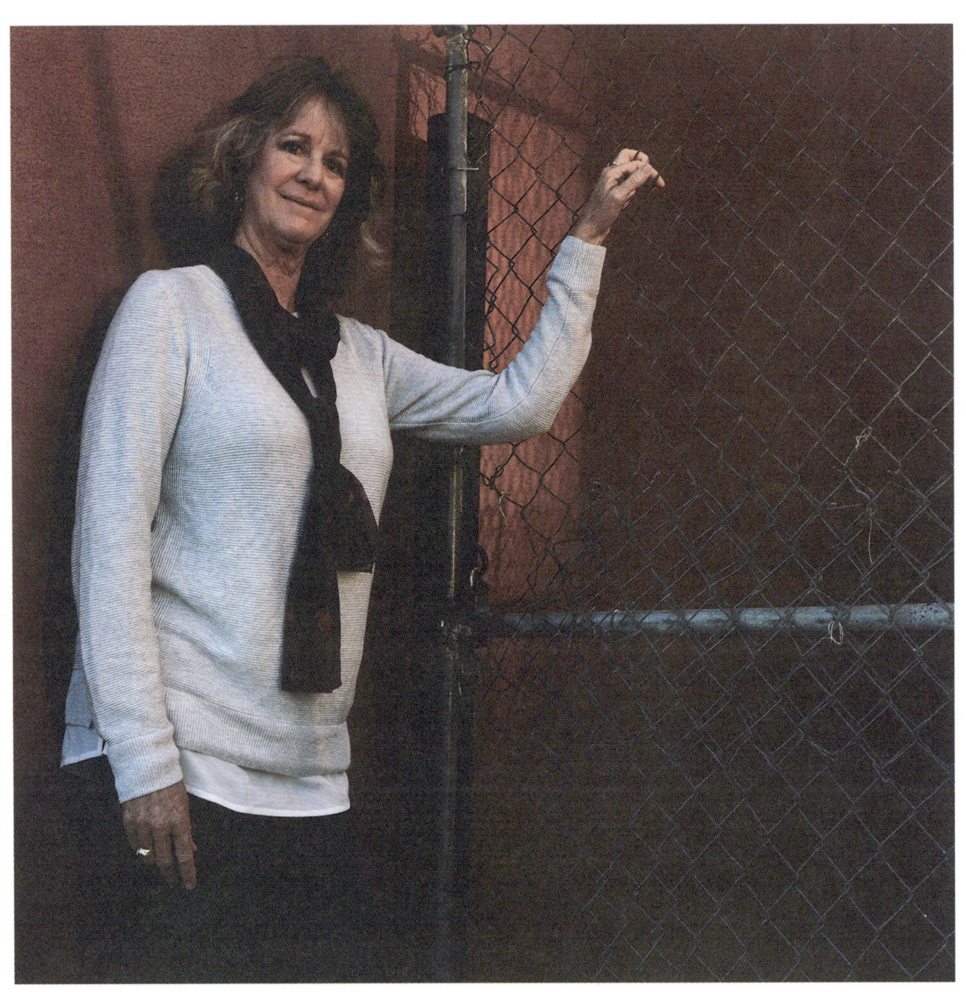

I feel free when
I'm independent!

Paula Schwartz

FREE means to me, is my peace and happiness and loving, all the time and doing things with kidness.

Pauline's Barber Shop

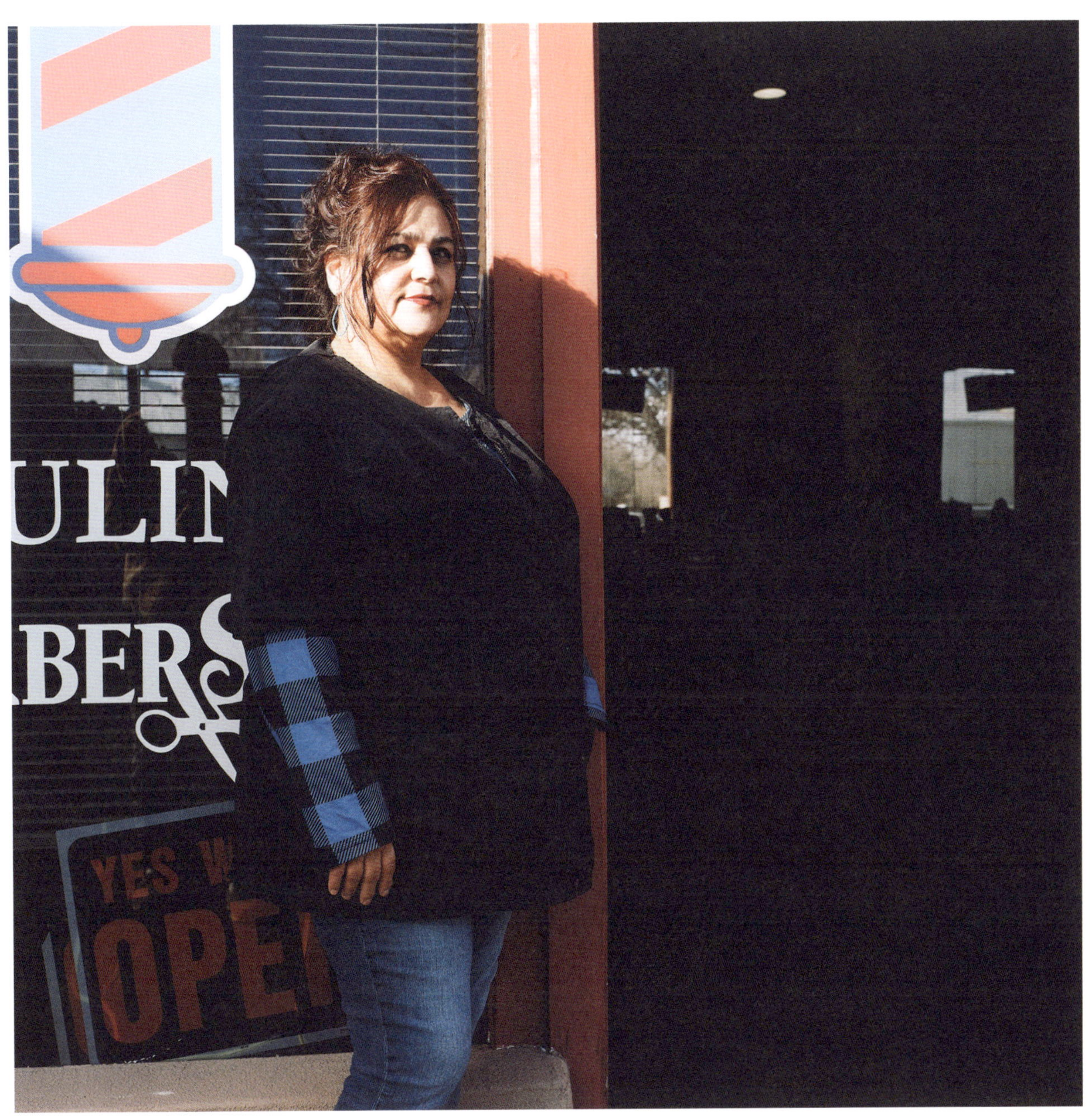ULI
BER
YES W
OPE

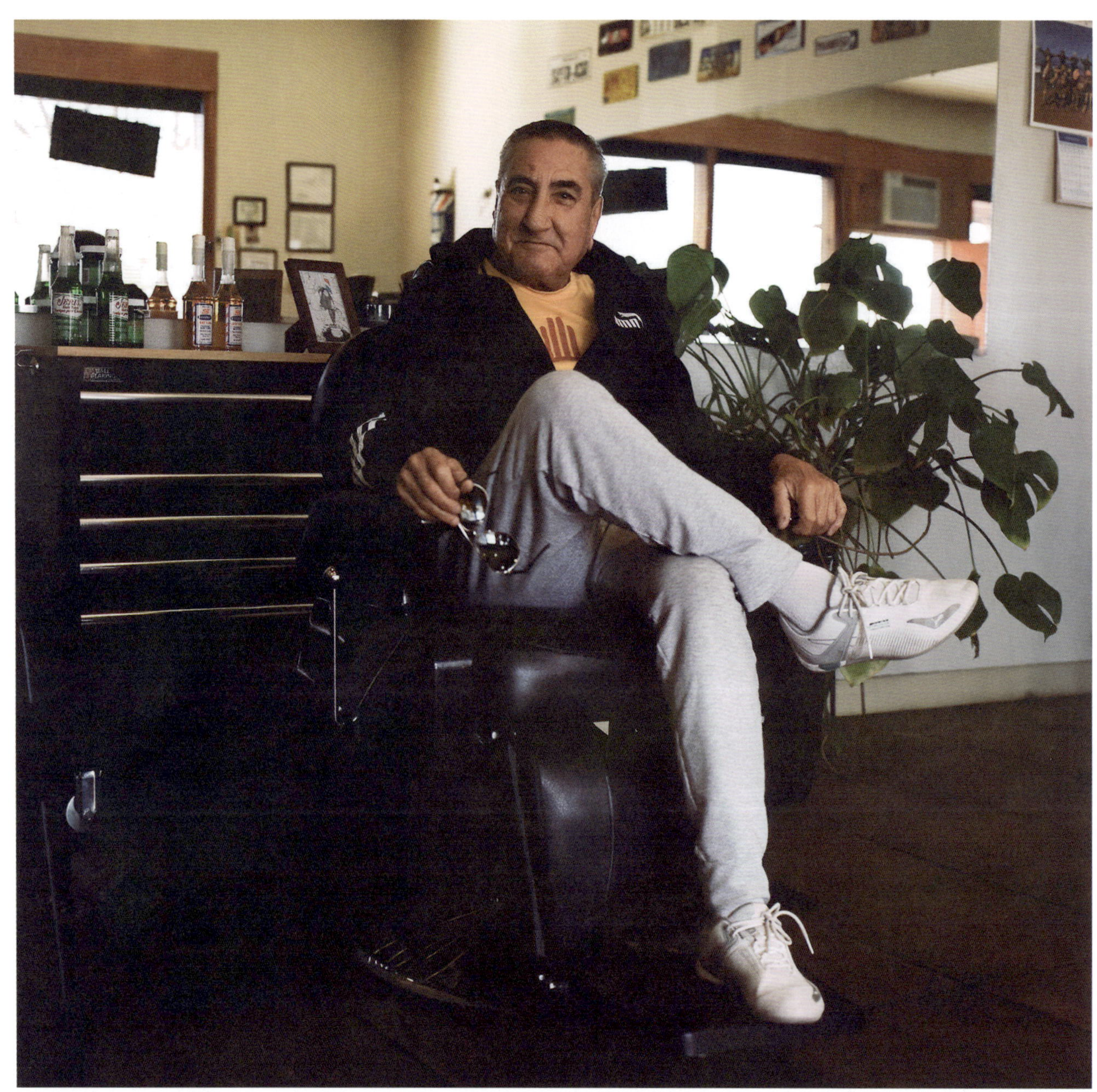

① When I
Lost my
FRIST LoVe,
I FELT FREE!
____
SINGLE

David D. Smith

Santa Fe, New Mexico · January 2022

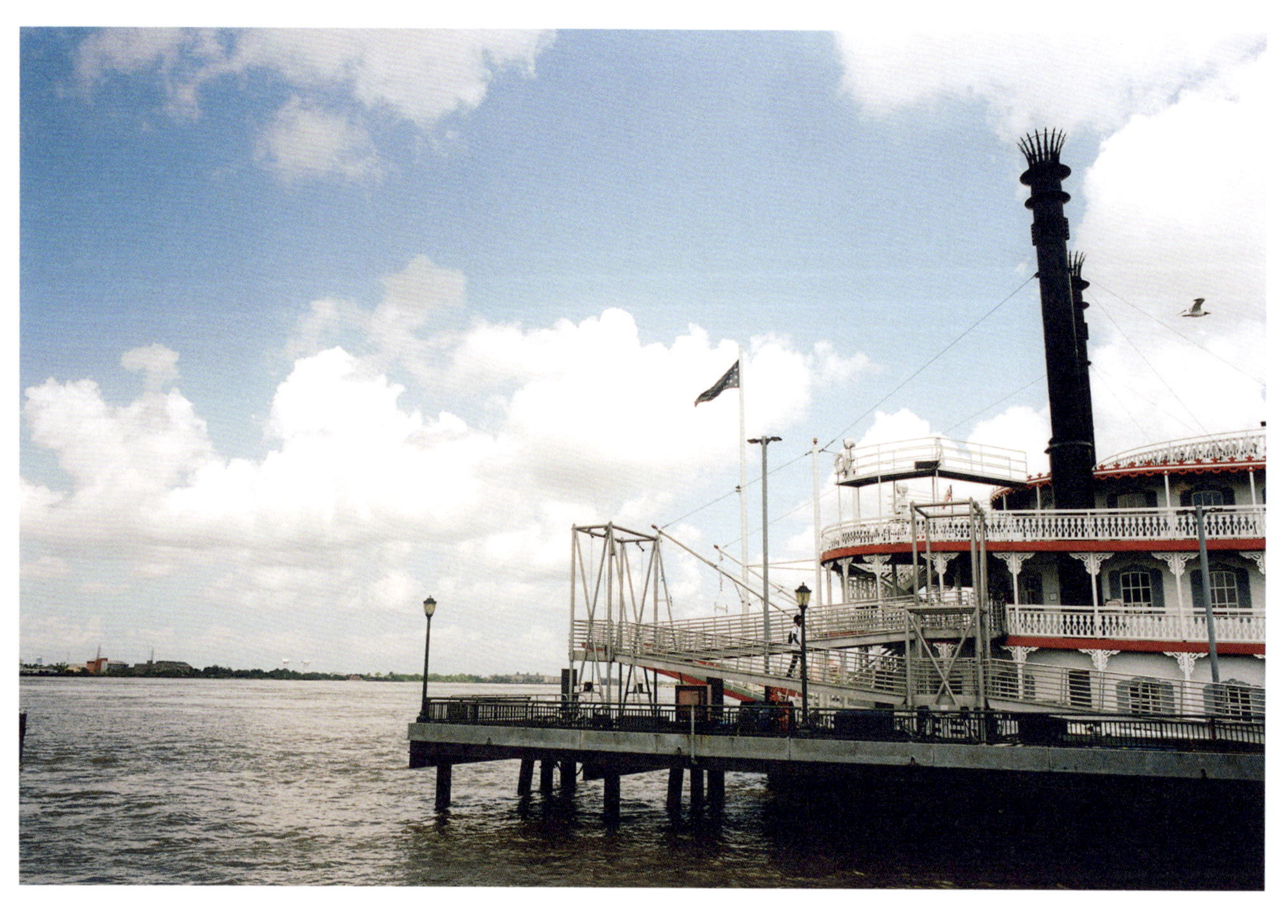

When I help
Someone else...

When I leave the toilet
seat up!

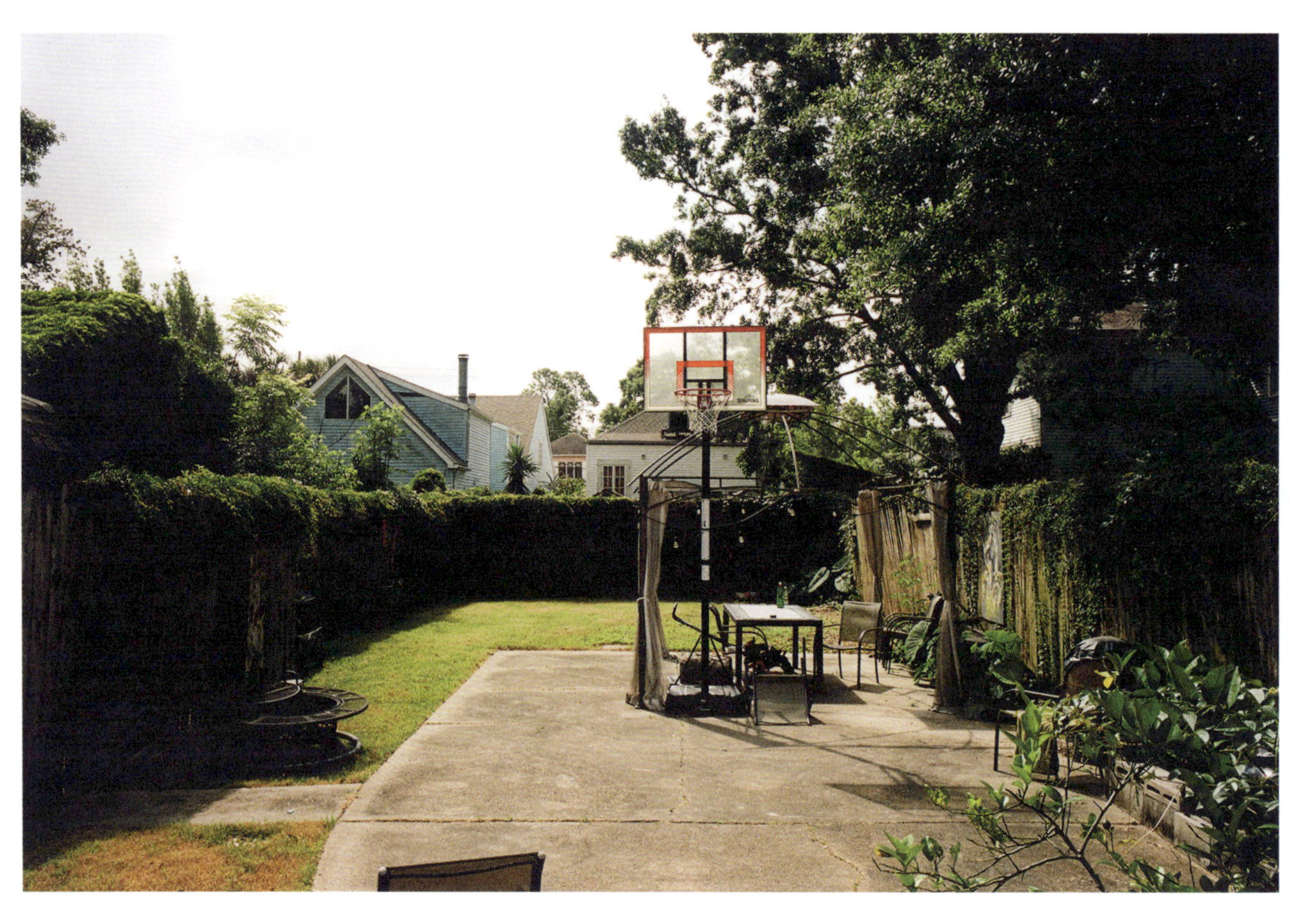

On weekends with
no school.

Friday

Night !

When I've faced the truth.

When I act like a child.

Brett

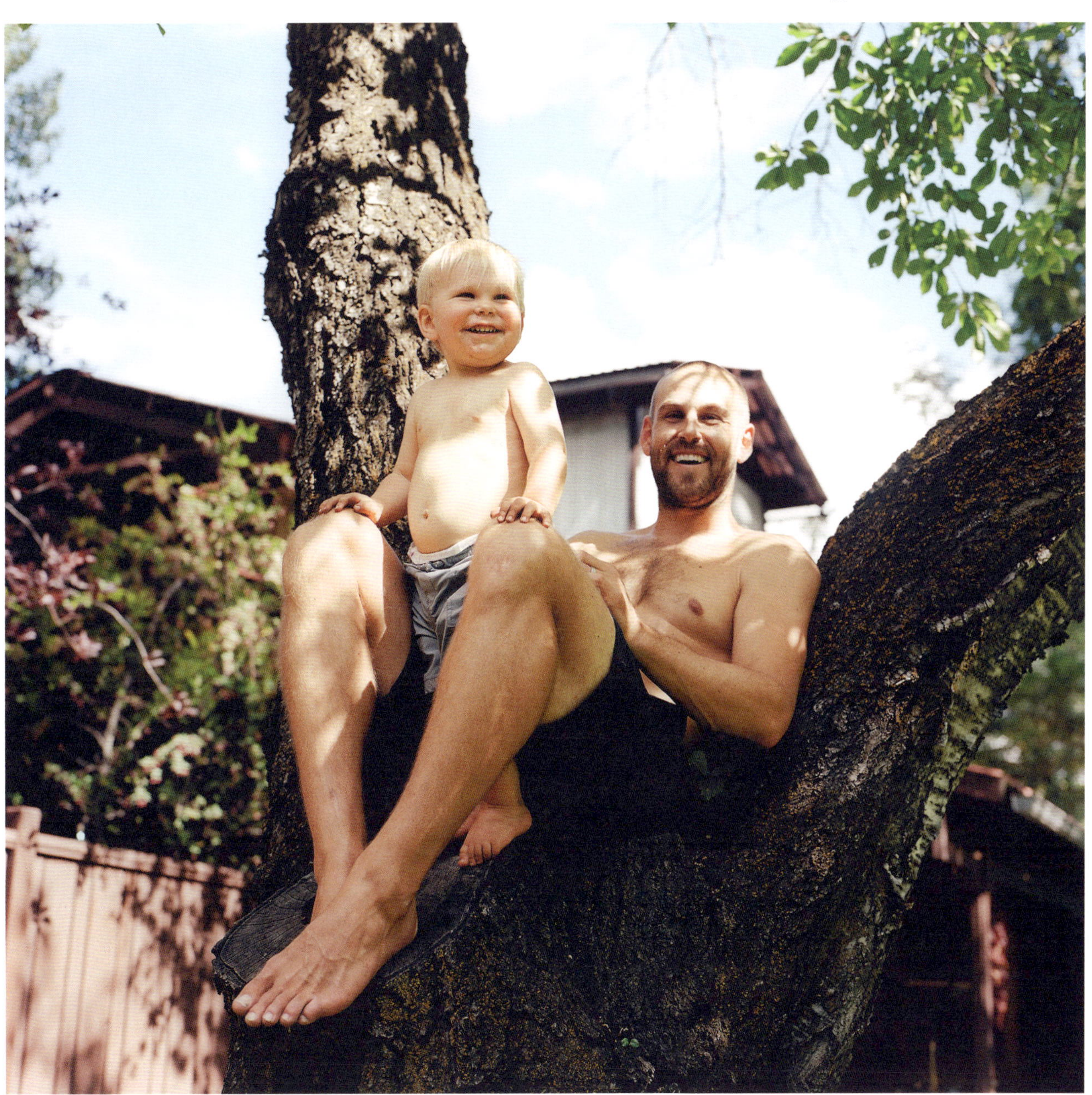

Durango, Colorado · August 2022

When I'm Playing my Guitar

Tommy Mal[...]

Edgard, Louisiana · May 2022

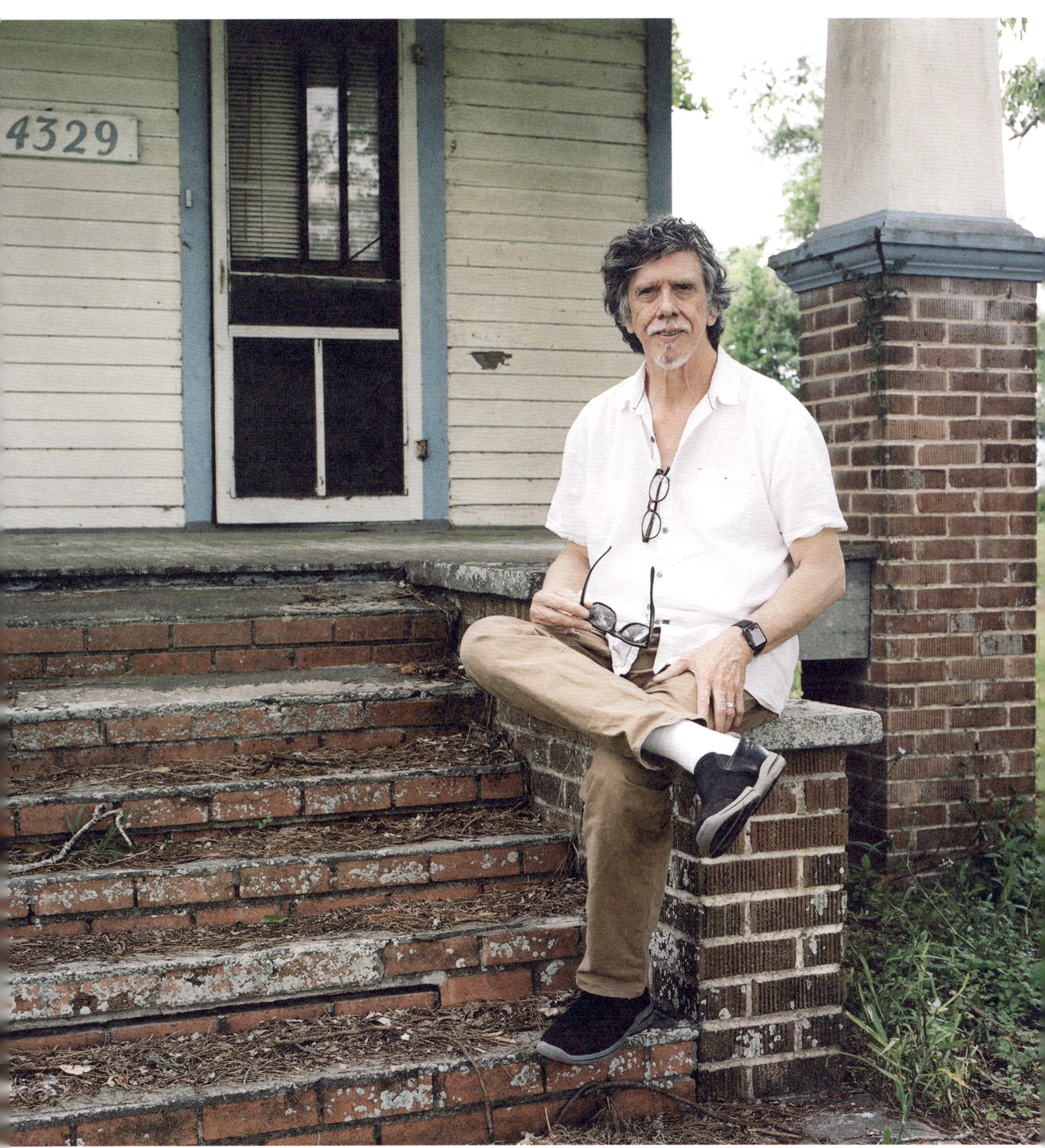
4329

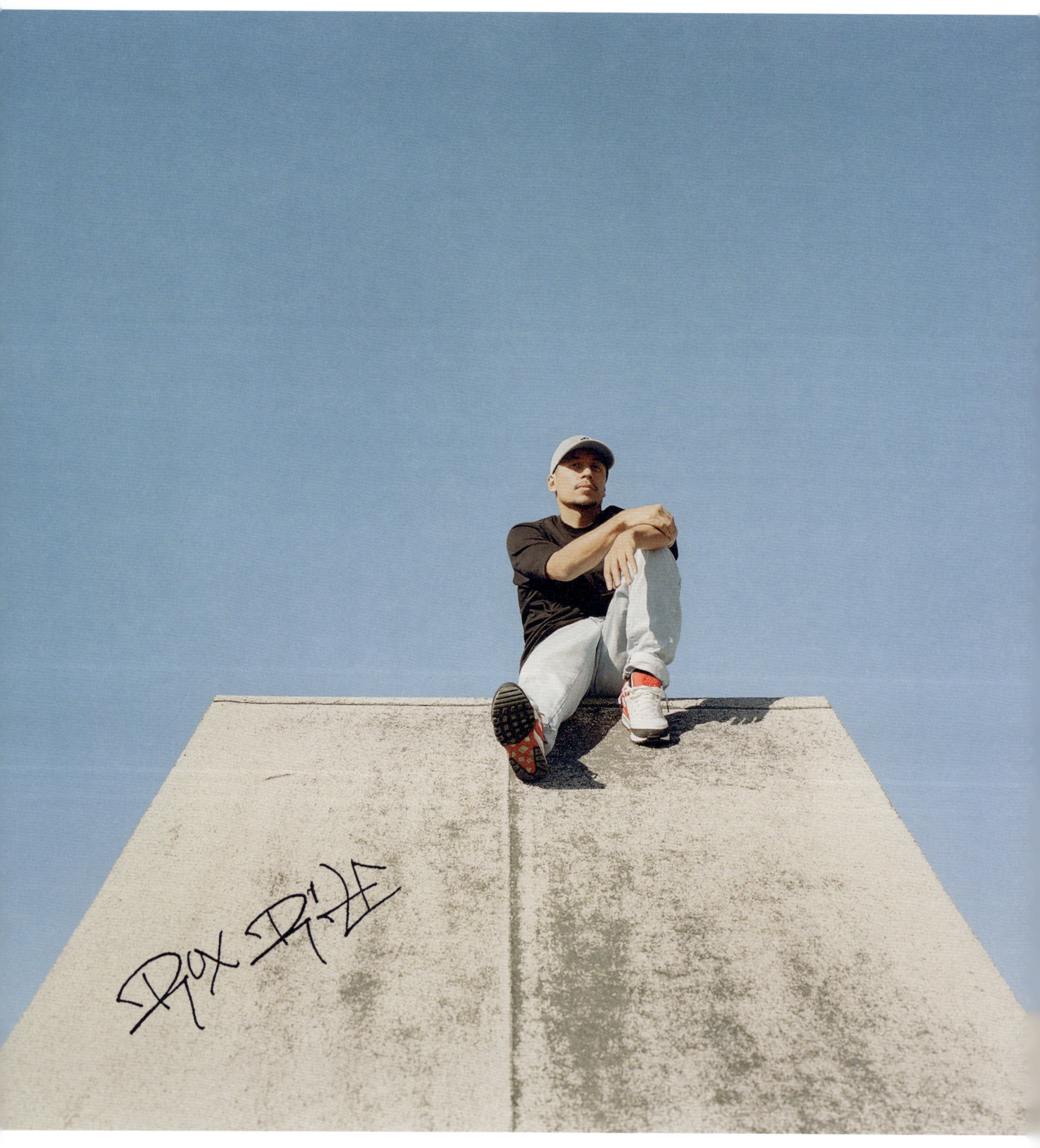

AS A BREAKING PRACTITIONER
FOR 27 + YEARS. I FEEL MOST
FREE WHEN I CAN EXPLORE
MOVEMENT TO MUSIC I ENJOY
WITH NO ONE WATCHING.

I feel free when I
listen to what my soul
wants

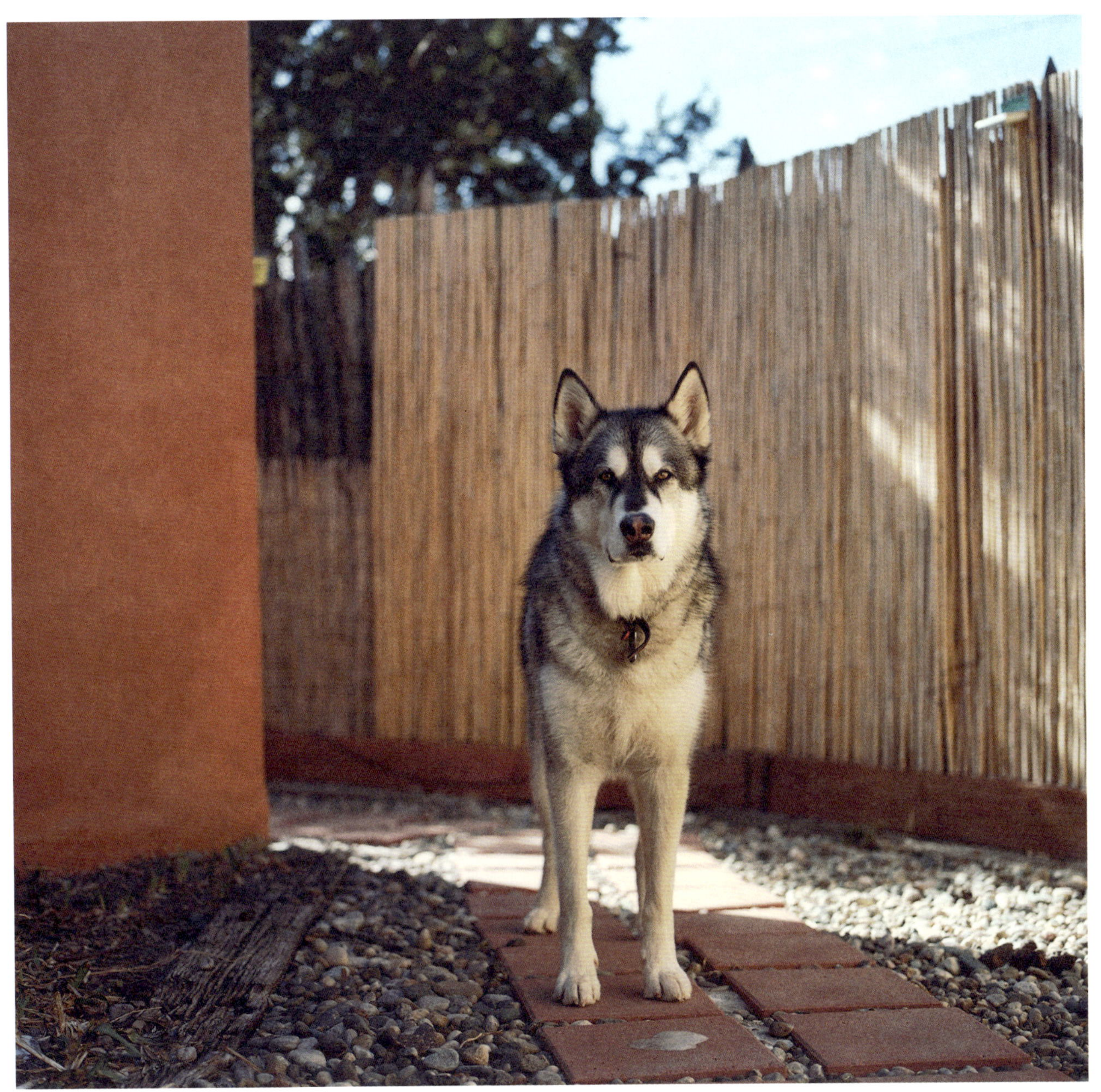

Anonymous

To every person in this book, thank you for trusting me.

I began developing the idea in March 2021. It took me almost two years to complete the work. There are so many people that helped and supported me along the way. People who let me crash on their couch, set up interviews, spent hours discussing the project, lifted me up when I was down and so much more. Simply put, I could not have done this alone.

Although this was a solo project, I felt like I always had a team.

A SPECIAL THANK YOU
TO THE FOLLOWING PEOPLE:

WES, ANNIE, ELLA, MOM, POPS
ROBBIE, WILL, COURTNEY L.
AMIE, GRANBY, IAN, MARY
CIIS, CAROLYN, JOAN, CINDY
COURTNEY N., HEATHER, LILY
BRETT, DARBY, RHONE, EMILY
NORA + PHOTO WORKS SF, BRET
JASON, PAIGE, KAYLE, JOSH
THE TROPE TEAM, SAM L.
JACK, LINDY, MICHELLE, SCOTT
GEORGIA, BARKLEY, RASHEED
DARLINGTON, DAVID, NICKY
ANTHONY M., ALEX, KRISTA
KEVIN, IVA, CARL, MOOSE

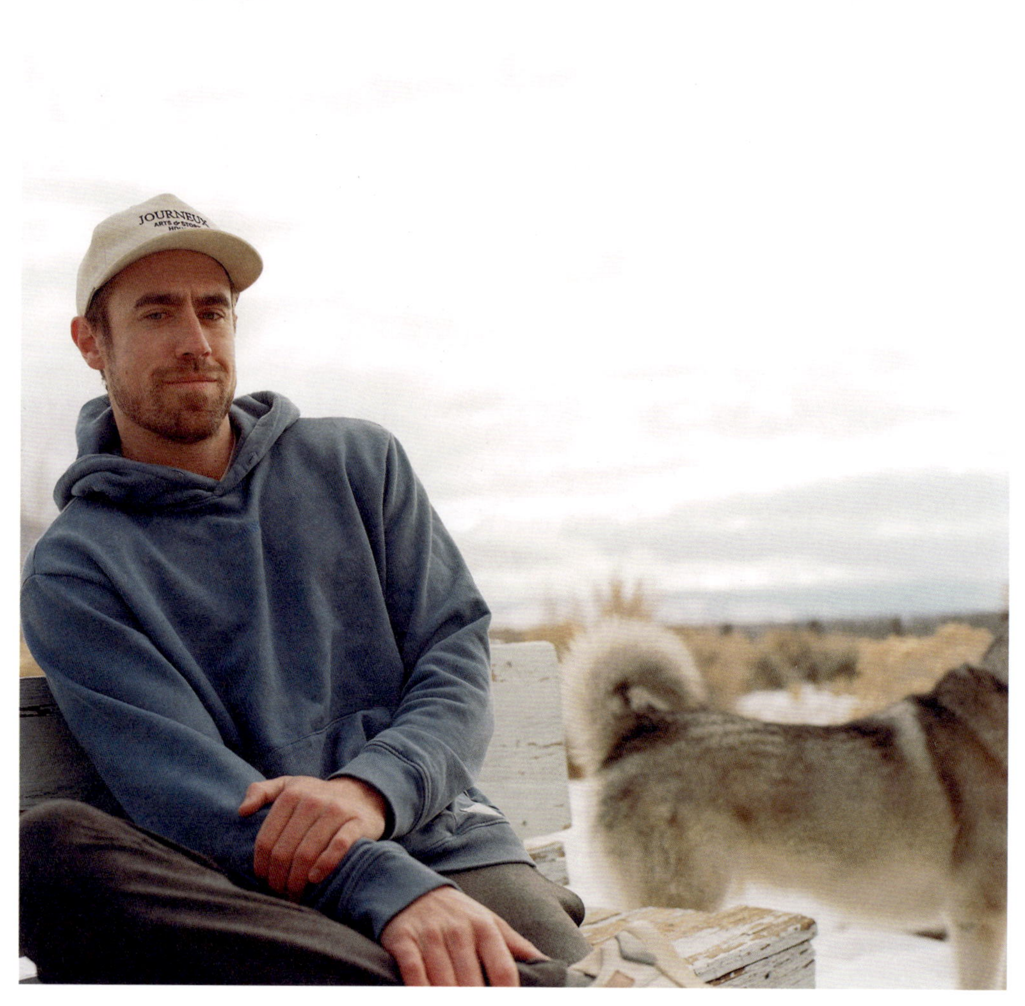

Born and raised in the iconic Haight Ashbury neighborhood in San Francisco, Ryland's passion for photography began just as his college soccer career was ending. Realizing athletics had an expiration date after sustaining a series of injuries, he yearned to dive into a new pursuit, one that he could sustain and would complement his lifestyle. The camera was the right path to both. What started as a hobby slowly grew into a professional career. He has worked in both the commercial and documentary space and his photography was first published in *Trope Chicago*. Today, Ryland describes his approach to shooting as loose and free, striving to listen, remain in the moment and not let preconceptions get in the way. He sees the camera as a bridge—connecting to a new realm of life. Aside from his photography projects, he designed and led an Artist Incubator Program with the non-profit TA98, is a co-host of the Live Better Retreats, is producing his first documentary film and holds an MFA degree from California Institute of Integral Studies. He lives on his boat in the Bay Area with his dog Moose and is on a mission to create work and experiences that connect people with themselves and others.

LCCN: 2022951416
ISBN: 978-1-951963-13-2

Printed and bound in China
First printing, 2023

+ INFORMATION:
**For additional information
on our books and prints,
visit trope.com**